The Palais des Beaux-Arts, Lille

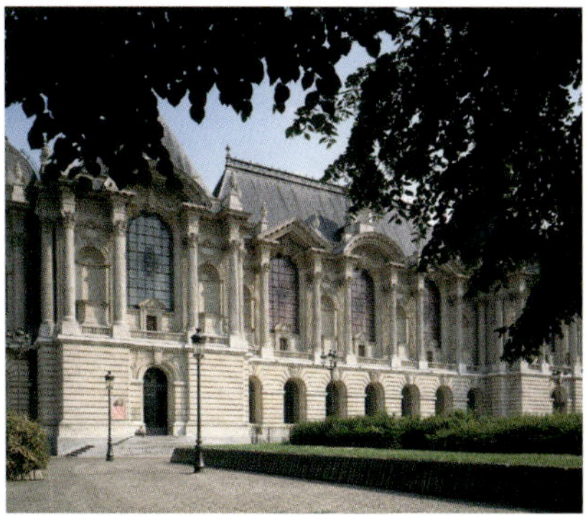

Place de la République
59000 Lille-France
Tel : +33(0)3 20 06 78 00
Closed on Tuesdays
Open from 10 a.m to 6 p.m
On Mondays, from 2 to 6 p.m

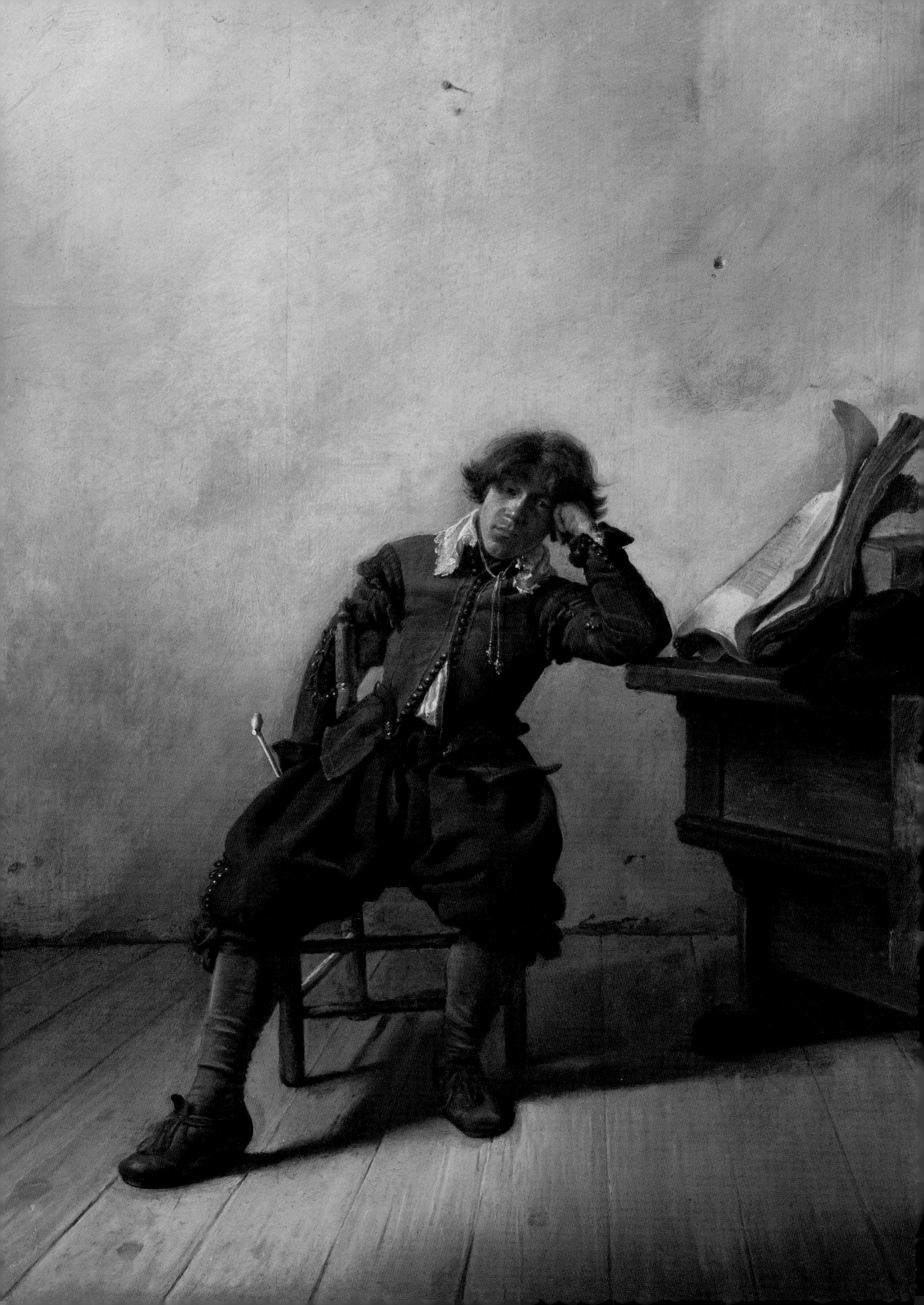

The Palais des Beaux-Arts, Lille

Alain Tapié
Chief Curator

Marie-Françoise Bouttemy, Annie Castier, Elisabeth De Jonckheere, Dominique Delgrange, Alexis Donetzkoff, Donatienne Dujardin, Alain Gérard, Florence Gombert, Michèle Moyne, Delphine Rousseau, Annie Scottez–De Wambrechies, Isabelle Warmoes

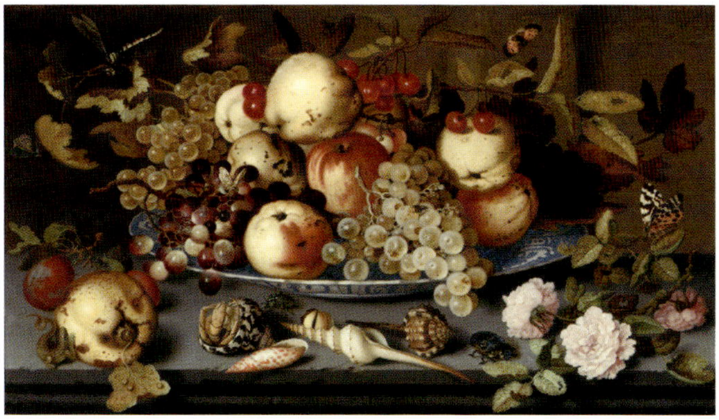

Fondation BNP PARIBAS
Le Palais des Beaux-Arts de Lille
Réunion des Musées nationaux

On the cover:
Alfred Agache 1843–1915
Vanity. Oil on canvas, 160 x 130 cm
Gift of the heirs of Edouard Agache, 1924. Inv. P. 1670

Inside front cover:
Faience statuettes depicting Chinese men,
Lille, 18th century

Frontispice:
Pieter Codde 1599–1678
Student in His Study. Oil on panel,
46 x 34 cm
Antoine Brasseur donation, 1885. Inv. P. 240

On page 3:
Balthasar van der Ast 1593/94–1657
Fruit and Shells, 1623. Oil on panel,
37 x 65 cm
Purchased 1977. Inv. P. 1937

Foreword

The generous patronage of the Fondation BNP Paribas has made this publication possible just in time to highlight the tenth anniversary of the renovation of Lille's Palais des Beaux-Arts. Since its founding in 1892 and its restoration in 1997, this institution has exemplified Lille's cultural vocation through its continuous presence and influence.

Considered one of the foremost museums in France, the Palais des Beaux-Arts houses many works that hold a significant place in art history. The array of masterpieces in the permanent collection – from Donatello, Dürer, Raphael, Brueghel, Rubens, Van Dyck, Peter Codde, Philippe de Champaigne, Chardin, Goya, Géricault, Delacroix, Carolus-Duran, Monet and Picasso to Poliakoff – constitute an incomparable voyage through time and the human geography of the European spirit that has served artists as a common territory.

The Palais des Beaux-Arts in Lille is also a site of creation where contemporary and classical meet, and visitors are invited to explore unaccustomed and surprising artistic interconnections.

Beyond the constant care expended on the works permanently and temporarily on display, the museum is characterized by a policy of openness that aims to facilitate access by all segments of the public, not only to the exhibition galleries but also to the meetings, debates and conferences held there.

The Palais des Beaux-Arts, in the heart of the city, furthermore possesses many architectural assets, such as its impressive Second Empire-style façade, designated a historical monument, and its tall ceilings, with their arresting play of light.

I warmly invite you to discover, or rediscover, through the pages of this book the uniqueness of the Palais des Beaux-Arts of Lille.

Martine Aubry
Mayor of Lille

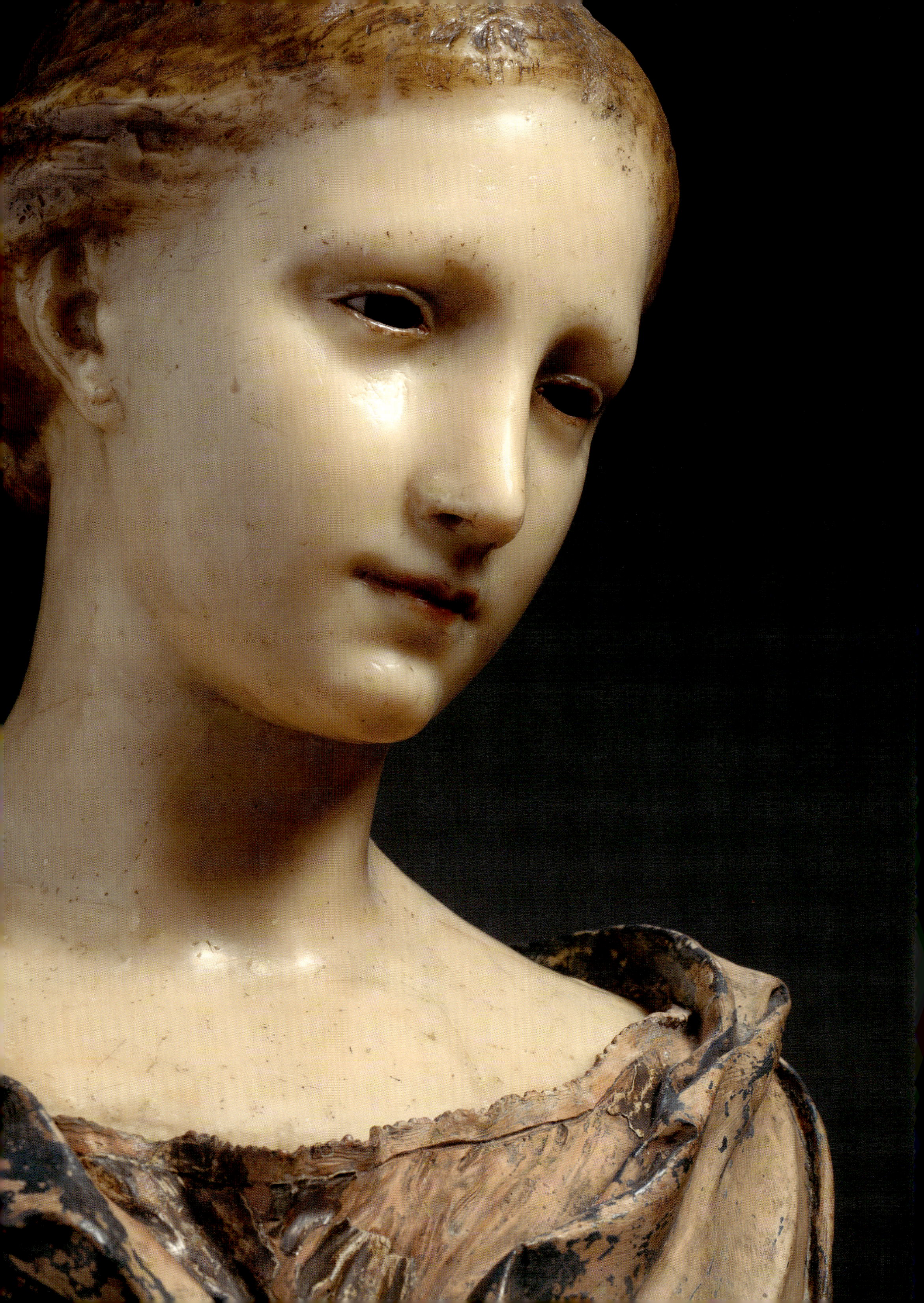

The History of the Museum

The Underlying Idea of a Museum

The concept of the museum, before it applied to a collection of objects, originally referred to a community of men. In Aristotle's time and even at Plato's Academy, the cult of the muses served the philosophical quest for truth. The space that housed them, the *mouseion*, was erected around a meeting room where scholars would engage in discussions and share moments of fellowship while their wants were supplied by royal patronage. We might do well to recall that what we now know as a museum began as a community of thinkers whose minds were turned toward the questions of the world. In ancient times, the temple dedicated to the cult of the muses received offerings: some, in the form of ex-votos, were displayed and viewed in conditions that favoured their safekeeping; others, painted effigies on *pynakes* (tablets), would become the pinacotheca; still others were kept carefully sheltered and thus formed the first storage reserves. There were also *hieropes*, caretakers who ensured the objects' maintenance. The Middle Ages contributed to the phenomenon with the notion of the treasury, the vestiges of which may still be found in churches, through the precious objects preserved there as well as ecclesiastical furnishings. But it was in the 16th century, with the distinction of the liberal arts, in particular painting and sculpture, that the modern concept appeared in the form of galleries.

In 1543, enthusiasm for the sculpture and medals of the ancient world led Paul Jove to give his collection the name 'museum', which had formerly been the prerogative of the muses. By 1551, the cabinet of curiosities appeared, especially in Germany. One of the most celebrated of these was perhaps that of the *collegio romano* belonging to the Jesuit Athanasius Kircher in the early 17th century. All sorts of rare and unusual objects from distant lands – shells and fossils, strange petrified formations – took their place alongside antiquities to form a wondrous microcosm devoted to study and meditation. In Italy, the cabinet of curiosities took the form of a *studio* where, on the model of ancient houses, the walls were covered with imitations of man's fine inventions, scientific instruments and architecture. Like a world theatre, these intellectual decors were integral to the collections, from the *studiolo* of Isabella d'Este (1474–1539) to the *Kunstkammer* of the Elector of Bavaria. The cosmogonic dream was reborn in the unity of a place that began as an ancient temple.

On the threshold of the 17th century, a major upheaval took place that saw collections, particularly painting collections, become autonomous in the context of prestigious diplomatic and commercial exchanges. These groups quickly took on the identity of their collector, especially when they abruptly changed hands. A well-known case is the masterpieces owned by the Dukes of Mantua, which in 1627 became the property of King Charles I of England and, after his execution, were dispersed to Philip IV of Spain, Christina of Sweden, Cardinal Mazarin and a German banker-cum-collector named Everard Jabach

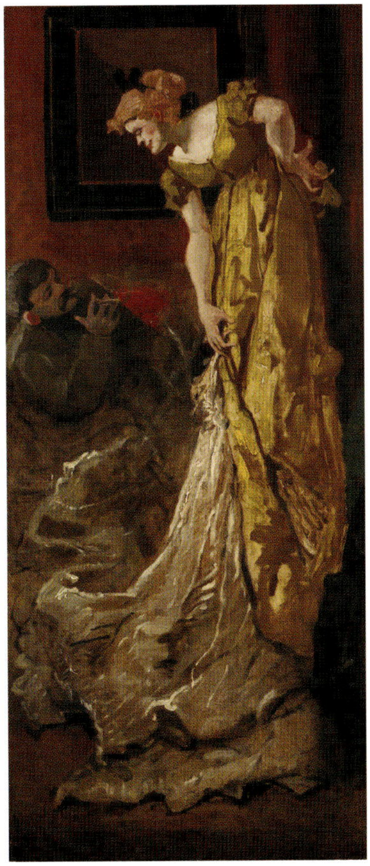

2. Henri de Toulouse-Lautrec 1864–1901
In the Studio: the Model's Pose,
(after Alfred Stevens's *The Studio*).
Oil on canvas, 137.5 x 61.5 cm
Gift of Mrs Malle and Mrs d'Epenoux, 1975. Inv. P. 1897

1. France or Italy, 16th–18th century
Wax Head. Wax and clay,
height 45 cm
Wicar bequest, 1834. Inv. Pl. 1

in 1671. Colbert pressured the latter to yield the better part of his collection to his king, Louis XIV. The vanity motivating these accumulations was counterbalanced by a growing feeling of the works' essential didactic mission. In 1667, Oxford's Ashmolean Museum would be the most apt illustration of this. The generating principle of transmission was born and has remained the very reason for a museum in our time. The passage from private to public goods throughout the 18th century, which contributed to the advent of art lovers and connoisseurs, had no other basis than this.

In 1727, Caspar F. Neickel's treatise on museography modernized the cabinet of curiosities. In 1752, the British Parliament bought the collection of Dr Sloane, which laid the foundation for the British Museum. In 1769 in Florence, the Medici collection became the Uffizi Gallery. Monasteries turned into museums and even cultural centres. Simultaneously, museographical classification and arrangement appeared. To orient visitors, chronological presentation gradually became the norm, while, to favour the principle of presenting examples for artists, the notion of schools and stylistic characteristics won out over place of production, at the risk of oversimplification. In line with this same movement, drawing schools appeared in the 1740s. Following the model of the Renaissance academies, they combined learning and collecting as repositories and models of Antiquity.

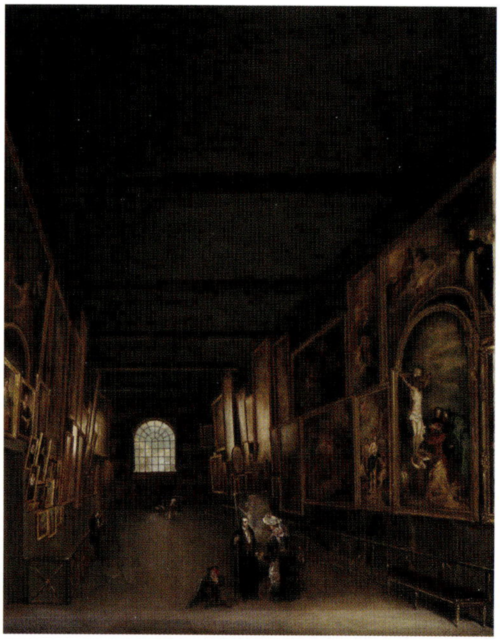

3. Isidore Bonnier de Layens 1792–1877
Interior view of the Recollects chapel serving as a painting gallery, c. 1825.
Oil on canvas, 84 x 65 cm
Gift of Mr Bonnier de Layens. Inv. P. 871

With the installation of the royal collections at the Louvre in 1747, the principles of maintenance and restoration reinforced each other. Historical knowledge of styles and subjects also served artists who, in surpassing their models, transcended them to forge, for political ends, the idea of beauty and its public necessity. The grand gallery divested itself of its scale models of fortified cities and, in pure and innovative overhead lighting, was given over to the flowering of the fine arts. By the time of the French Revolution, the museum as an institution had made considerable strides.

In 1789, the arrival of the clergy's property in the public domain was based on the fact that they had been acquired 'in the interest of persons and not to serve a function'. This shrewd point of view paved the way to the major consideration for the coming centuries: artistic value and didactic content, which now took priority over art's political and religious function. This approach would have a major effect on the perception of art history as an autonomous practice often too far removed from the context of the works' production. In 1792, the installation at the Louvre of large numbers of celebrated or highly decorative works from the royal buildings highlighted the general movement of conservation and inventory that now separated art and history from science and technology. Heritage enrichment linked to military campaigns in Europe after 1794 brought to its height the idea of a relationship between the greatest masterpieces meant for the major demonstration of France as a 'haven of freedom' that was reflected in the mirror of aesthetics. This is why the Napoleonic wars, particularly in Italy in 1797, included a heritage component. The Revolution's confiscation of paintings, sculpture and scientific instruments found its legal justification in the Treaty of Tolentino of 1797.

These properties' triumphal entry into France in 1798 revived old memories of trophies accumulated in the Roman period and thereafter. The protests of Quatremère de Quincy in his letters to Miranda raised the philosophical question of the removal of these works from their context. But this judgement was an opportunity for future museums. As shreds detached from their history, these works acquired a new status. Their destiny suspended, they attained a new eternity, as deposits from Paris enriched the future provincial museums through a decree proposed to the Consulate in 1801 by Jean-Antoine Chaptal, chemist, politician and Minister of the Interior under Napoleon I from 1801 to 1804. They were distributed among fifteen cities: Lyons, Bordeaux, Strasbourg,

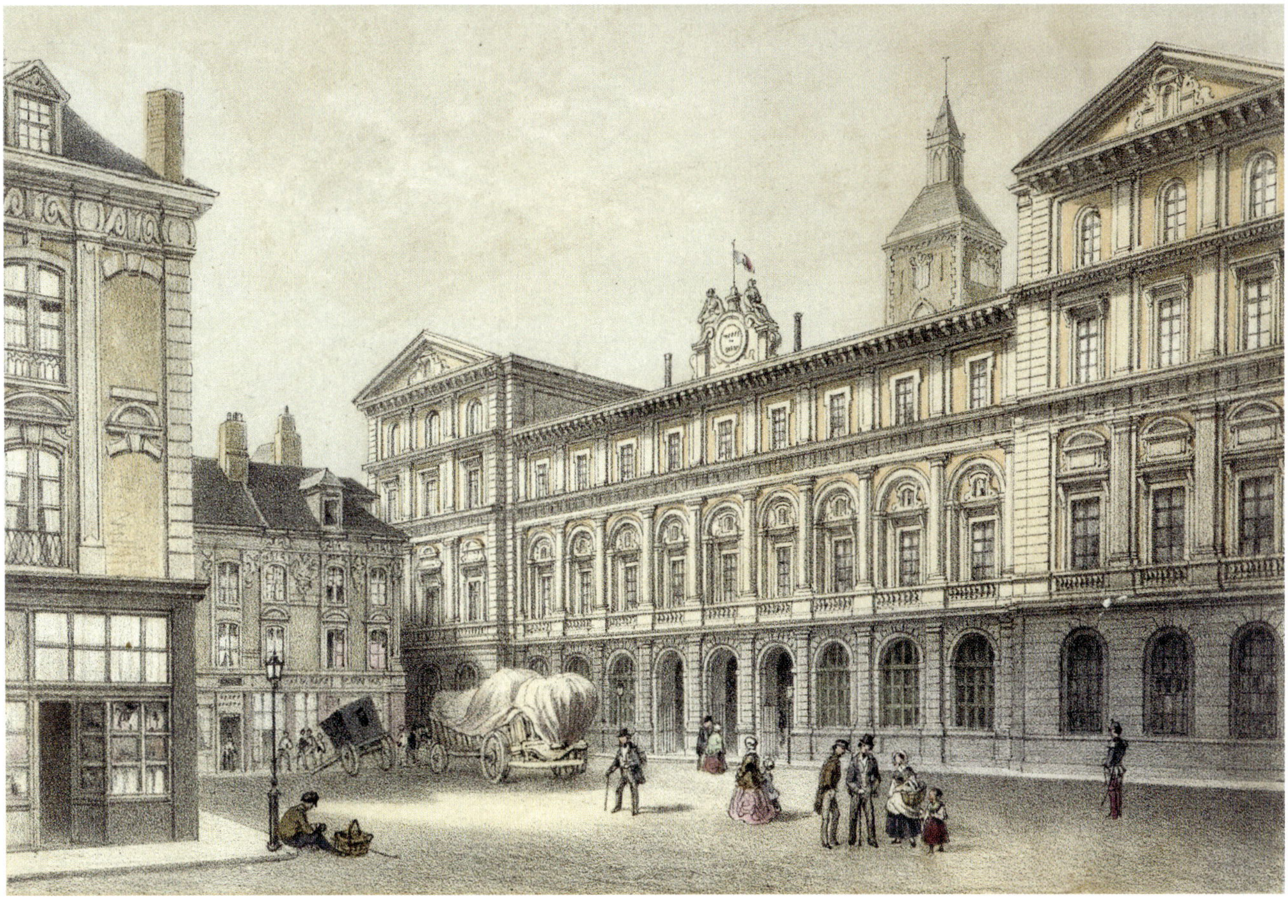

4. Façade of Lille City Hall as rebuilt by the architect Benvignat (1805–1877). The museum was on the second floor. Lithograph by Deroy
Private collection

Brussels, Marseilles, Rouen, Nantes, Dijon, Toulouse, Geneva, Caen, Lille, Mayence, Rennes and Nancy. Their drawing schools, directors and teachers mobilized to choose paintings from 'all the masters, all genres, all schools' for the purpose of founding a museum. AT

The Museum and Municipal Institutions of Lille

Before the Revolution, Lille had no museum. Anyone wishing to admire works of art could do so in churches, convents and the homes of the well-to-do.

The Monastery of the Augustinian Recollects, Lille's First Museum, 1791–1847
Works of art, essentially paintings, confiscated from the convents after the adoption of the Civil Constitution of the Clergy in 1790, were assembled at the Recollects monastery (Rue des Arts) and entrusted to the keeping of the 3
Lille painter Louis Watteau. In late 1793, he proposed to the Directory for the district of Lille that a museum be founded. In 1795, a selection of 197 paintings among the 646 removed was 'deemed worthy to be kept for teaching'. This was the embryonic nucleus of the city's future museum.

On 1 September 1801, Bonaparte signed the decree prepared by Jean-Antoine Chaptal to divide among fifteen cities 846 canvases 'seized' in the conquered countries to serve as the basis of as many museums. Lille received forty-six, of high quality, which were exhibited in the Recollects chapel. The municipality assumed the costs of restoring and setting up this first museum, theoretically opened in 1805 and officially inaugurated on 15 August 1809. Its first curator, Henri Joseph Van Blarenberghe (1750–1826), more concerned with teaching than with serving the public, let the museum drowse. It was aroused from its slumber by three events: in 1834, the Wicar bequest, through the Société des

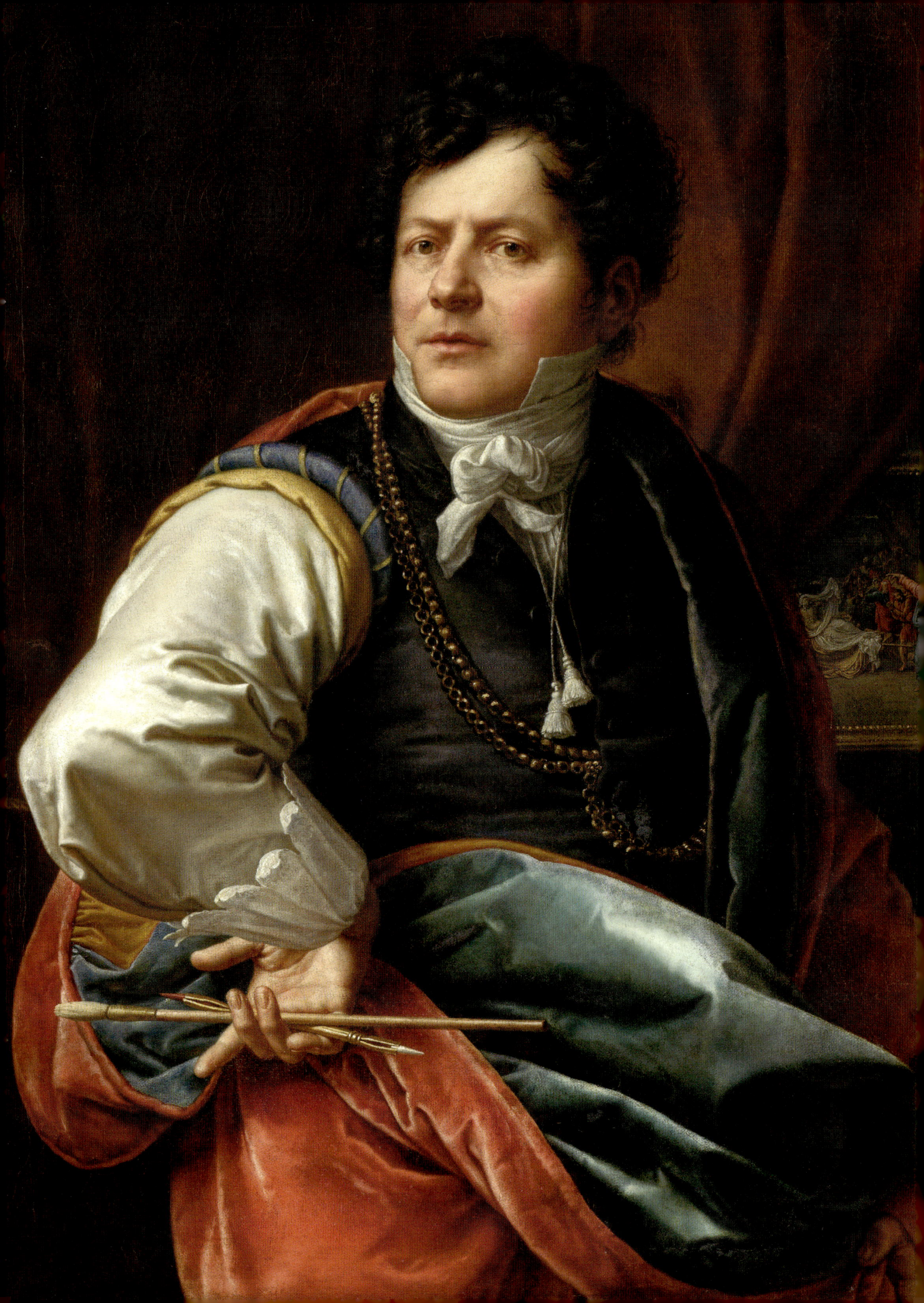

Sciences et des Arts, considerably enriched the collections; in 1838, the state transferred Delacroix's *Medea* to the museum; and in 1841, a new curator, Edouard Reynart, was appointed.

The Musée Rihour (1848–1880) and the Curator Reynart

The arrival of Edouard Reynart (1802–1879), promoted to chief curator in 1841
after ably assisting his predecessor for several years (the arrival of the *Medea*), 103
caused a revolution at the museum. The new head, a good amateur painter, was endowed with exceptionally sound taste and had a remarkable network of connections.

His comfortable financial situation allowed him to devote his time to the improvement of 'his' museum without restraint. His ceaseless activity alarmed Mayor Bigo-Danel, who decided to oversee it with the help of a museum administrative commission, formed in 1845. The tactful Reynart found support in this structure, which made relationships with Lille's cultural milieu easier for him, in particular the very active Société des Sciences et des Arts. The Société inherited the magnificent collection of drawings bequeathed by the painter Wicar; in 1836, management of the collection was entrusted to the museum, which enlarged it significantly.

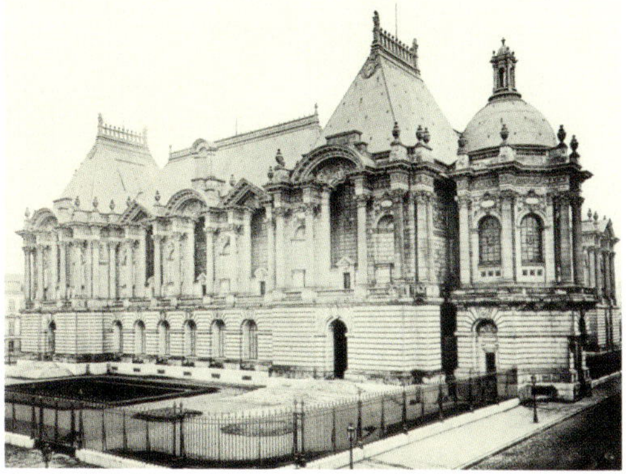

6. The Palais des Beaux-Arts in 1892, Facade facing the Place de la République

Reynart's activity was prodigious in all realms of art. The number of paintings increased from 188 in 1841 to 715 in 1875, essentially with additions of fine quality, but the curator's research extended to many other sectors as well. Purchases, donations and state transfers required the opening of new sections, overseen by as many specialized administrative commissions: Medals (1824), Ethnology (Moillet donation, 1849), Ceramics (1865), Archaeology and Numismatics (1860), Antiquities and Archaeology (1882), Decorative Art (1884), Sculpture and Prints (1887).

The size of these collections made it necessary to move them into much
larger premises: upstairs at the town hall built to plans by Benvignat on the 4
ruins of the former Palais Rihour. The move was carried out in several stages from 1848 to 1860. The quality and presentation in the new quarters were the object of a very laudatory report published in 1853 by the Director of National Museums, Philippe Jeanron.

The Palais des Beaux-Arts and Its Problems, 1881–1945

In 1879, Auguste Herlin succeeded his colleague and friend Reynart and continued his work. The need for an art museum was apparent to all; the idea took form after the election in 1881 of Mayor Géry Legrand, who was enthusiastic about cultural matters. He organized a lottery that raised 1,800,000 gold francs, making it possible to hold a competition to design a 'palace of fine arts'.

The competition was won by the Parisian architects Bérard and Delmas, who proposed a highly ornate palace that was, however, less satisfying from a museological standpoint. Its construction from 1885 to 1892 entailed many disappointments: the finished building was half the size planned. The inaugural festivities could not disguise the latent difficulties, which became apparent from the 'round' of curators: six, one after another, until 1913. Simultaneously, serious heating problems closed the brand-new palace from 1895 to the beginning of 1898. A certain administrative disorder resulted from these facts, which were denounced by a financial inspector's severely critical report in 1911.

Calm returned in 1913 with the appointment of a man of order and a lover of art, Emile Théodore, to the post of curator. He courageously shouldered the daunting task of protecting the museum from 1914 to 1918. Despite severe bombardment (seventy-five rockets over the buildings), flooding and the depredations of a traumatic military government, he limited losses to only a few

5. Jean-Baptiste Wicar 1762–1834
Self-portrait in Spanish Costume, c. 1825–1830.
Oil on canvas, 99 x 75 cm
Inv. P. 887

objects. The effectiveness of his difficult management was recognized on 14 July 1919 with the official recognition of the museum's merits through its *citation à l'Ordre de la Nation* (honourable mention).

The reopening of the galleries in 1924 was followed by remarkable expansion from 1933 to 1935. The covered atrium was bordered by additional galleries. But despite this, space was still insufficient. The curator appointed in 1939, Pierre Maurois, could not proceed to the modernization he desired. The declaration of war restricted him to supervising the safeguarding of the collections.

Growth and Renewal after 1946

Repatriated after their exile, the collections benefited from a renewed presentation. Beginning in 1946, the curator was assisted by the Société des Amis du Musée, headed by Max Crépy. Works by contemporary artists appeared on the walls.

Appointed in 1962, Albert Châtelet was the first curator who was a professional art historian. He did a great deal to raise the museum's profile. Hervé Oursel, who succeeded him in 1969, had at his disposal financial means and a staff that allowed him to present quality exhibitions. As a regular visitor of these exhibitions, Mayor Pierre Mauroy became convinced of the necessity of a sweeping renovation of the museum.

The occasion was provided in 1987 by negotiations between the Mayor of Lille and Jacques Chirac, Prime Minister at that time, which ended the 'saga' *10-12* of the scale relief models: those representing the fortified towns along the northern border remained in Lille; the rest returned to Paris. As a consequence, the necessary funds were allocated to display them in an enlarged and renovated museum. In concert with the municipal services, the new curator, Arnauld Brejon de Lavergnée, oversaw the construction entrusted to the architects Jean-Marc Ibos and Myro Vitart.

The museum closed on 1 May 1991 and was reinaugurated 7 June 1997. Enthusiasm for the renovated and enlarged museum was unanimous, although it quickly appeared that space problems persisted. As soon as the new curator, Alain Tapié, arrived in Lille, he was confronted with delicate questions of how best to utilize the available space.

The museum's history continues. AG

The Palais des Beaux-Arts Today

Thus, an external event of great cultural importance lay behind the renovation and enlargement of the Palais des Beaux-Arts. Mayor Pierre Mauroy wanted to present in his city the sixteen models and relief plans that represented the defensive system of the cities of the North. The Palais des Beaux-Arts, in its multiple vocation, was the site chosen to preserve this new heritage. It was around these models that the various layouts referred to below were designed and carried out, in the knowledge that the emergence of postmodern culture today has led to a new regard for eclectic architecture.

The 1980s' spirit of cultural enterprise and renovation was expressed in Lille by the will to redeploy the richness of the collections of archaeology, *objets d'art* and, above all, 19th-century painting and sculpture. However, the spectacular way the building faces onto the prefecture did not foster a feeling of openness toward the city. Two further questions were submitted for the architects' reflection: What function to assign to the monumental Wicar Hall – storage reserve or exhibition gallery? And what role should the atrium created in 1935 play? In view of museum visitors' new needs, establishing a bookstore, museum shop, auditorium, restaurant, public library, educational studios and a temporary exhibition gallery seemed imperative, as well as im-

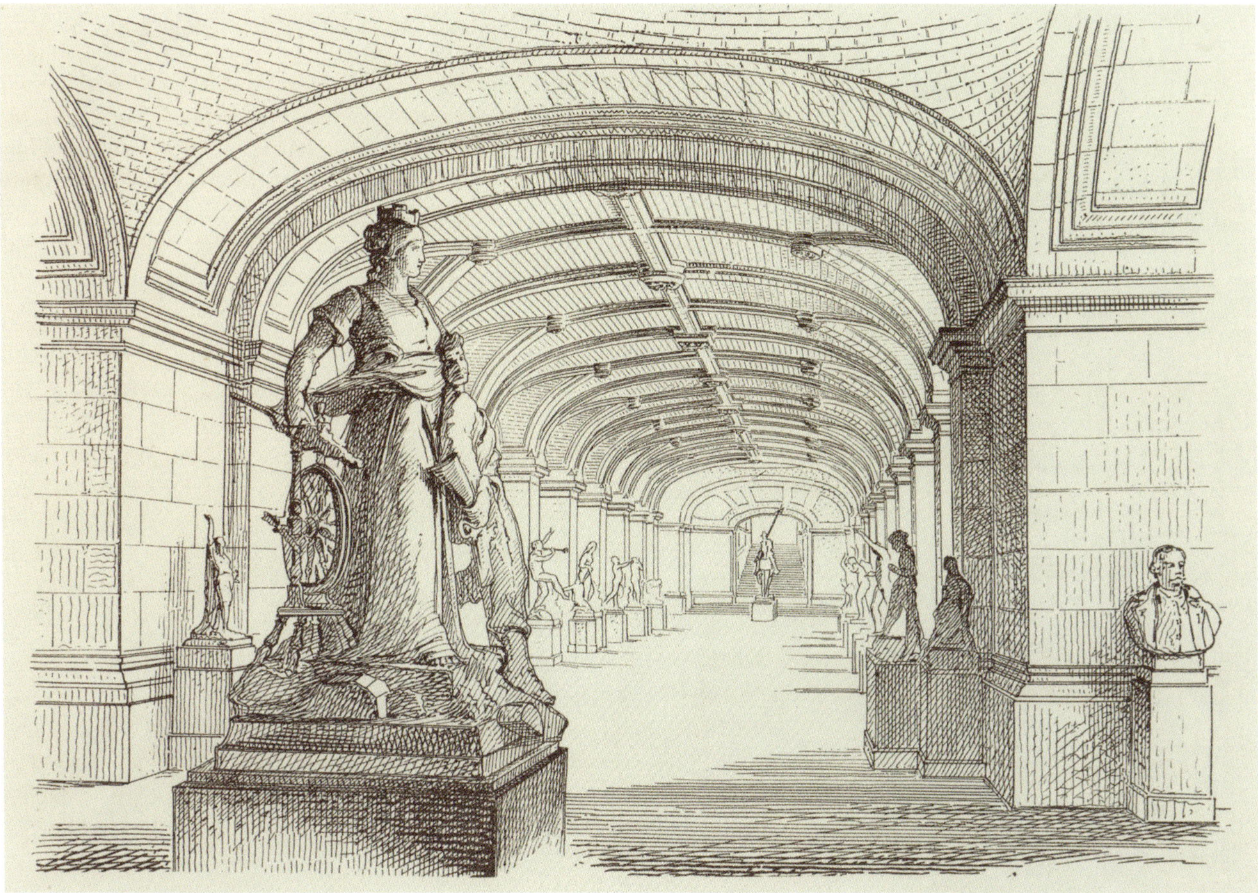

7. View of the sculpture gallery at the Palais des Beaux-Arts' inauguration in 1892
Documentary Department

proved exploitation of the lower levels, whose vaulted architecture is a happy instance of the Flemish tradition, even if for a century the proximity of the water table had made the collections vulnerable to flooding.

The winning project, by Ibos and Vitart, daringly broke ties with the 19th-century building and its references to the past to introduce into the available space a wedge-like service building, whose façades evoke the modernist rigour of Frank Lloyd Wright. The inner façade, which looks onto the old building and acts as a mirror, has a subtle geometry of line that plays on gold and the renovation's emblematic red. The ground-floor restaurant was to be a bastion of taste, symbolizing the urbanity and friendly atmosphere of the museum block. Glass bricks leave the visual field between the two buildings open and cover a temporary exhibition gallery lit by natural light from above. On either side are the educational and technical studios, the auditorium and the library. The vaulted brick galleries now house the Antiquities, Medieval and Renaissance Departments. The relief models are in the atrium, at the heart of the museum, where the interplay of the black panels and glass walls that protect them uses light to re-create the striking effect of these reconstructions of cities, with their fortifications and surrounding scenery. In its spareness – the large monumental stairway has disappeared – compensated in height by a strong presence of large gold-leaf rectangles arranged regularly over the blind sections of the galleries, the atrium promotes circulation between the front and back of the museum. The entrance gallery facing the Place de la République façade has metal furniture with pure lines, while in the rotundas hang two chandeliers designed by the artist Pesce, a baroque counterpoint that 'contains fragments of everyday objects'. The walls of the painting galleries on the upper levels give the 17th-century collections their due of the renovation's emblematic red.

The design of any museum display will evolve in accordance with successive architectural approaches and in light of new didactic functions, stylistic and thematic comparisons that arise in the course of the curators' research, and new chromatic and volumetric necessities intended to favour the individual perception of each work as part of a whole. The destiny of every work is suspended, for the works have often been plucked from their original context and either placed on a pedestal or hung on the wall to participate in a microcosm, or else set on an isolated support to emphasize their remarkable nature or their capacity to serve as a vector and motor for interpreting the whole. Spurred by the renovation carried out between 1992 and 1997, the museum augmented its public programmes and scholarly and cultural activities through a lively and inventive use of the available space. The atrium, a crossroads and meeting place, can also accommodate large, in-depth international exhibitions designed to enter into dialogue with the museum's new architectural spirit while preserving the sense of transparency and freedom of circulation. Like pendants, the library and cloakroom are now housed to the fore of the two galleries on either side of the atrium.

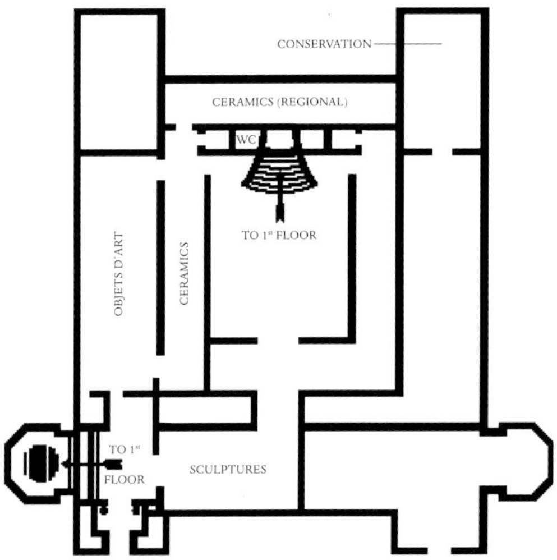

8. Plan of the ground floor, in 1970

The Antiquities, Medieval and Renaissance Departments evolved museographically in pace with research on German sculpture, early Netherlandish and Italian Renaissance painting. This section includes a study gallery that presents the museum's 'painters' paintings'.

On the painting level, the programme sets out with the 16th century, the century of Netherlandish Mannerism dominated by Italianate imagery and figures, with Van Hemessen and Van Heemskerck, and by the landscape in its Northern form, with Brueghel and his school. The next two galleries highlight the relationship between Lille and Antwerp, based on the major figure of Rubens, his studio and collaborators, Van Dyck and Jordaens. Then comes a Flemish gallery that focuses on the works' iconic (Teniers) and symbolic affinities. The 17th-century French painting collection provides a double view of its sources: Flemish (Philippe de Champaigne), then classical, based on the academic spirit and literary texts (Stella and La Hyre). For the 18th century, a fruitful juxtaposition occurs between refined research in the spirit of the Enlightenment (Raoux and Robert) and the persistent influence of Rubens (Boucher) and Rembrandt (Chardin). Five galleries are devoted to 19th-century French painting. The first features preclassical works, both pre-Revolutionary ('Watteau de Lille', Boilly) and post-Revolutionary (Jacques-Louis David). The second features academic works – some Romantic in inspiration (Géricault), others literary (Delacroix). The third gallery encompasses Realism, be it idealized (Duval and Millet), sociological (Carolus-Duran, Courbet) or Orientalist (Constant). In the fourth, naturalism is seen through the spirit of the Barbizon School (Corot and Daubigny) and Impressionism, born of English influence (Michel) and fuelled by the physical depth of an attachment to the land, in particular Normandy (Monet, Boudin, Lepic). In the fifth gallery, the diversity and admixture of Symbolist (Puvis de Chavannes, Redon) and academic (Carolus-Duran) currents are deployed, certain of which herald Nabis intimism as represented above all by Vuillard. The inner galleries surrounding the atrium house Dutch painting, reigned over by Ruisdael, Pieter de Hooch and examples from Rembrandt's entourage; Italian painting, dominated by Venice with Bassano, Tintoretto and Veronese; and the celebrated Spanish collection, with El Greco and Goya. In this same group of rooms are the Palais des Beaux-Arts' galleries of contemporary art and prints and drawings, which display the drawings of the Wicar collection in rotation. Each geographical area (Flanders, France, Holland and so on) is identified by a colour, sometimes conferring upon a well-known or little-known masterpiece its power of influence. Partitions – in the form of porticoes, so as to retain the openness of the space – can be arranged in the centre of the galleries.

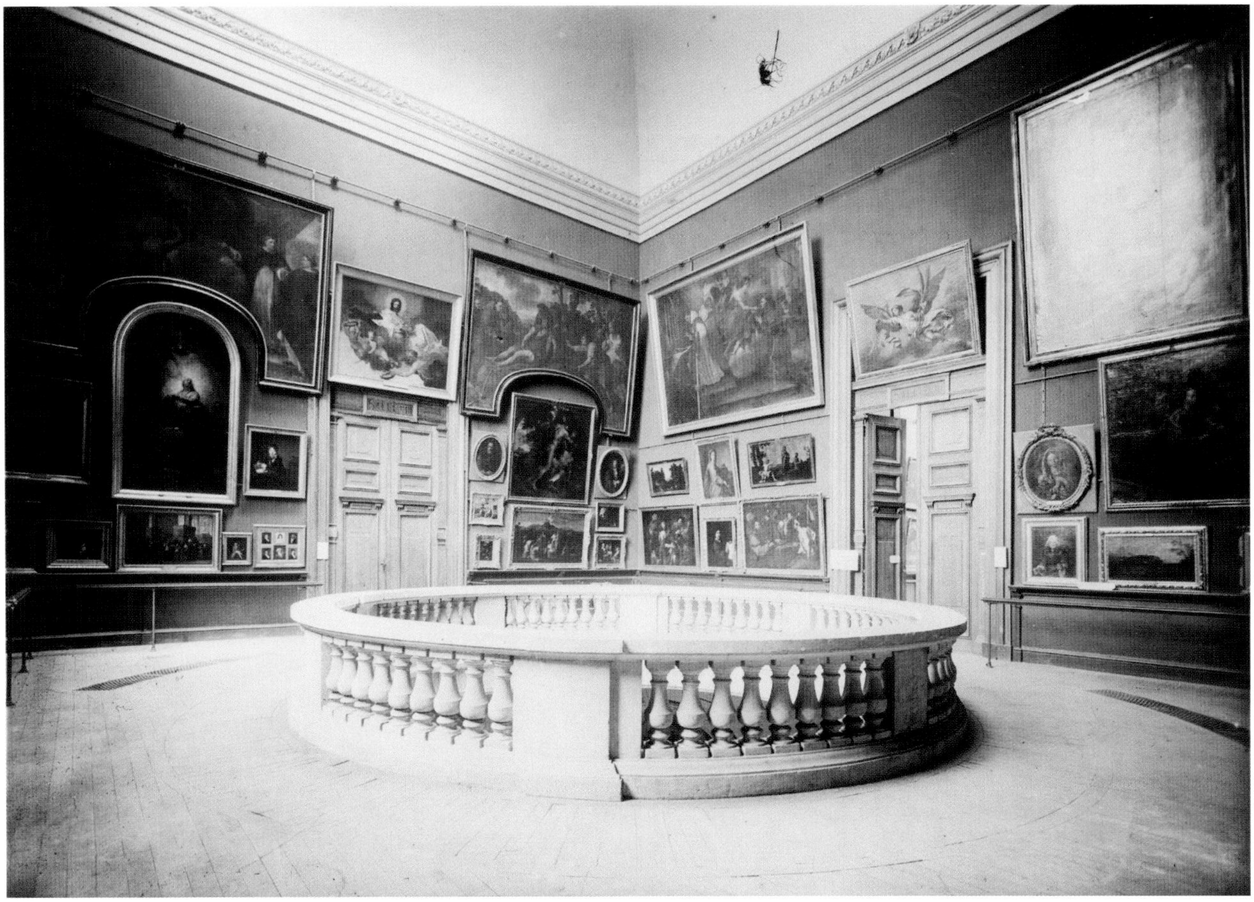

9. View of the French paintingrooms (17th–18th centuries) after World War I

Palais des Beaux-Arts, Cabinet des dessins

Despite its size, the Palais des Beaux-Arts cannot claim to give a complete picture of a culture or an artistic milieu, though its Flemish and Dutch collections are not far from achieving this dream. These riches are most often the product of the happenstance of confiscation. The signs of the subjectivity of taste shown by gifts and bequests are tempered only through purchases. The arbitrary and violent aspect of cession and confiscation haunts the gallery walls like a ghost, over and beyond the new harmonies created by the hanging. Between temporary projections and the quest for permanence, the installation design allows the invention of history through fragments and the suggestion of hypotheses, rather than certainties. To mitigate the discontinuities that occur when a whole cannot be reconstituted, the display is designed to compare, set in perspective and construct a discreet yet impressive theatre that, far from letting itself be overwhelmed by the decor, makes the paintings speak like actors whose lines grow richer in dialogue. AT

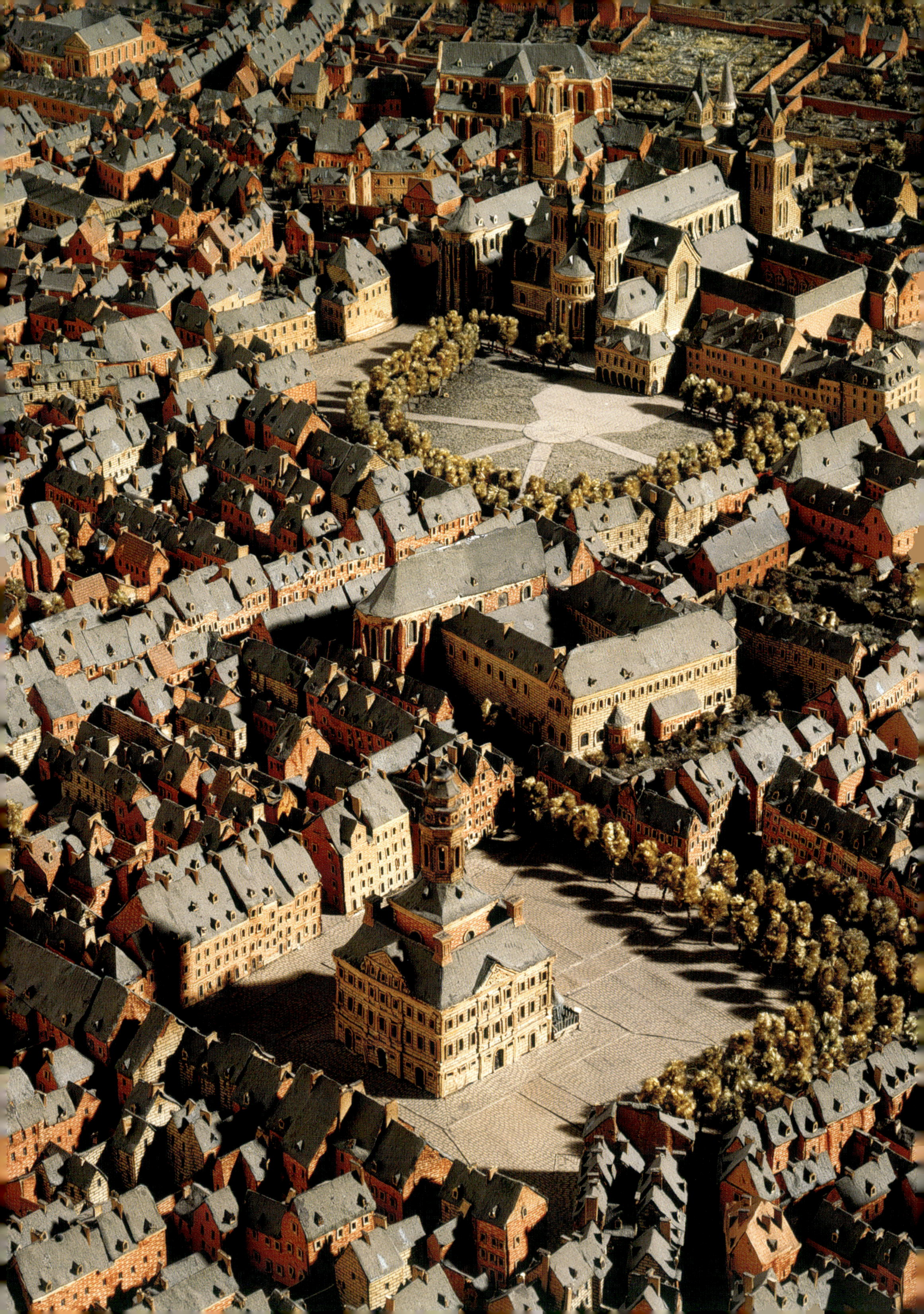

The Scale Models of the Former French Netherlands, Seventeenth–Nineteenth Centuries

Calais, Lille, Namur, Maastricht, Tournai: the basement of the Palais des Beaux-Arts takes the visitor back in time to discover the old cities of the French Netherlands. Fifteen models executed between the late 17th century and the 19th century represent the fortresses built and bitterly disputed by France, the Spanish Netherlands, Austria and the Dutch Republic during the European conflicts of the 17th and 18th centuries. They attest to the golden age of siege warfare and bastioned fortifications, a means of defence implemented in the 16th century throughout Europe to resist artillery power.

In 1668, Louis XIV's Minister of War, Louvois, had scale models made so that from Paris he could follow the work of fortification in progress in the strongholds newly conquered in the Spanish Netherlands. These simple, summarily executed tools for showing the state of the projects' development quickly became prestigious objects glorifying the king's territorial and military might. In the 1680s, their execution became extremely detailed, as shown by the relief models exhibited.

Masterpieces of Miniaturization

The military engineers in charge of building the relief plans of the king's fortified towns sought the materials most suitable for a realistic treatment of the campaigns and architecture. At the same time, they adopted a scale of 1 *pied* to 100 *toises* (1:600), deemed the most apt for legibly representing the detail of the cities and fortifications, as well as the surrounding territory within the firing range of the assailants' artillery. The relief models' status as art objects increased when, in 1700, Louis XIV decided to install the collection in the Bord-de-l'Eau Gallery at the Louvre.

The care lavished on the construction of the relief models was made possible first through the specialization of several men in charge of their realization, then by the creation of specialized workshops. The models were built on site, in the city represented. When finished, they were crated and taken to Paris for presentation to the king. In 1743, two workshops were established, one in Béthune, the other in Lille, for the sole purpose of building models. In 1756, they were merged into a single workshop at the Louvre, where the collection was housed. This workshop was transferred to Les Invalides along with the collection in 1777.

The first step in creating a relief model was to sketch plans and elevations of the entire city to be represented, with the surrounding countryside. Everything was carefully noted, with colour codes for rendering the materials. An overall plan of the site cut in several pieces, a kind of 'working drawing', served as a pattern for creating tables for each relief model. The models, which are quite large, are composed of various wooden tables assembled like a giant jigsaw puzzle. The tabletops are shaped so as to re-create the curves of the relief. The texture of the ground's surface is obtained by pulverizing fine sand

10. Scale model of Maastricht (1750): City Hall on the market square, and the Vrijthof with the episcopal palace complex

over a layer of glue. Finely cut dyed-silk flocking represents fields, prairies and green spaces. Fine silk chenille wrapped around brass wire is used for trees. Water is represented in oil paint. The buildings are composed of small blocks of wood covered with paper printed or painted to imitate the texture of the building materials. The openings are cut with a punch.

Scale models were valued cartographic tools because, well in advance of the aerial view available from hot-air balloons and aircrafts, they provided an overall measurable view of a fortified city in one's territory. The collection's great success continued through the reign of Louis XV, was renewed under Napoleon I and lasted until 1879. Between 1668 and 1870, 260 relief plans of 150 sites were made – technical tools and works of art in the service of the apparatus of the state for the implementation and study of the territory's defences.

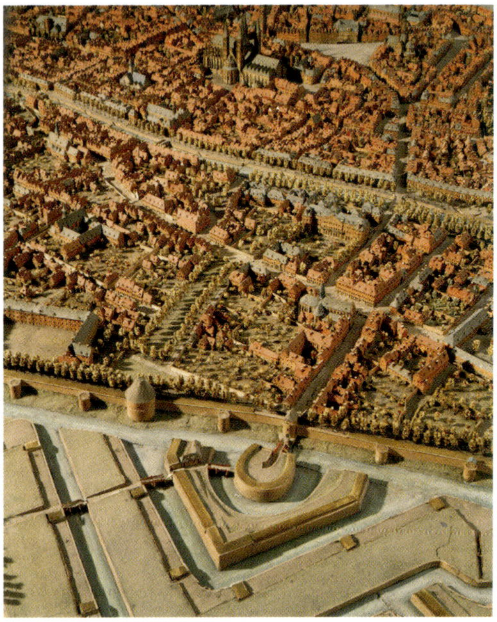

11. Scale model of Tournai (1701): the ramparts, the ravelin of the castle gate and the great tower of Henry VIII. The cathedral is in the background

Outstanding Tools for Studying the History of the Fortified Cities

Today, there are a hundred relief models at the Musée des plans-reliefs (Hôtel national des Invalides, Paris). The fifteen scale models at Lille's Palais des Beaux-Arts were deposited in accordance with an agreement made on 2 October 1987. Having lost its military vocation, this collection of minutely detailed masterpieces of miniaturization, classified as a historic monument in 1927, became an outstanding tool for studying a past that has in large part disappeared or been greatly altered.

Because of the collection's original vocation, the relief models provide a wealth of information on the history of fortifications from the Middle Ages to the 18th century. The trace of the old cities' medieval ramparts, modernized by the addition of bastioned fortifications beginning in the 16th century and above all in the 17th, is particularly visible on the relief models of Bergues,
10 Tournai and Maastricht. Generally, the models allow the study of the trace of the fortifications and their impact on the surrounding area. The omnipresence of water on all the scale models exhibited cannot escape the visitor's attention. This major feature of the defensive principles implemented in this region of the former French Netherlands derives from Dutch know-how. In these flat expanses, extensively irrigated by bodies of water or bordering the sea, 16th-century military engineers learned how to channel water in order to strengthen
12 the defensive fortifications by flooding the ditches, as well as in the cities' outskirts, to prevent or slow the advance of the enemy.

The relief models are also an exceptional documentary source of urban history. In addition to the layout of the streets and the nature of land allotment, they reveal the burgeoning of religious buildings in the cities under the *ancien régime* and the importance of gardens in the urban fabric. These models are also rich in information on the nature of the building materials used for houses and represent in a fairly precise manner the architectural details of large private houses and religious and civic buildings, many of which have been destroyed or considerably reworked. On some of the relief models, like
11 the one of Tournai, the main religious buildings were executed to a more detailed scale: these sumptuously decorated constructions stand out, expressing all the cities' richness.

The models' degree of detail also provides a wealth of information on the countryside under the *ancien régime*. Farming practices, land division, industrial equipment (canals, mills, quarries, lime kilns and so forth) and the location of abbeys and châteaux are clearly distinguishable.

Visitors familiar with old maps will enjoy observing how the scale models borrow codes of representation from two-dimensional maps, for example a cartouche with the city's name, or a compass indicating the cardinal points.

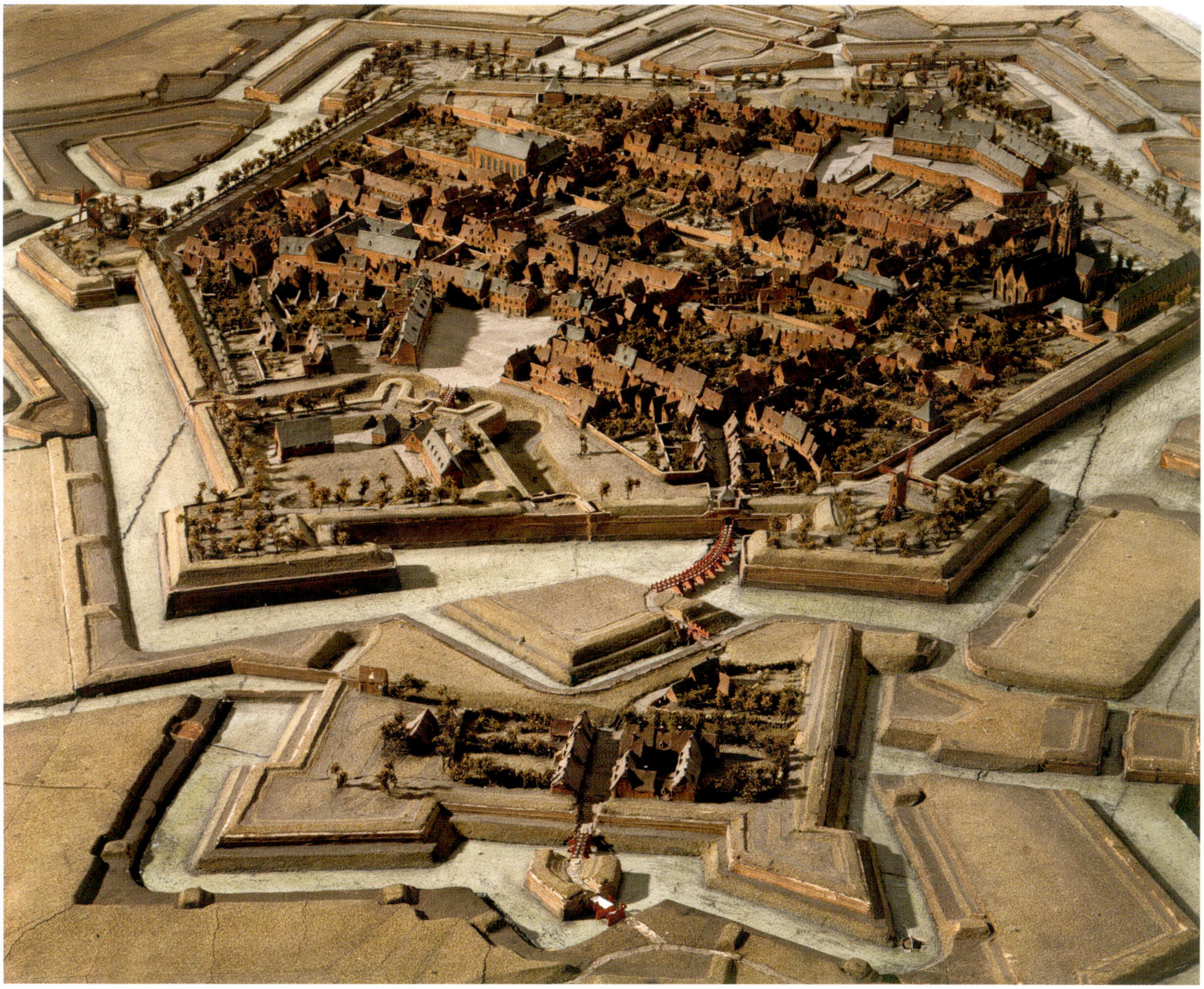

12. Scale model of Gravelines (c. 1750–75): view from the south, with defensive flooding

Village names were given on small brass plaques, now blank on the Lille model, but still visible on the model of Oudenaarde – a fine example of the collection's value, with its blue and gold frame and rococo cartouche, characteristic of the Louis XV style. IW

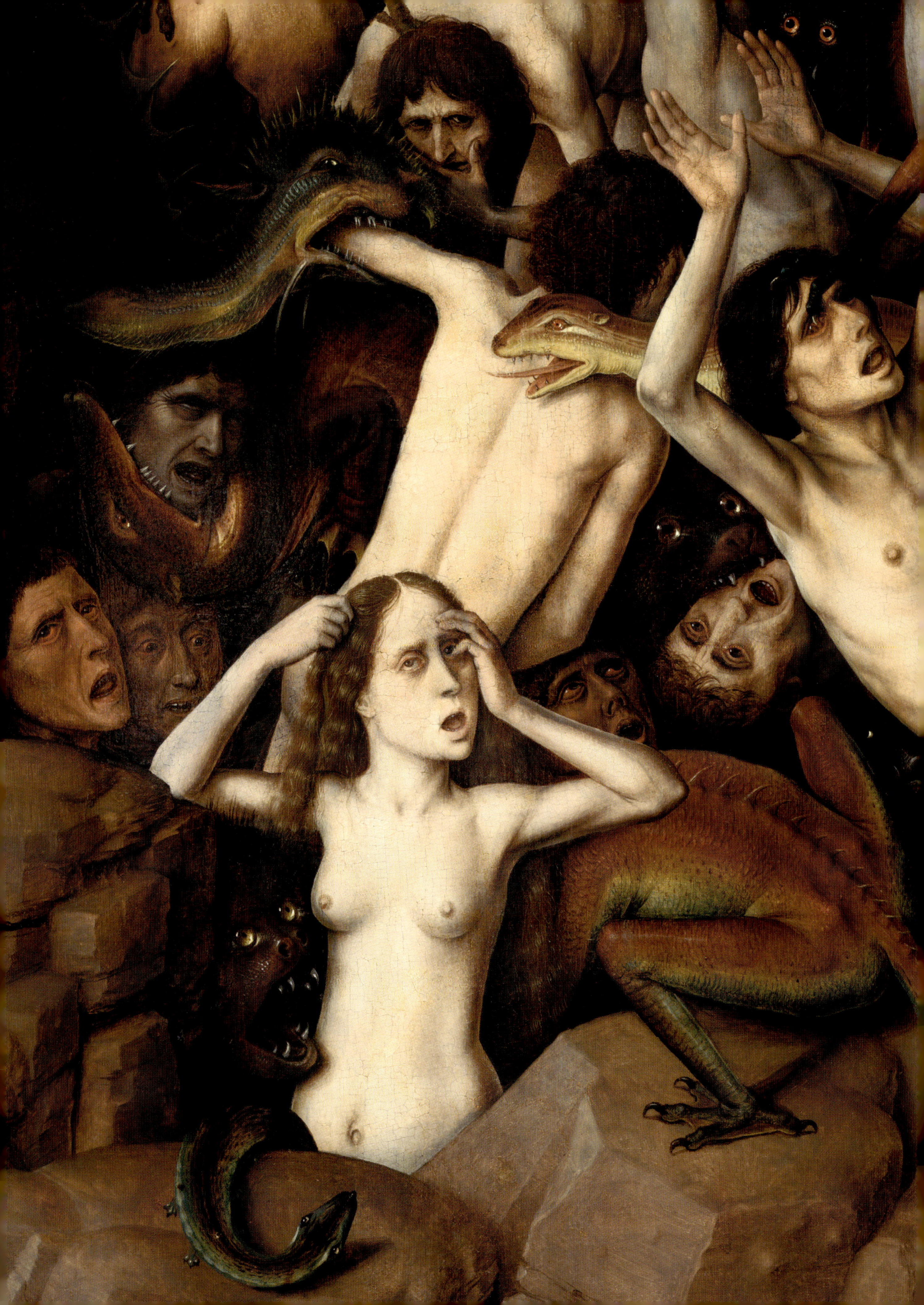

From Antiquity to the Renaissance

Nothing can more accurately express the spirit of the collections than the manner in which they were amassed. The museum's Antiquities, Medieval and Renaissance Departments date back to 1824. At that time, the 'museum of archaeology and numismatics' in the old Recollects monastery of Lille housed the medieval sculpture, coins and medals, art objects and ceramics that the Société des Sciences et de l'Agriculture et des Arts had begun acquiring in 1802 and ceded to the city in 1865. This first museum, which reflected the tastes of the refined and at times erudite collectors, held the collections that academic thought excluded from the realm of the fine arts. By definition, it encompassed everything that predated the 17th century, with the exception of some paintings, as well as all *objets d'art*, even those postdating the 17th century.

When this archaeology museum was installed in new premises in the city hall in 1860, complementing the painting gallery that had been set up there in 1848, there were more than four thousand Greek, Roman, medieval and modern objects. The first state consignment of antiquities was added to these in 1863. Under the direction of the eminent Edouard Reynart, at the museum's head from 1841 to 1879, the growth of the collections was exceptional. He secured the Gentil donation in 1868, which brought the museum some of its most outstanding 15th-century sculptures and many wood-carvings.

In 1881, the archaeology museum was installed in a wing of the restored Palais Rihour that had formerly been the oratory of the Duchess of Burgundy. A lapidary museum was also set up in the guardroom of the palace of the Dukes of Burgundy. Large donations were made – Benvignat, Jules de Vicq (1881) and Ozenfant (1894), among others – and the museum's organization and cohesiveness posed a growing problem. It was not until 1912 that inventories were systematically carried out in retrospect, under the watchful eye of Emile Théodore, who was the museum's general curator from 1913 to 1937. The antique, medieval and Renaissance works were distributed in three inventories: an inventory of antiquities; an archaeological inventory that included sculpture, art objects and all objects of different materials and techniques, regardless of date; and a lapidary inventory, now lost but whose existence may be surmised from surviving catalogue entries that have come down to us.

The archaeology galleries closed in 1945 and were reopened in 1954 as a 'gallery of art objects' from the 12th century to the early 19th century. Many more pieces of a historical or documentary nature were presented than is the case today.

The chronological arrangement designed for the museum's renovation in 1997 illustrates 'the main movements in art'. It falls within the tradition of the encyclopaedic museum, while avoiding the academic thinking that, from the 17th to the 19th century, granted pride of place to painting and accorded art a status quite distinct from craft. In the Middle Ages, metalwork, ivory sculpture and illuminated manuscripts were major forms of artistic expression, of a

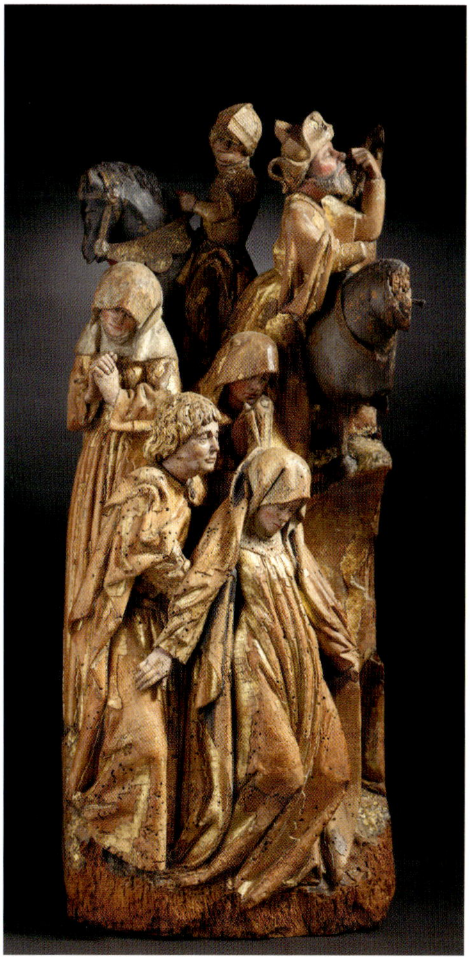

14. Brussels?, c. 1460
The Swooning of the Virgin. Walnut, polychromy, 56.5 x 23 x 12 cm
Gentil donation, 1868. Inv. A. 478

13. Dirk Bouts, c. 1420–1475
The Fall of the Damned, c. 1470.
Detail of ill. 32

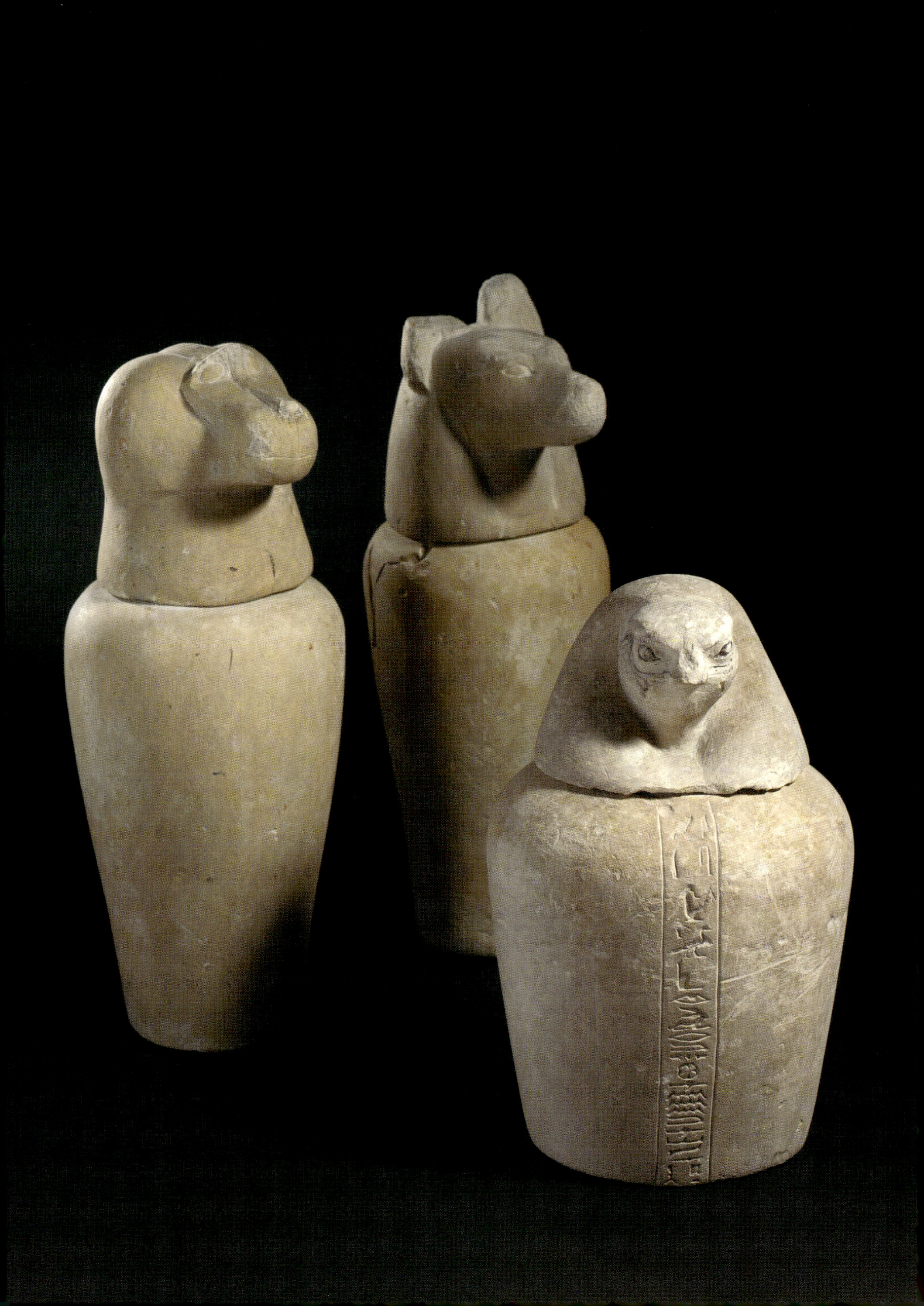

rank equal to sculpture and painting. Furthermore, the painters and sculptors of this period were still members of craft corporations.

Antiquities

The museum's Egyptian collection, which includes steles, amulets, canopic jars, ceramics, shawabtis, bronzes, statuettes, a cat sarcophagus, mummies and mummy bandages, entered the museum through private donations (Gentil, Rigaux, Jouguet), purchases and, above all, the state consignments of 1907 and 1908. As in many provincial museums, a portion of the objects sent by the state was from the excavations supervised by Albert Gayet from 1896 to 1910 at the Middle Egypt site of Antinoopolis. This is the case with four mummies from the Christian era (4th–8th century). The costumes they are still dressed in are exceptional. The most remarkable grave goods consist of a child's sarcophagus containing a mummy, fragments of a painted shroud, bandages from the Ptolemaic and Roman periods, and a fine painted sarcophagus of a cat. There is also a limestone canopic jar that belonged to the priest Nesy- *15*
Ptah, *Unro* in Letopolis (Ausim), dating from the Late Period (664–332 BC).

The collection of classical archaeology does not differ substantially from those found in other provincial museums, being made up essentially of ceramics from the dispersal of the Campana collection and other private collections, in large part deposited by the state in 1863 and 1895. Ownership of the collection was transferred to the city of Lille in 2005, the year it was published

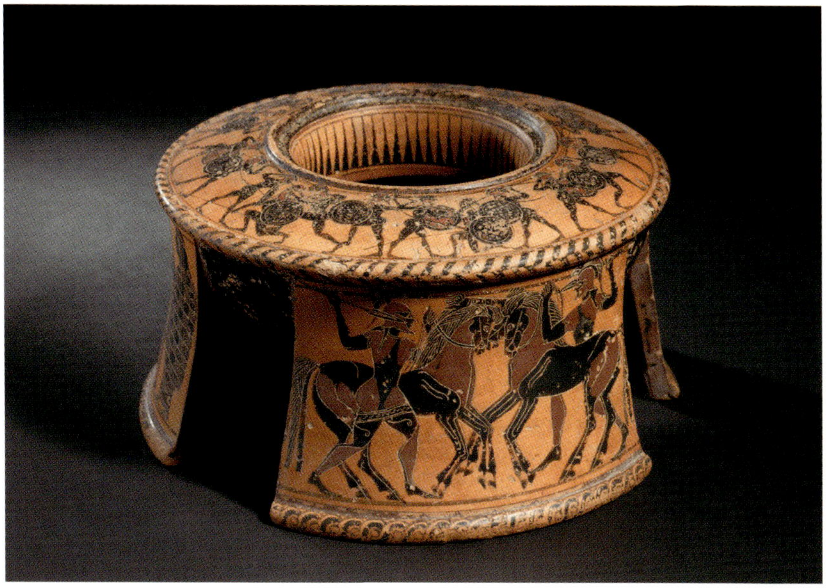

16. Painter C, Athens, *c.* 580–570 BC
Tripod vessel. 12 x 22 cm
Ant. 763

in the *Corpus vasorum antiquorum*. Some Punic items – steles, bronzes and urns from various excavations – round out the view of the Mediterranean basin under the Roman Empire. A skyphos, a drinking vessel used at men's banquets, was decorated by the Lewis Painter (Athens, *c.* 460/450 BC) in the red-figure technique. The outlines left in reserve in the clay before firing, the details of which have been heightened with the paintbrush, stand out against a black glazed background. The best-preserved face depicts the god Eros, nude and winged. Noteworthy among the collection's black-figure ceramic ware is a tripod vessel, probably for holding perfume, whose lid is missing. *16*
It is attributed to Painter C, active in Athens about 580–570 BC. The Judgement of Paris is represented on one side. The other sides depict heroes in hand-to-hand combat.

15. Egypt, 664–332 BC
Canopic jars of the priest Nesy-Ptah.
Painted limestone, 22 x 13 cm
Ant. 2796

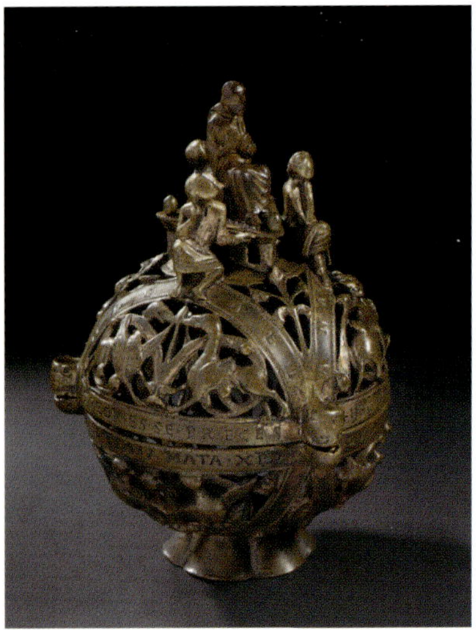

17. Meuse Valley, *c.* 1160
Censor with Hebrews in the Furnace.
Chased and gilded cast brass,
16 x 10.4 cm
Benvignat donation, after 1874. Inv. A. 82

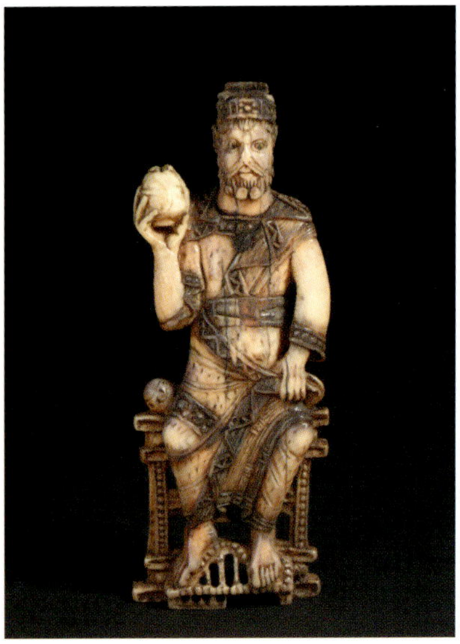

18. Saint-Omer, *c.* 1100
Old Man of the Apocalypse.
Walrus tusk and glass beads,
12 x 4.6 x 0.15 cm
Acquired 1885. Inv. A. 94

19. Lille region?, *c.* 1150
Torso of Christ. Limestone, traces of polychromy, 50 x 34 x 27 cm
Leroy purchase, 1881. Inv. LAP. 14

Romanesque Art from the North of France and the Meuse Region

The monuments of northern France were rebuilt many times between the late Middle Ages and the end of World War I, making the oldest examples of architecture all the more valuable. Urban development in Flanders and Artois (then in the kingdom of France) and in Hainaut (under the rule of the Holy Roman Empire) made them the richest regions in Europe.

The museum has several early-medieval frieze fragments with plant and animal decorations that are among the rare surviving elements of the Romanesque cathedral of Cambrai, the nave having been rebuilt in 1148. A
19 limestone *Torso of Christ* that entered the collection thanks to Charles Leroy, the architect in charge of many 19th-century projects in the Lille area, is an invaluable example of the region's statuary about 1150. This fragment would have been part of a group representing the Deposition, a subject rarely treated in 12th-century monumental sculpture. It is complemented by two other fragments, one of them a *Bust of Joseph of Arimathea* (?), with what most probably represents the long, thin hand of Christ resting on the figure's shoulder. The polychrome sculpture of a *Head of a Woman* dating from the last third of the 12th century is also remarkable in the regularity of the fine, almost abstract folds of the veil and its solemn frontality, attenuated by the harmony of the volumes.

Firm and solid stylization that moves away from Byzantine art is common to all the arts in the Romanesque period, including ivory. A binder plaque representing the Deisis – St John and the Virgin to either side of Christ on the Cross, interceding for humanity – offers a fine example of the revival of ivory production after the Byzantine iconoclastic crisis in the late 10th cen-
18 tury. *The Old Man of the Apocalypse* carved in walrus tusk about 1100 – judging from analogies with manuscript illumination – is one of the most beautiful Romanesque ivories. The old man, crowned and holding a perfume flask, was probably applied to a reliquary casket along with figurines of twenty-four other old men, four of which have survived and are now at the Metropolitan Museum, New York; the British Library, London; and the Hôtel Sandelin museum in Saint-Omer, a city that is noteworthy for the impressive collegiate Church of Saint-Bertin (now the cathedral), where the figurines seem to have come from.

If architecture and its sculptural ornamentation dominated the aesthetics of the time, metalwork also held a front-rank position. The chased and
17 gilded cast-brass *Censor with Hebrews in the Furnace*, datable to about 1160, is considered one of the finest creations of Mosan *dinanderie* (brassware) from this period. The hemispheres are composed of animals skilfully interlaced among foliage. The choice of subject is unusual for a censor: three young Hebrews condemned to perish in the flames for having refused to worship an idol are saved by an angel in their midst. The martyrs' worship of God is thus combined symbolically with the smoking incense, which bears praise heavenward. The museum also has one of the earliest examples of Mosan enamelware, a copper champlevé plaque representing Gideon and the Fleece. Gideon, the fifth judge of Israel (Judges 6), armed like a 12th-century knight, contemplates the dew falling from the hand of God onto the patch of fleece, a prefiguration of the virginity of Mary. A small champlevé plaque from Limousin for a belt buckle or hook fastener is one of very few secular enamels from the late 12th century.

21 A magnificent reliquary cross, from the church of Wasnes-au-Bac near Valenciennes, in silver gilt and niello on a core of walnut, attests to the evolution of more and more sophisticated techniques about 1210. It reflects the

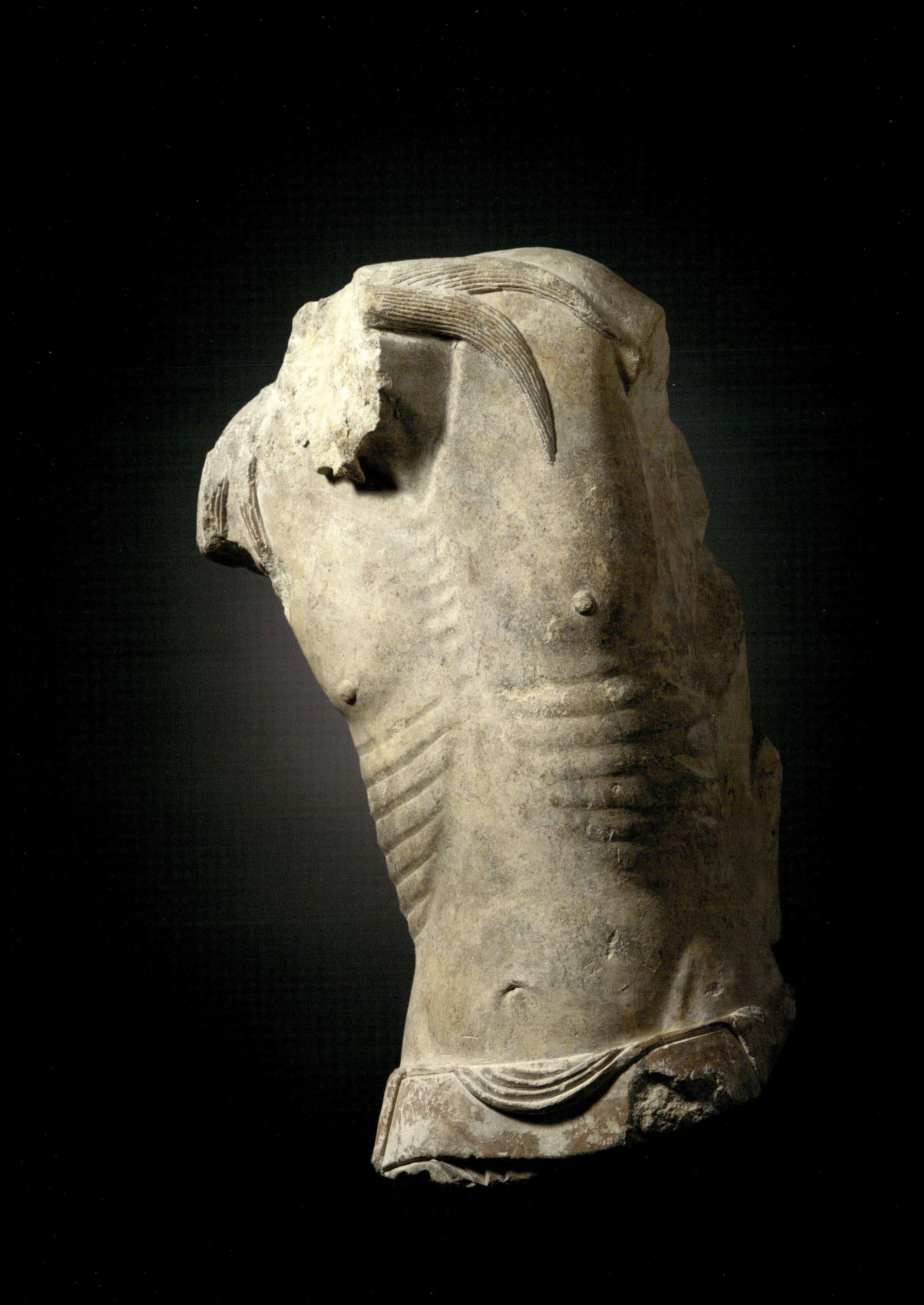

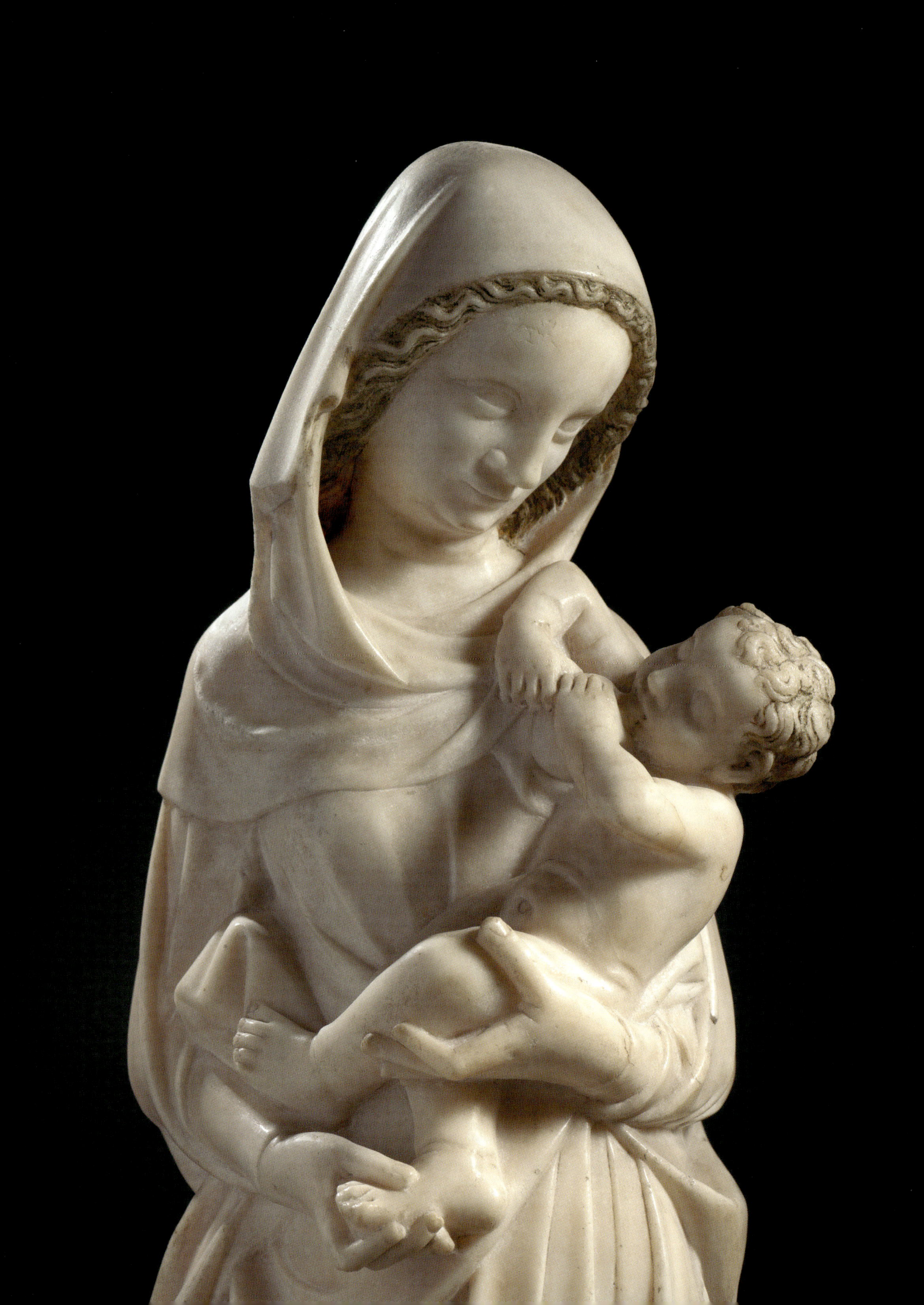

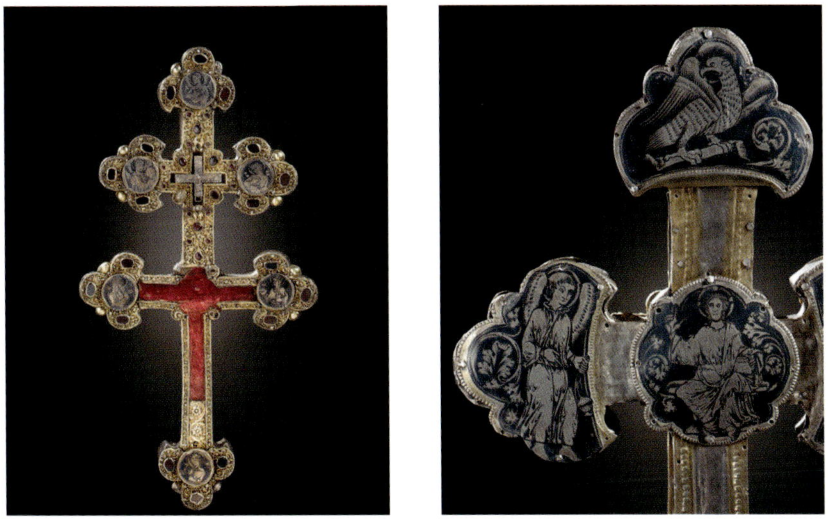

21. Valenciennes region, church of Wasne-au-Bac, *c.* 1210
Reliquary cross. Walnut core, silver gilt, silver niello, 40 x 18.5 x 2.8 cm
Purchased 1896. Inv. A. 97

brilliant era of Joan of Constantinople (1200–1244), countess of Flanders and Hainaut. Formerly attached to a pole, the cross with double crossbeam held in its upper part a relic of the True Cross brought back from the Crusades in the Holy Land, after the sack of Constantinople in 1204. On the obverse, the figures of St John and the Virgin, the Church and the Synagogue are inscribed in extremely beautiful medallions in silver niello.

Gothic Sculpture and the Precious Arts in Thirteenth- and Forteenth-Century France

The Gothic style that characterizes the architecture born at the Abbey of Saint-Denis, near Paris, applies to all the forms of the architectural vocabulary and to the tendency for graceful naturalism of this new art movement in the Île-de-France. The expressions are more human, often smiling, and the volumes of the figures are rendered with sensitivity.

The large wooden statue of *St Amand*, from the 1270s, is representative of the slender style fashionable during the reign of St Louis. It represents the bishop of Maastricht, who brought Christianity to Flanders and the North of France in the 7th century, treading the symbol of evil underfoot. Several statues of the Virgin slouching at the hips, holding the Child, allow one to admire the new sensitivity to volumes, such as the small boxwood statue produced by an excellent Paris workshop about 1280.

In the 14th century, the development of patronage by the great royal and princely courts, like that of Charles V, attracted artists. At the close of the century, the princes' desire to outdo one another led to a precious and ornate trend, known as the International Gothic style, that played on shimmering colours. Despite political rivalries that cast the king's power in doubt, about 1400 under Charles VI, the precious arts underwent a full expansion.
The *Virgin Suckling the Child* by the Master of the Mosan Madonnas, active *20*
about 1330–50, is carved in marble and heightened with gilt in the manner of ivory carvings from the same period. The folds of the robe, deep toward the bottom and tighter at the bodice, the Virgin's maternal gesture, her lost and melancholy look, and the very theme of nursing make of this statue a perfectly proportioned work and a milestone of Marian iconography. From about 1340, the *Diptych of the Life of Christ and the Virgin*, created by an Île-de-France workshop, also presents gold highlights that emphasize the delicateness of the sculpture, while there is a greater shimmering effect in the polychromy of the fine freestanding *Virgin*, still flanked by two panels decorated with scenes

20. Master of the Mosan Madonnas, act. Meuse Valley *c.* 1330–50
Virgin Suckling the Child. Marble, traces of gilding, 65.5 x 21.5 x 13.5 cm
Planquart collection, Mr Houret purchase, 1888. Inv. A. 0

from the Childhood of Christ, that was created in France or Italy in the middle of the century. The silver reliquary dedicated to the goldsmith Jean Nicolas by Marie de France on the Feast of the Assumption in 1414 is another of the collection's sophisticated smaller pieces.

The Quattrocento

In 15th-century Italy, art was an instrument of prestige for the nobility and reflected profound changes in society, the perception of the world and the
22 triumph of humanism. The marble relief representing *The Banquet of Herod* by Donatello marks a milestone in art history. Acquired in 1834 through the bequest of the artist Jean-Baptiste Wicar, a connoisseur of Italian art, it had been owned by Lorenzo de' Medici, who died in 1492. Using the technique of *rilievo schiacciato* (a finely graded low relief), which he invented, the sculptor

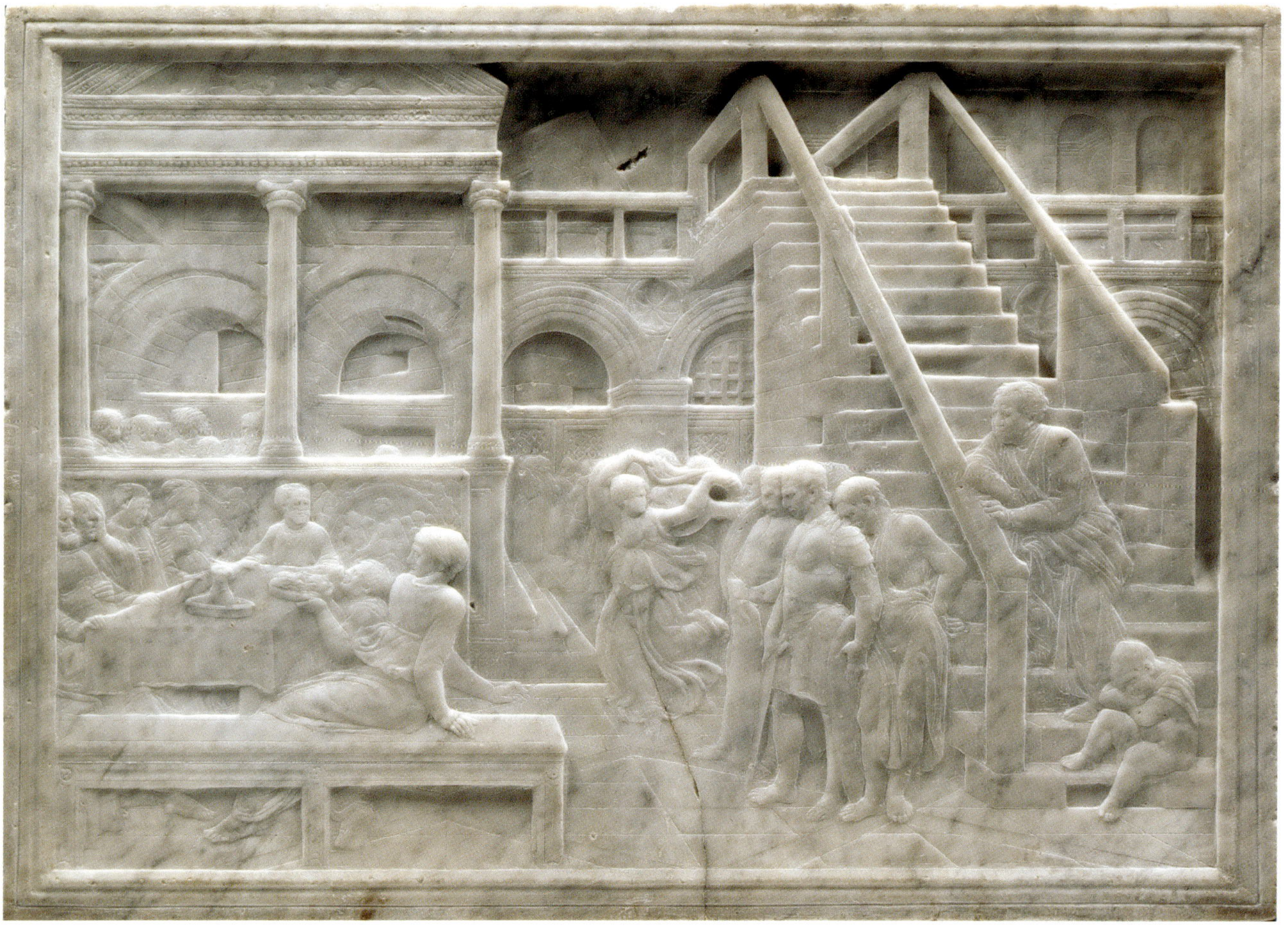

22. Donatello (Donato di Niccolo di Betto Bardi) *c.* 1386–1466
The Banquet of Herod, *c.* 1435.
Marble, 50 x 71 cm
Wicar bequest, 1834. Inv. Pl. 1912

implemented the principles of perspective set out in Leon Battista Alberti's treatise of 1435. Alberti was the first to take the art of Antiquity as a basic reference, in particular for architecture. In his relief, Donatello skilfully constructs the narrative in several architectural planes, from Salome's dance in the centre and background to the tragic denouement: the presentation of the head of John the Baptist in the middle distance and, in the foreground, the pained realization of Salome, represented a second time, who turns away from the scene.

It was also in Florence, in the first decades of the 15th century, that a new rendering of light, volume and space developed in painting, although panel painting still remained under the influence of the International Gothic style.

23. Bastiano Mainardi *c.* 1460–1513
Virgin of the Briar Roses, *c.* 1485. Oil on panel, 60 x 34.5 cm (unframed)
Salomon purchase, 1878. Inv. P. 779

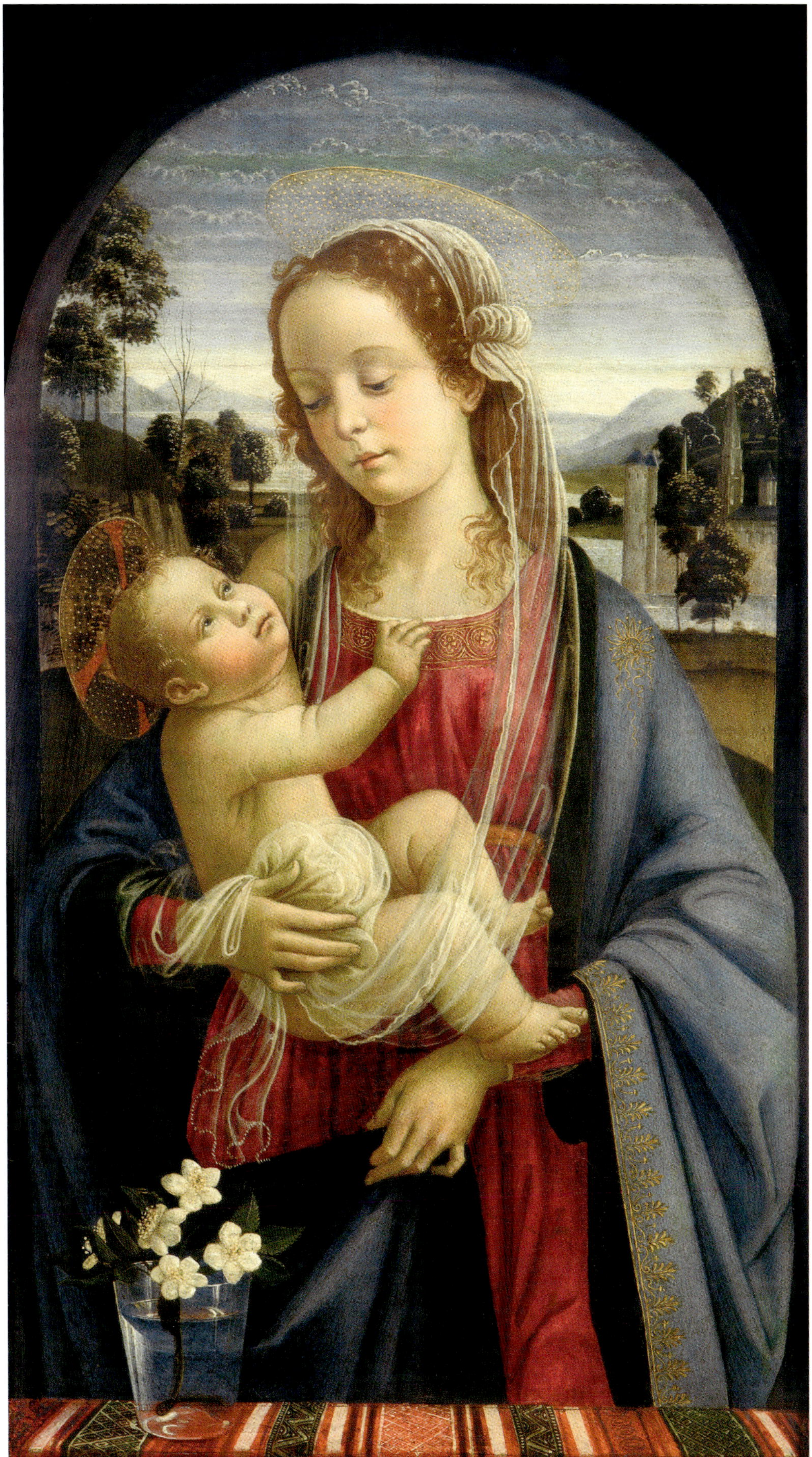

The Florentine painter Ambrogio di Baldese (?1352–1429) introduced iconographic innovations in *The Virgin and Child in Glory with St John the Baptist and St Peter, Two Angels and God the Father Blessing*, such as the perspective effect of the floor tiles and the figure of God, bending down from the sky opened by three cherubs. The *Christ on the Cross and the Virgin and Child Surrounded by Saints*, executed in the circle of Cristoforo Moretti (1486–1530) in Cremona, with a traditional iconography inspired by the apocryphal story from the *Golden Legend* of Jacobus de Voragine, still adheres to an ornate style.

Some Florentine painters of the second half of the 15th century were influenced by Botticelli (1445–1510), who derived an idealized graphic schema of the Virgin and Child based on realistic observation of anatomy. The Master of the Fiesole Epiphany, in the *Mystic Marriage of St Catherine, with St John the Baptist, St Benedict and St Bartholomew*, is not indifferent to the lessons of the great master, nor is Bartolommeo di Giovanni, in his painting of the Virgin and Child shown at half length and in three-quarters view beneath an arch. The sensitive modelling, calm regularity of the drapery and softness of the lighting suffuse the painting with a gentle, collected atmosphere. The *Mary Magdalene* attributed to the same painter draws upon the expressive contrast between the volumetric figure and the sober background. Sebastiano Mainar-
23 di's *Virgin of the Briar Roses*, painted about 1485, formerly in the gallery of the Directors of the Mint in Florence, falls within the subtle intellectual tradition of Florentine art but also evinces a sensitivity to Flemish painting, in its feeling for detail in the flowers and the carpet in the foreground and in its panoramic landscape, which is related to the art of Hugo van der Goes (*c.* 1435–1482). Van der Goes, who had demonstrated the possibilities of oil painting, a Flemish invention, was known in Italy for the famous triptych commissioned by the great Portinari family of bankers, who were the Medicis' agents in Bruges.

In contrast, the *Virgin and Child with St John* painted by Antoniazzo Romano in Rome about 1500 has an abstract gilt background, from which the figures seem to stand out three-dimensionally. The *St Sebastian* by Francesco, active in the Marches between 1460 and 1500, shows a taste for precision inherited from his father, Gentile da Fabriano, while the dark background and tight framing introduce a new dramatic intensity. The composition of the figures and their interaction would become the object of much attention on the part of the great masters of the following generation, for example Raphael (1483–1520).

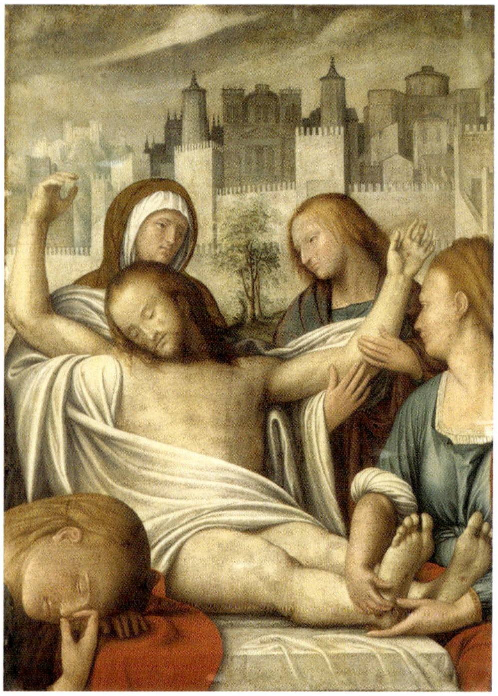

24. Bramantino (Bartolomeo Guardi)
act. Milan *c.* 1465–1530
Lamentation, *c.* 1520. Tempera on canvas, 100 x 80.5 cm (unframed)
Gift of Mlles Cottini, 1879

The Cinquecento

The 16th-century *Christ in the Tomb* by Girolamo Marchesi (*c.* 1480–about 1550), formerly the top of an altarpiece, conveys an almost sculptural sense of volume that betrays the influence of Tuscan art and the assimilation of the influence of Raphael. The theme of the Lamentation provides an oppor-
24 tunity for daring compositions. About 1520, Bramantino executed a replica in tempera on canvas, meant to be easily transported, of an original panel painting of the subject (Bucharest Museum). Although pushed dramatically into the foreground, the composition is suffused with a metaphysical depth. The
25 *Lamentation* by Luca Penni, from the Church of the Holy Sepulchre in Paris, evokes Florentine Mannerism and the art of Primaticcio in the rich palette and the tight framing, which has been accentuated by the later cropping of the painting's sides and top. It is close to a *Deposition* by the same artist (Amiens Cathedral).

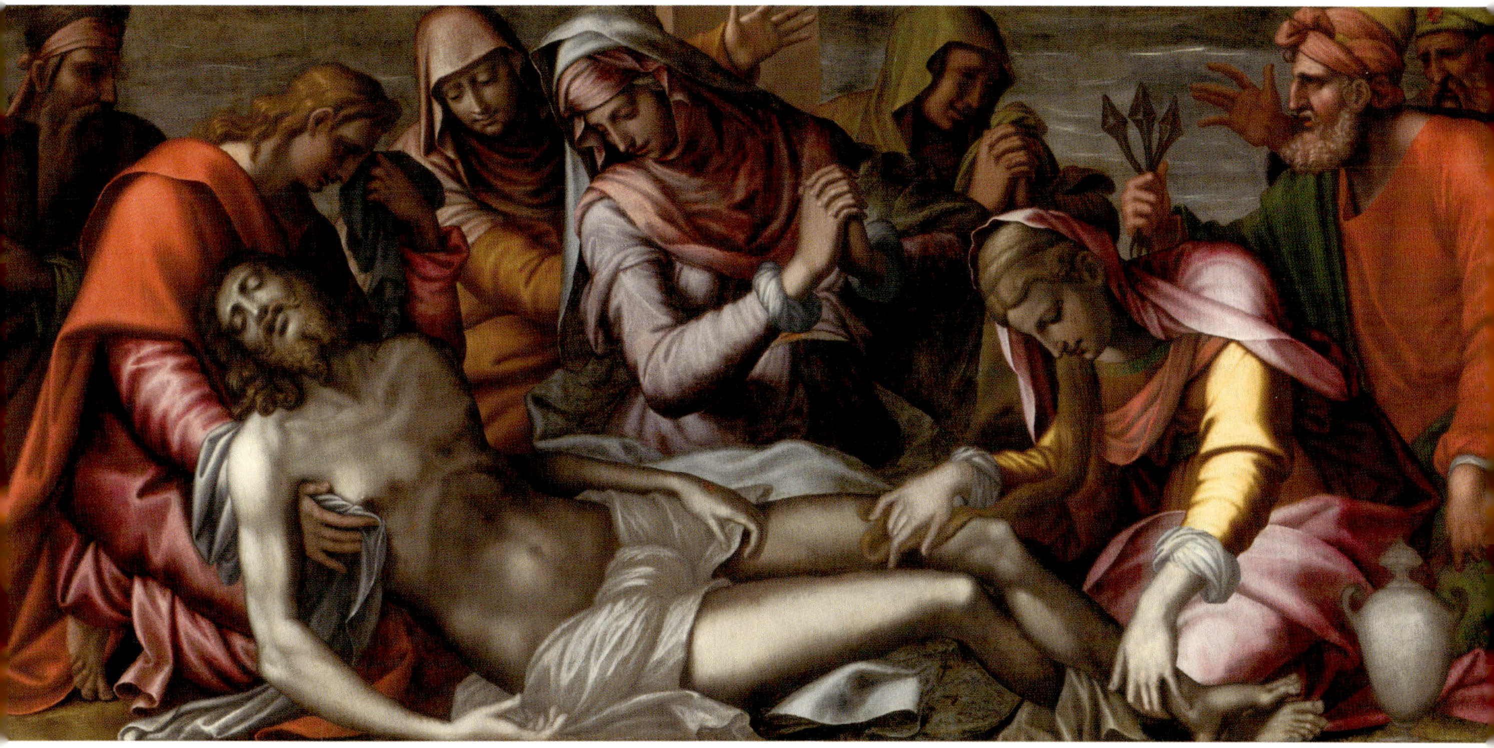

25. Luca Penni *c.* 1500–1556
Lamentation. Oil on panel,
59 x 140 cm

Church of the Holy Sepulchre, Paris, state consignment, 1801. Inv. P. 770

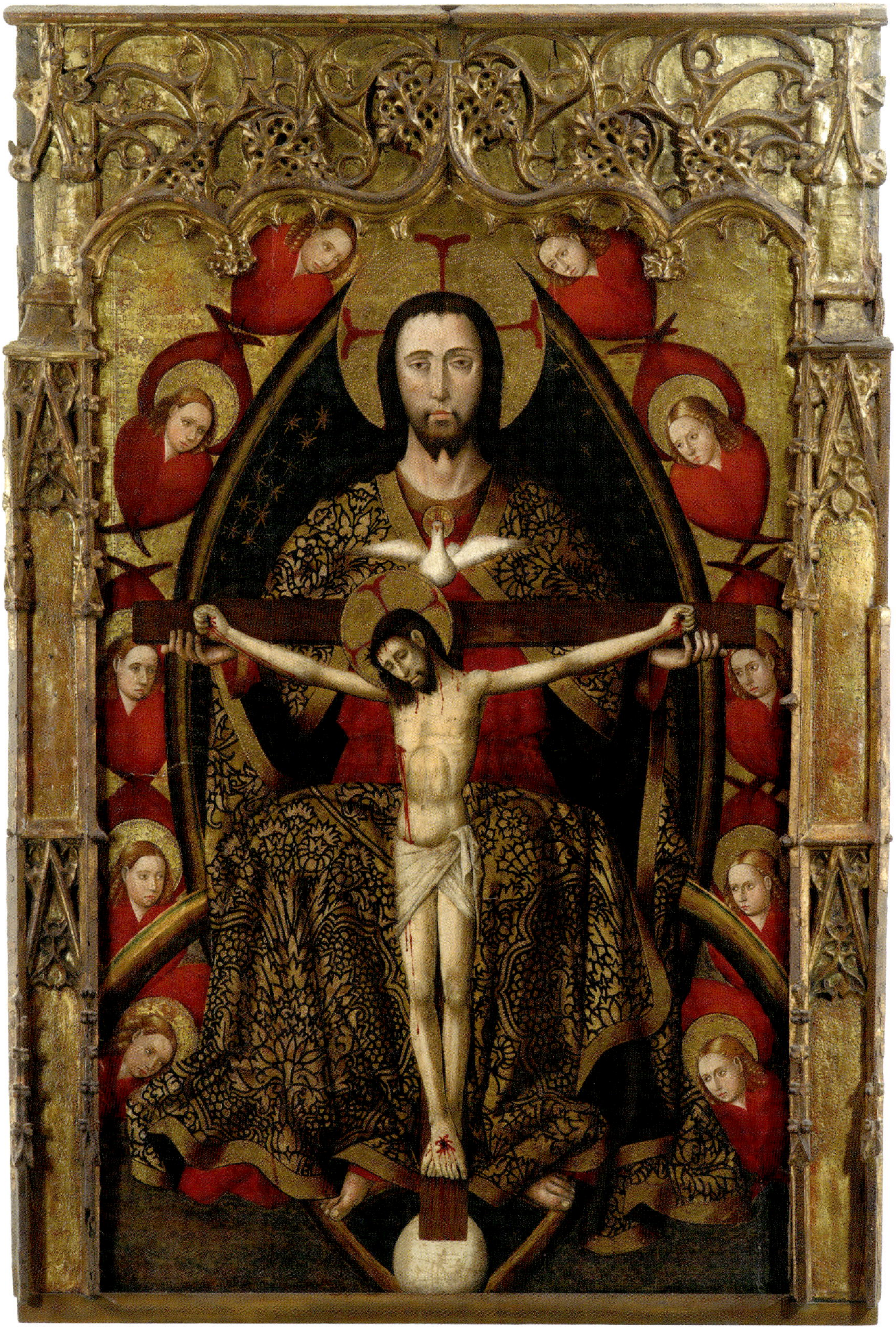

26. Jacomart (Jaime Baço), *c.* 1413–1461
Trinity. Oil on panel, 160 x 110 cm
Lampe purchase, June 1901. Inv. P. 1446

Fourteenth- and Fifteenth-Century Catalan Painting

Lively art centres developed in Spain. In the early 14th century, they looked to Italian art; in the 15th, they turned toward Flemish art. The panels of *St Paul, St Matthew* and *St Jude* by Ramon Destorrents, the principal painter and illuminator at the court of Catalonia and Aragon, attest to the strong influence of Florentine and Sienese art in the second half of the 14th century. Figures of other apostles belonging to the same series now in the museums of Cracow and Barcelona were originally placed on either side of a painting (now lost) representing the Virgin.

In the 15th century, chapel walls were adorned with monumental altarpieces. The *Trinity* of Jaime Baço, called Jacomart, the official painter to King 26
Alfonso V of Aragon and then of John II, was at the summit of a polyptych. It owes a great deal to imported Flemish art in the sensitive treatment of the figures painted in oil but remains faithful to solemn Byzantine severity. The 'Throne of Grace' or Trinity Pietà, an image of Salvation *par excellence*, is crossed by a rainbow, a symbol of God's alliance with the earth. The dove of the Holy Ghost links the Father and the crucified Son. There is a very similar composition at the museum in Amiens.

Late Fifteenth-Century German Sculpture and Painting

The *St George Altarpiece* is among the collection's signal works. According to graffiti inscribed on the back by worshippers, we know that for a time it was installed in the Church of Sankt Georgen an der Ahr (Southern Tyrol). It was reworked in the 16th century. The main figures – St George, the Princess of Trebizond, St Andrew and an unidentified saint – are from the workshop of the painter Simon Mareigl von Taisten, while the Christ as Man of Sorrows and the two apostles of the predella are attributed to excellent studios in Brixen (Bressanone). The rendering of drapery folds breaks sharply with the Germanic sculptural canons of the time.

In Cologne, painting gave its own interpretation to the Flemish contribution. Gilding is still very much present. In the *Glorification of the Virgin* by the 27
Master of the Lyversberg Passion, the Mother of God appears in glory on a timeless gold background, her feet resting on a crescent moon. This image of a vision refers to the Immaculate Conception, the Assumption and the Apocalypse. The Virgin's pale complexion can be likened to Stephan Lochner (*c.* 1400–1451), but the apostles are closer to Flemish art (Rogier van der Weyden and Dirk Bouts). About 1480, the *Crucifixion with a Donor* by the Master of the Life of the Virgin hung over a tomb in a church. The donor, almost certainly a canon from the Abbey of St Anthony in Cologne, is flanked by two patron saints, St Andrew and St Matthew, at the sides of the Virgin and St John. The Virgin's eyes, reddened with tears, are in accord with the taste of Germanic expression. The shading of the light in the distance is in the Flemish spirit.

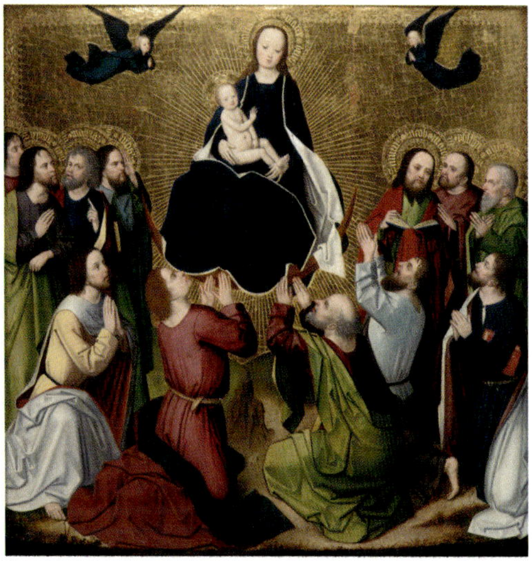

27. Master of the Lyversberg Passion, act. Cologne *c.* 1460–80
The Glorification of the Virgin, *c.* 1470. Oil on panel, 78.5 x 78 cm
Antoine Brasseur donation, 1880. Inv. P. 743

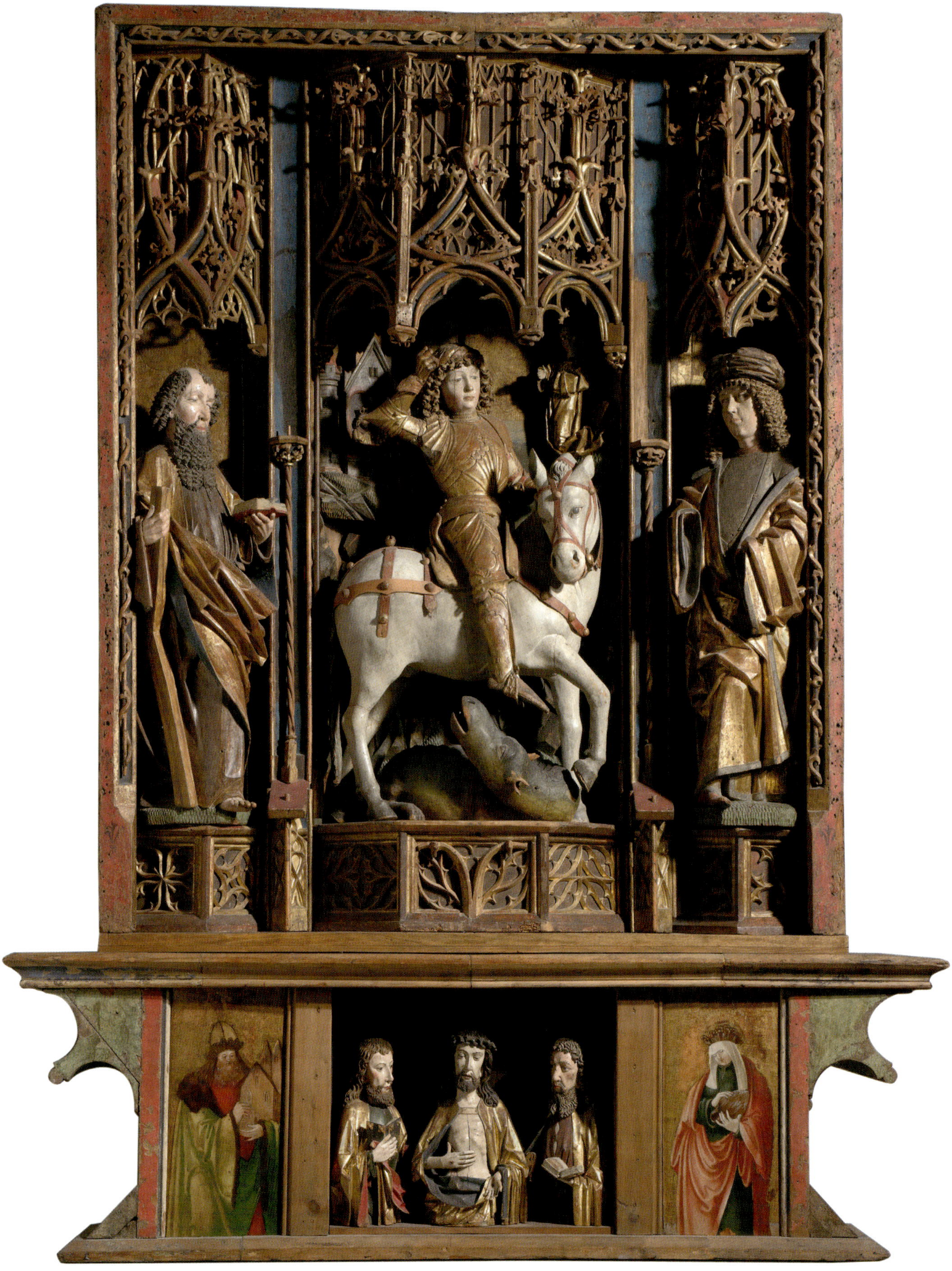

Fifteenth- and Sixteenth-Century Netherlandish Art

Rich in works of the late 15th and early 16th centuries, the collections of the Lille museum attest, most especially for the Low Countries, the subtle passage from late Gothic to Renaissance art, suffused with a new humanism.

At the death of the Count of Flanders, Louis of Mâle, in 1384, Flanders was attached to the Duchy of Burgundy. The arts flourished under Philip the Good (1419–1467), when the duchy extended to Hainaut, Brabant, Luxembourg, Holland, Zeeland and Frisia. But at the end of the century, following rivalries between the dukes of Burgundy, the kings of France and the Habsburgs, the Netherlands came under the control of the Holy Roman Emperor Maximilian I of Habsburg. Through the marriage of his son Philip the Handsome to Joan of Castile, he extended his realm to Spanish territory. From this marriage, Charles V was born in 1500. Throughout the 16th century, this strengthened

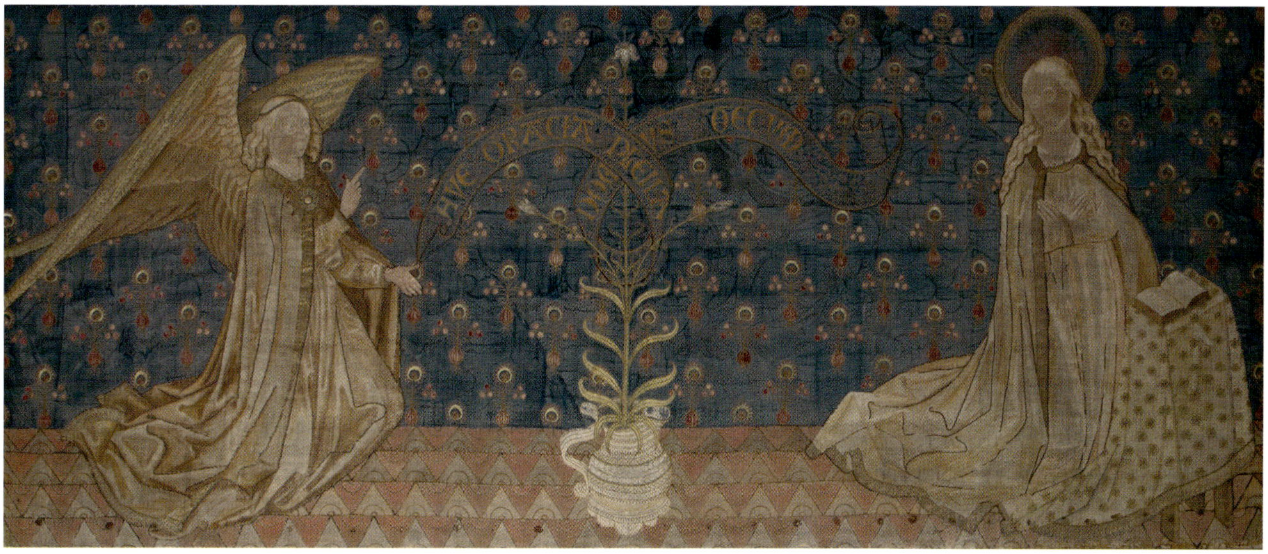

29. Circle of Robert Campin
1378/79–1444
Annunciation, *c.* 1450.
Embroidered silk, 87 x 200 cm
Gentil donation, 1868. Inv. A. 25

artistic and intellectual exchanges within the immense empire that Lille and Flanders lay at the heart of.

Fifteenth-century monumental sculpture from the Lille region is magnificently represented by a *Virgin and Child* from the second half of the 15th century, in limestone from Hordain (Nord). According to oral tradition, it comes from the Gothic Church of the Holy Saviour (destroyed in 1896). Thanks to the original polychrome, uncovered in 1997, the work's sensitivity is shown to advantage. The statue, which was perhaps flanked by two angels, adorned either the trumeau or the tympanum of a church portal. *30*

At the end of the 15th century, large wooden crucifixes like Lille's group of *Christ and the Two Thieves* in polychrome wood were often placed at the entrance to the chancel of a church, on the rood beam or the rood screen. The lengthening of the upper body, the sketchy modelling of the muscles and the treatment of the faces, imbued with inner suffering, place it among the most remarkable Crucifixions of the period.

Many paintings and sculptures were intended for private devotion and the founding of masses characteristic of the late Middle Ages. Tomb sculptures in chapels represented donors introduced by patron saints, kneeling in prayer on either side of an image of divine grace, either the Virgin and Child or the Trinity. Sculpted in Tournai stone between 1470 and 1474, the monument of the celebrated polyphonic composer Guillaume Dufay (1397–1474), the papal composer at the court of Savoy, is organized around an image of the Resur-

28. Southern Tyrol, near Brüneck, *c.* 1480–90
St George Altarpiece. Pine and linden, polychromy, oil glaze, original gilding, 313 x 245 x 61 cm
Church of Sankt Georgen an der Ahr. Acquired 1885. Inv. A. 34

rection. It comes from the cathedral of Cambrai. Estate records attribute the work to the 'marble cutter Alart Génois of Tournay'. The inscription specifies, 'Here lies the venerable man Master Guillaume Du Fay, musician, bachelor of law, formerly a choirboy then a canon in this church, canon of the Church of Sainte-Waudru in Mons, who died in the year of our Lord 1474, on the 17th day of November.'

Polychrome carved altarpieces are one of the most original creative forms produced in the Low Countries. They are made up of small sculptural components forming scenes comparable to the painting of the period. Two versions
14 of the *Swooning of the Virgin*, probably made in a Brussels workshop in the second half of the 15th century, were originally part of large altarpieces, in scenes of the Crucifixion. The poses of the Virgin and St John are patterned after models in the *Triptych of the Seven Sacraments* (Antwerp) by Rogier van der Weyden (*c.* 1399–1464). Domestic altarpieces of smaller dimensions were often polychromed with great refinement, for example the *Altarpiece of the Lamentation*, carved in oak about 1500–1510, and the small sculpture of the *Virgin and Child with St Anne* produced in Malines (Brabant), in walnut with a white preparatory coating, an orangeish bole covered with gold and silver leaf with stamped decoration, with translucent glaze highlights and relief brocade. The painters responsible for the polychromy worked separately from the carvers. The overall quality of the end product was ensured by the strict regulations of the guilds in every large city where these masters were registered.

The mastery of oil painting placed a realistic approach in the service of medieval symbolism. Aerial perspective was rendered by gradations of
29 shading. The approach to composition changed radically. The *Annunciation* embroidered on well-preserved blue silk damask was created about 1450 as an altar cloth for a chapel. The archangel Gabriel, barely touching the ground, announces his divine message to the Virgin with an oratorical gesture. The work's monumentality is the result of the clarity of the composition, which is comparable to a fresco executed about 1406 by the workshop of Robert Campin, in the Church of Saint-Brice in Tournai (destroyed in 1940), and the *Merode Triptych* by the same painter (The Cloisters, New York).

32 About 1470, Dirk Bouts executed the *Fall of the Damned* and the *Way to*
33 *Paradise*, two of his greatest masterpieces. These panels must have been the two wings of a triptych of the Last Judgement (a *Head of Christ* in Stockholm is also likely a fragment of it). The *Way to Paradise* illustrates how late Antiquity explained the geography of Paradise and access to it. The sense of detail, influenced by the style of Van Eyck (*c.* 1390–1441), makes it one of Bouts's most beautiful landscapes. In the *Fall of the Damned* the insistence on the physical and moral pain of the sinners cast into hell in their varied postures and facial expressions is characteristic of late-medieval religion.

In some respects, the composition of the late 15th-century *Crucifixion* painted in tempera on canvas by an anonymous master evokes another composition by Bouts, his *Crucifixion* in the Capilla Real in Granada. Fewer than a hundred Flemish works painted in tempera on canvas (also known as *Tüchlein*) from the period between 1400 and 1530 are extant; two are in Lille.

The practice of copying played a large role in the art of that period. Thus, the *Triptych of the Virgin and Child Surrounded by Angel Musicians* is based on works created by the official painter of the city of Brussels, Rogier van der Weyden. Four other versions placed in different settings are known of this type of the Virgin and Child in an enclosed garden (Bruges, Edinburgh, Minneapolis, Williamstown). Dated to 1490 by dendrochronological analysis of the wood of the panels, the Lille triptych probably originated in a Brussels workshop traditionally called the Master of the Embroidered Foliage, while the landscape, which continues into the wings, also recalls the pictorial

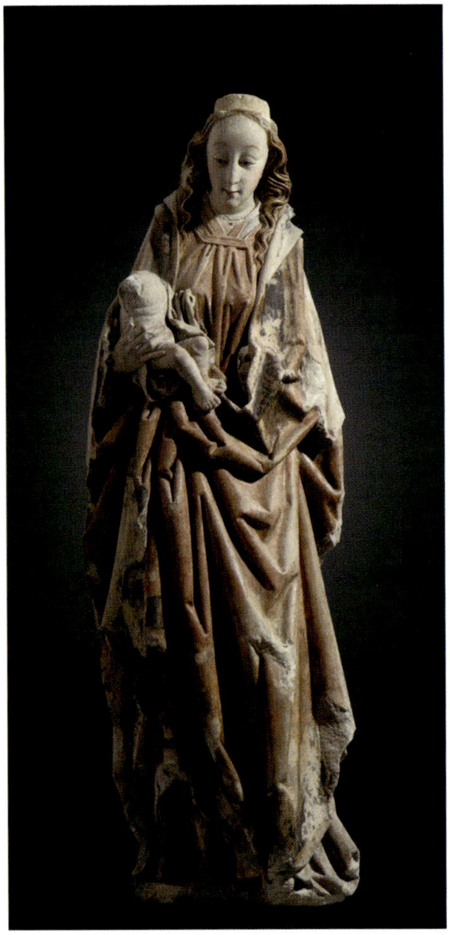

30. Lille?, last third 15th century
Virgin and Child. Hordain limestone, polychromy, 170 x 60 x 40 cm
Gentil donation, 1868. Inv. A. 1

31. Netherlands, *c.* 1500
Crucifixion. Wood, polychromy, 174 x 137 cm (Christ)
Gentil Crespel donation, 1936. Inv. SPBA 368

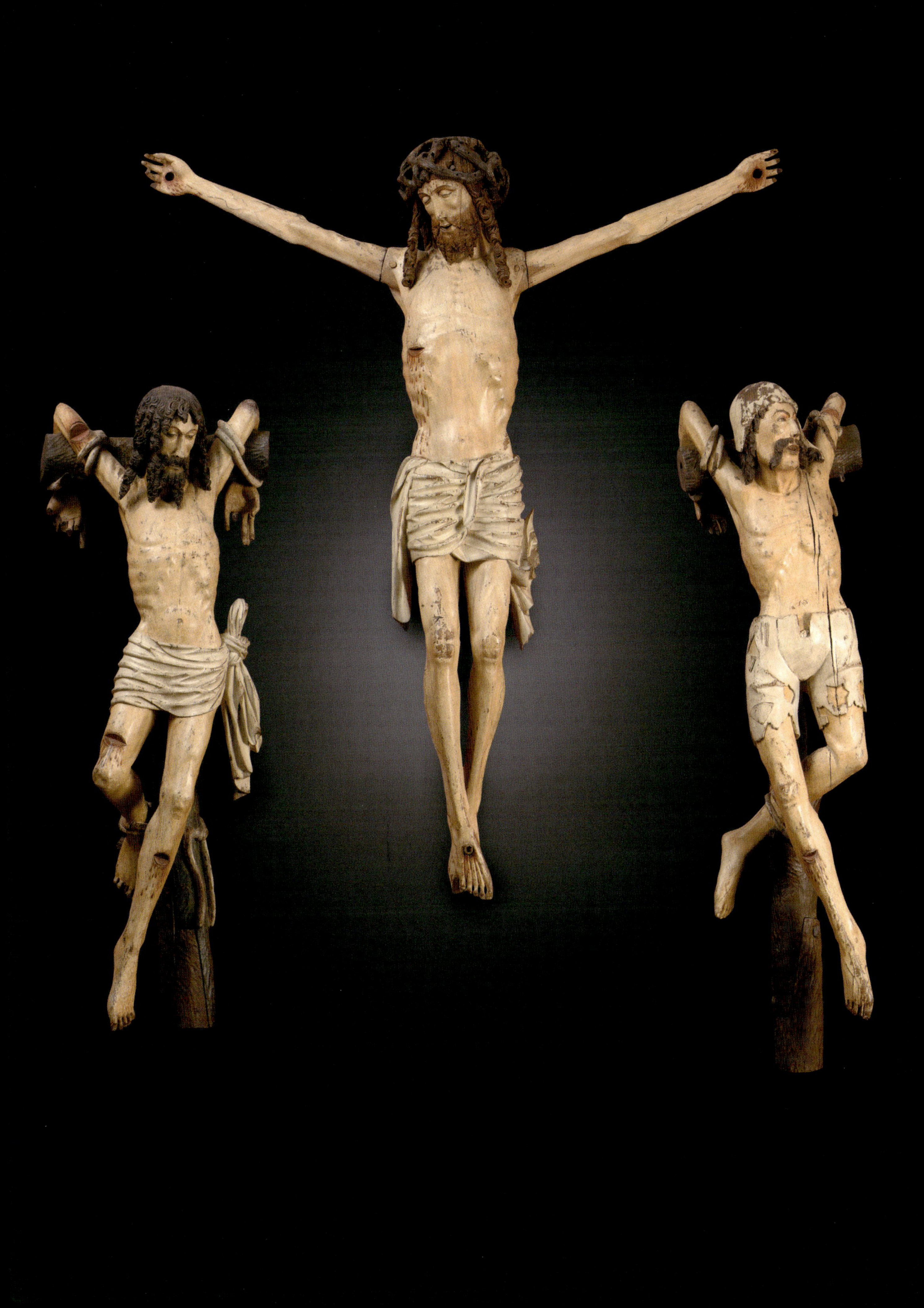

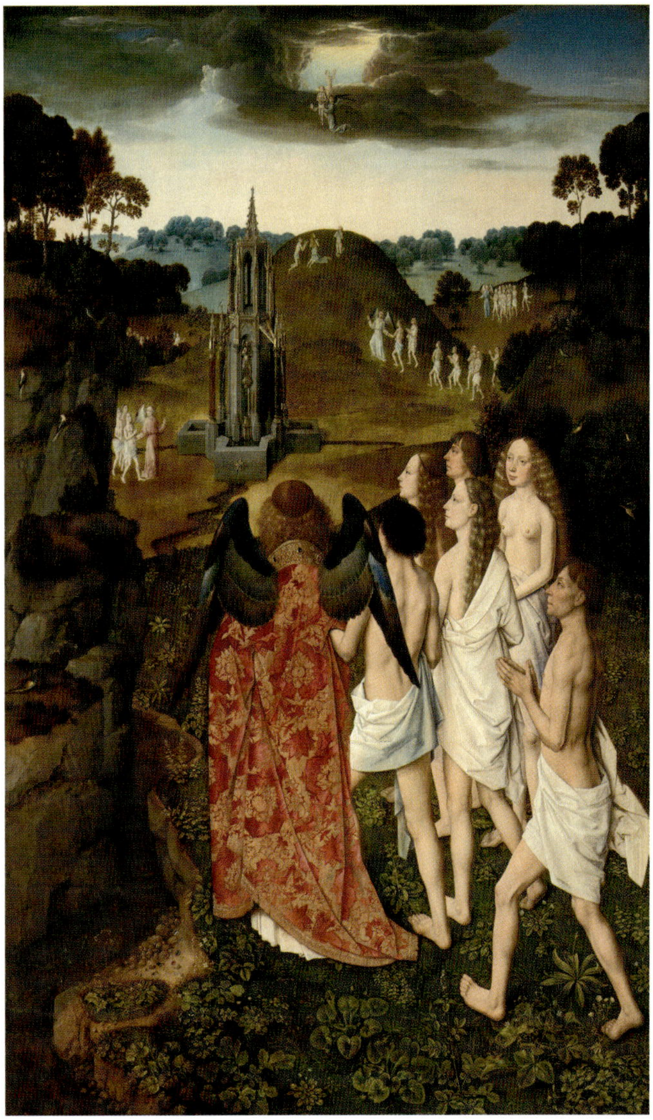

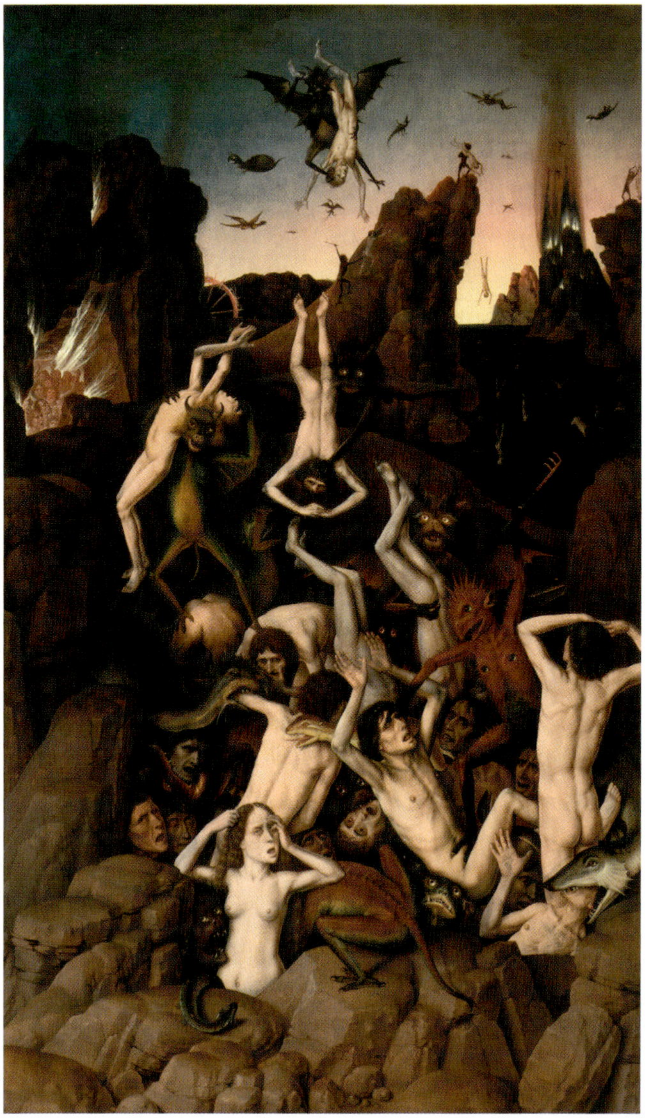

32–33. Dirk Bouts *c.* 1420–1475
The Way to Paradise and *The Fall of the Damned*, *c.* 1470. Oil on panel, each 115 x 69.5 cm (unframed)

Deposit from the state in exchange of an *Assumption* by Giambattista Piazzetta, 1957. Acquired 1863.
Inv. P. 1808 and P. 820

innovations of Bruges. However, copying models of the Virgin was more frequent in small formats intended for private devotion that usually included portraits of the donors. The donor portraits of *Barbe de Croesinck and Louis Quarré* framing a half-length *Virgin and Child* (private collection) were painted in Louvain or Brussels about 1480. Louis Quarré, lord of The Hague, was the receiver-general in Malines, treasurer of the Order of the Golden Fleece and master of accounts for the Duchy of Luxembourg in Brussels. Two other devotional panels also deserve special attention: *The Ascension with Two Donors Presented by St Quirin and St Amand* and *Christ Blessing the Virgin*, a commission from a Spanish patron in which the landscape, constructed in large harmonious planes, evokes the art of Hugo van der Goes.

In the early 16th century, landscape occupied an increasingly considerable place, with the figures becoming more lifelike and interacting with it. Transparency and the play of colours are used more freely, notably by the celebrated 'master of colour', Jean Bellegambe. The painter adapts his compositions perfectly to the theological subtleties of his patrons. The *Triptych of* *35-36*
the Mystic Bath combines the themes of the Mystic Winepress, the Fountain of Life and, in a more secular way, the Fountain of Youth. Hope and Charity lead man to the blood of the Redeemer, guided by Faith and an angel. Mary Magdalene and Mary of Egypt are already in the basin. Saints and religious join them on the right, the rest of society at the left. Isaiah and St John point to inscriptions referring to the salvation of the souls cleansed through Christ's sacrifice. On the back, two cherubs, a formula borrowed from Italian art, bear the coat of arms of Charles Coguin, abbot of Anchin (Nord) from 1511 to 1544. A second triptych by the master depicts two donors and Father Jacques Coëne of Marchiennes. Presented by their patron saints, they are shown in prayer before the Trinity. Bellegambe here borrows the composition of the *Trinity* in the large polyptych from the Abbey of Anchin (today at the museum in Douai) to create an imaginary Gothic and Italianate 'trinitarian' architecture.

The theme is also treated in sculpture. By 1500, God the Father is portrayed holding the dead Christ on his knees in accordance with the new iconography of the Throne of Grace, less hieratic than the type with the crucified Christ. As in painting, the faces' greater expressiveness and the suppleness of the drapery folds show a new relationship to space. This may be noted in two small limestone sculptures, formerly polychromed, of *St Luke* and *The Church* *34*
Triumphant, probably meant to decorate a monument, perhaps in Hainaut. The evangelist, his head raised expressively, is identifiable by the ox at his feet. The pose of the *Executioner*, carved in oak by the Master of Elsloo, is informed with a greater feeling of movement. It may have been part of a group representing the Carrying of the Cross executed about 1520, at the church of Heinsberg, Germany. Christ, carrying his cross with the help of Simon of Cyrene, is pulled by a rope held by the executioner. The face is treated with a great deal of expression, in a forced realism.

This is furthermore a characteristic of the *Adoration of the Magi* by Master *38*
M.S, active in Hungary in the early 16th century. The work is profoundly original. In its emphasis on detail and linear refinement, it is related to Germanic art, whereas the city in the background evokes an idealized Italian Renaissance architecture. It is possible that the youngest Wise Man, whose gaze is turned towards the beholder, is a self-portrait of the artist.

Between 1505 and 1535, the Antwerp Mannerists employed a multiplicity of figures, poses and fantastically rearranged architectural fragments. Particularly remarkable is the *Adoration of the Shepherds*, a well-regarded subject, with *37*
its skilful play of perspective and linear quality. It was long attributed to Dirk Vellert, active in Antwerp between 1511 and 1544, whose connections with the German painter Albrecht Dürer are known. (The false monogram AD and the

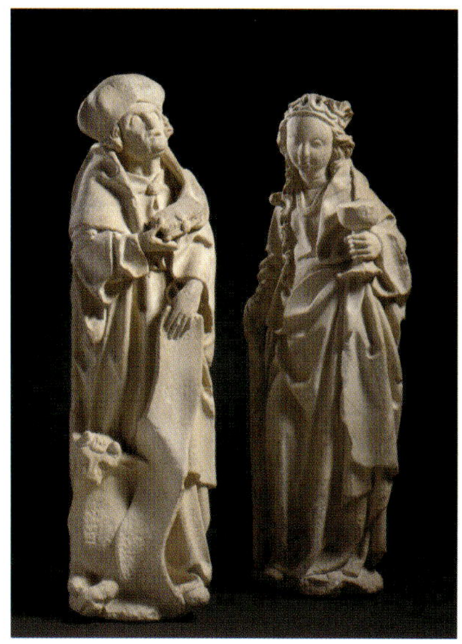

34. Hainaut?, early 16th century
St Luke and *The Church Triumphant*.
Limestone, formerly polychromed,
45 x 13.7 x 11.6 cm and 44 x 15 x 10.7 cm
Ozenfant donation, 29 June 1894. Inv. A. 328

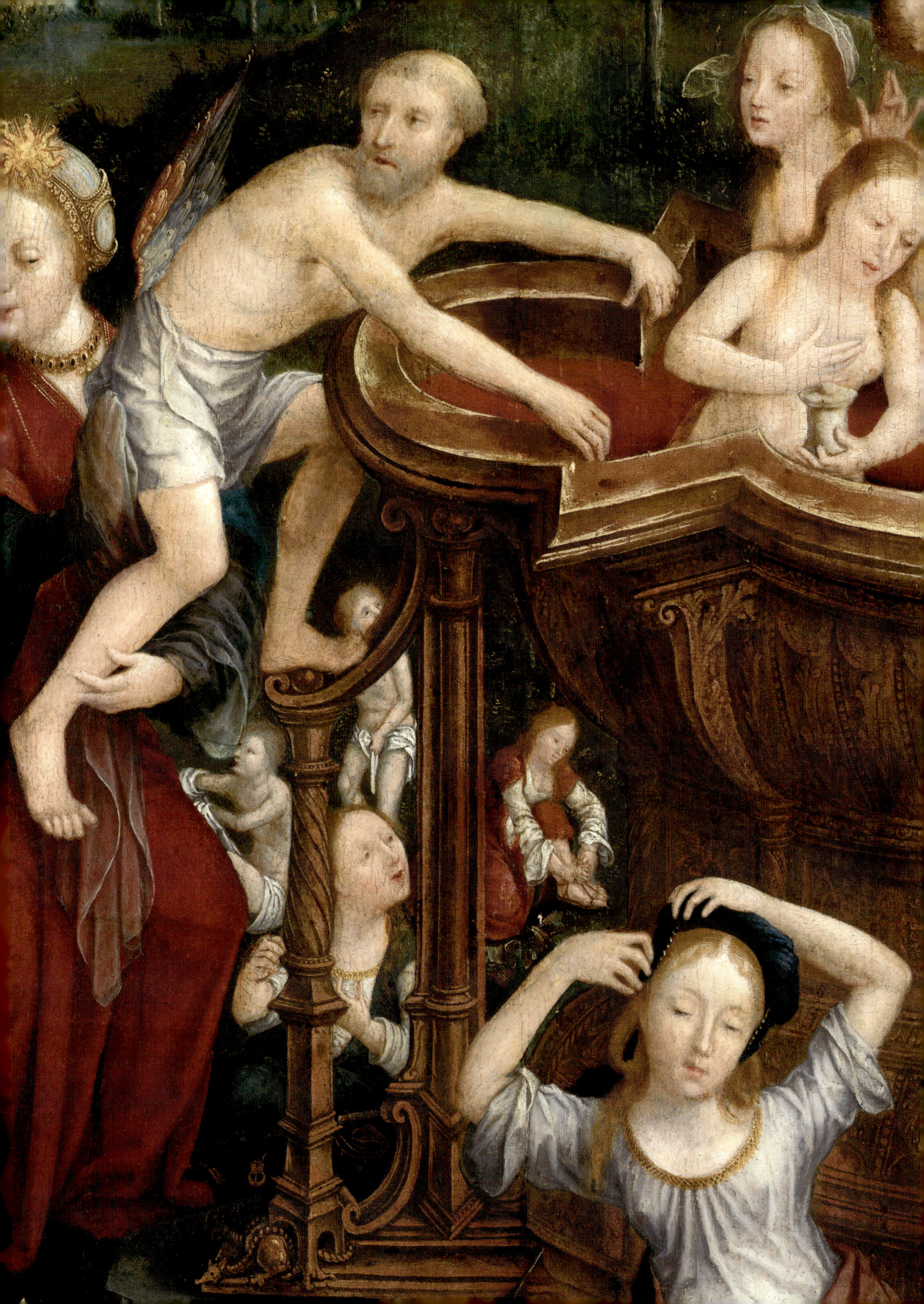

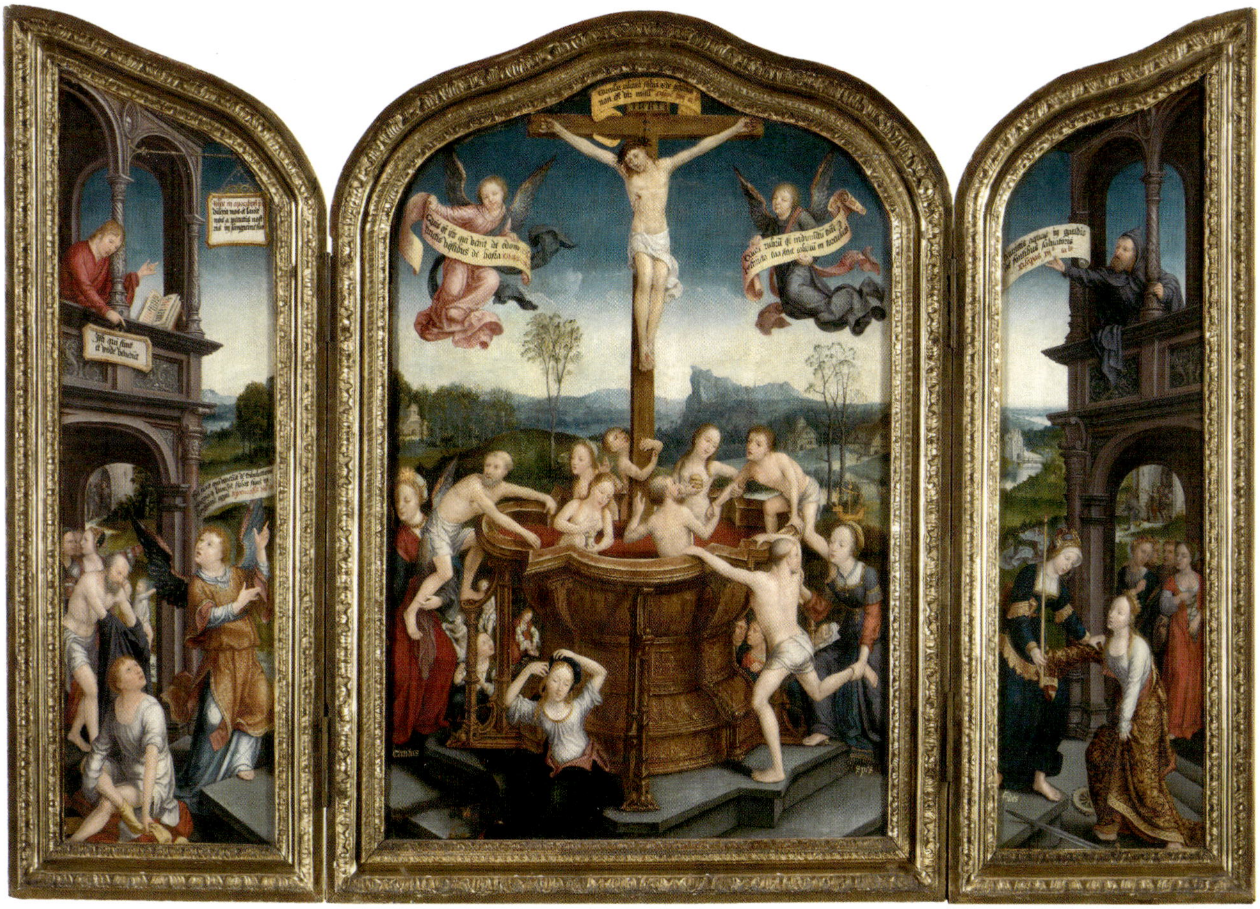

date 1512 on the pillar were added later.) But the style of the painting has been deemed so individual that it seems more plausible to attribute it to another great anonymous painter, the Master of the Lille Adoration. The Mannerists' flights bring to a close five hundred years of rich artistic exchange in the Middle Ages and Renaissance in the heart of Europe. FG

35–36. Jean Bellegambe *c.* 1470–after 1534
Triptych of the Mystic Bath, first third 16th century. Oil on panel, 92 x 141 cm
Purchased 1882. Inv. P. 832

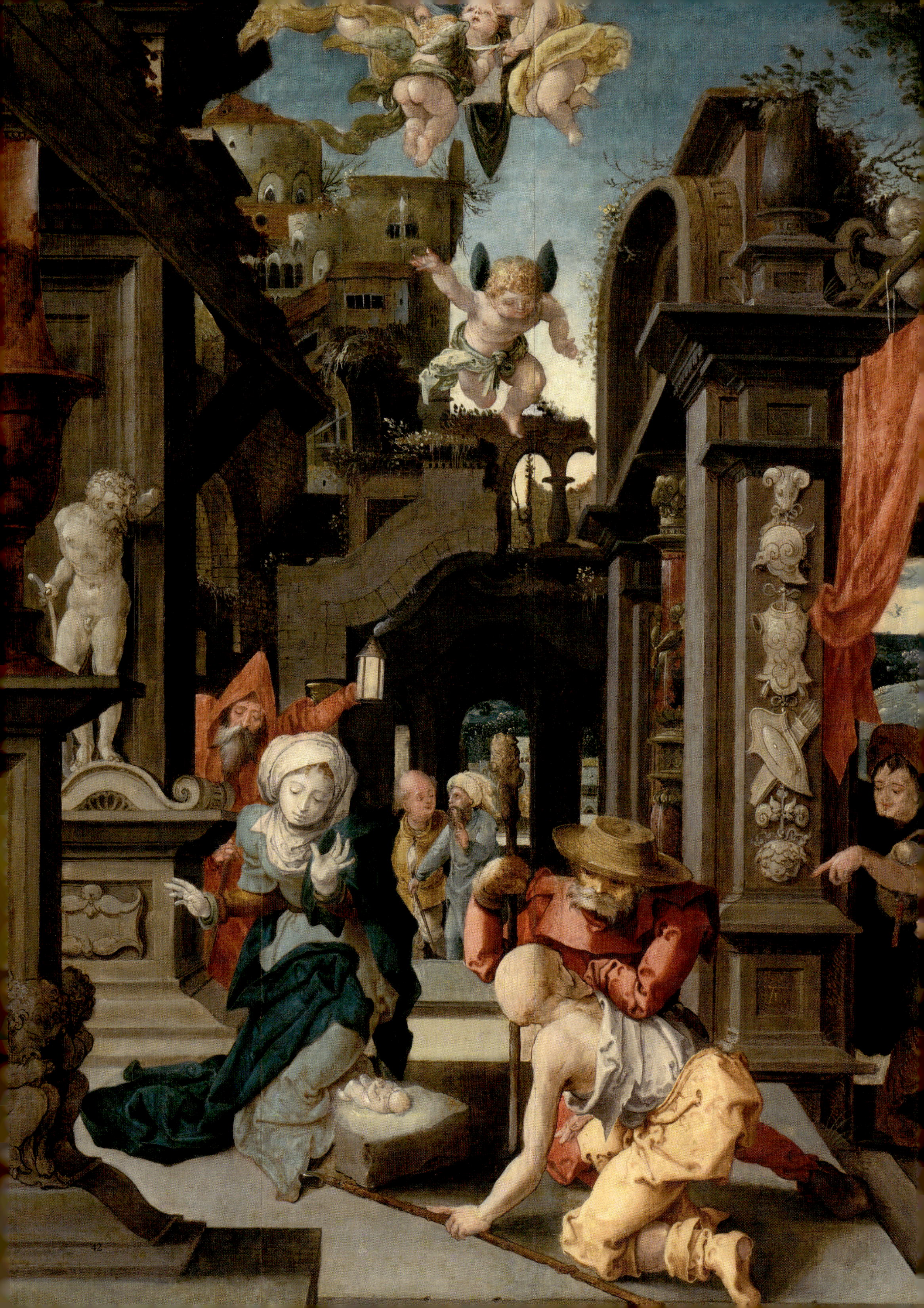

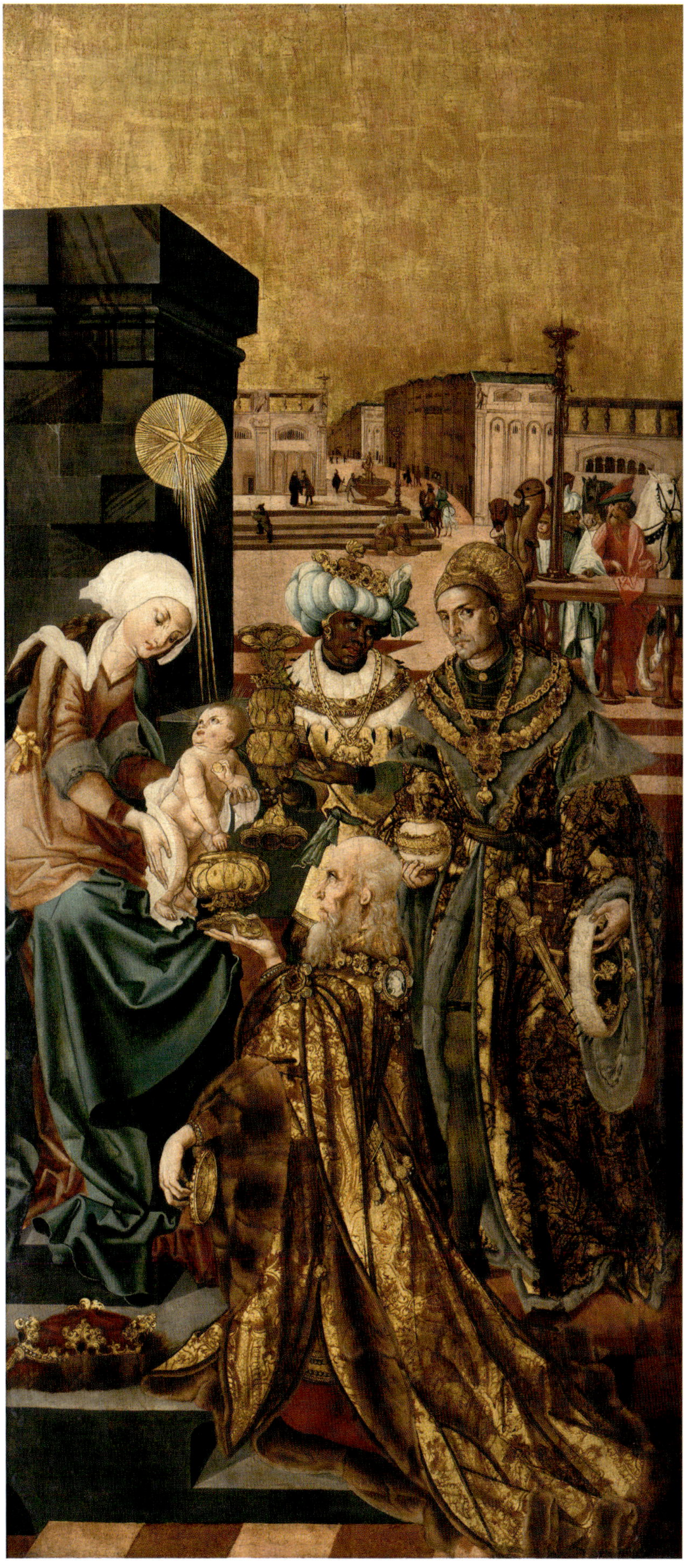

37. Master of the Lille Adoration
c. 1510–30
The Adoration of the Shepherds.
Oil on panel, 86 x 63.5 cm
Alexandre Leleux bequest, 1873. Inv. P. 739

38. Master M.S *c.* 1506
The Adoration of the Magi. Oil on
panel, 181 x 84.5 cm (unframed)
Antoine Brasseur donation, 1883. Inv. P. 748

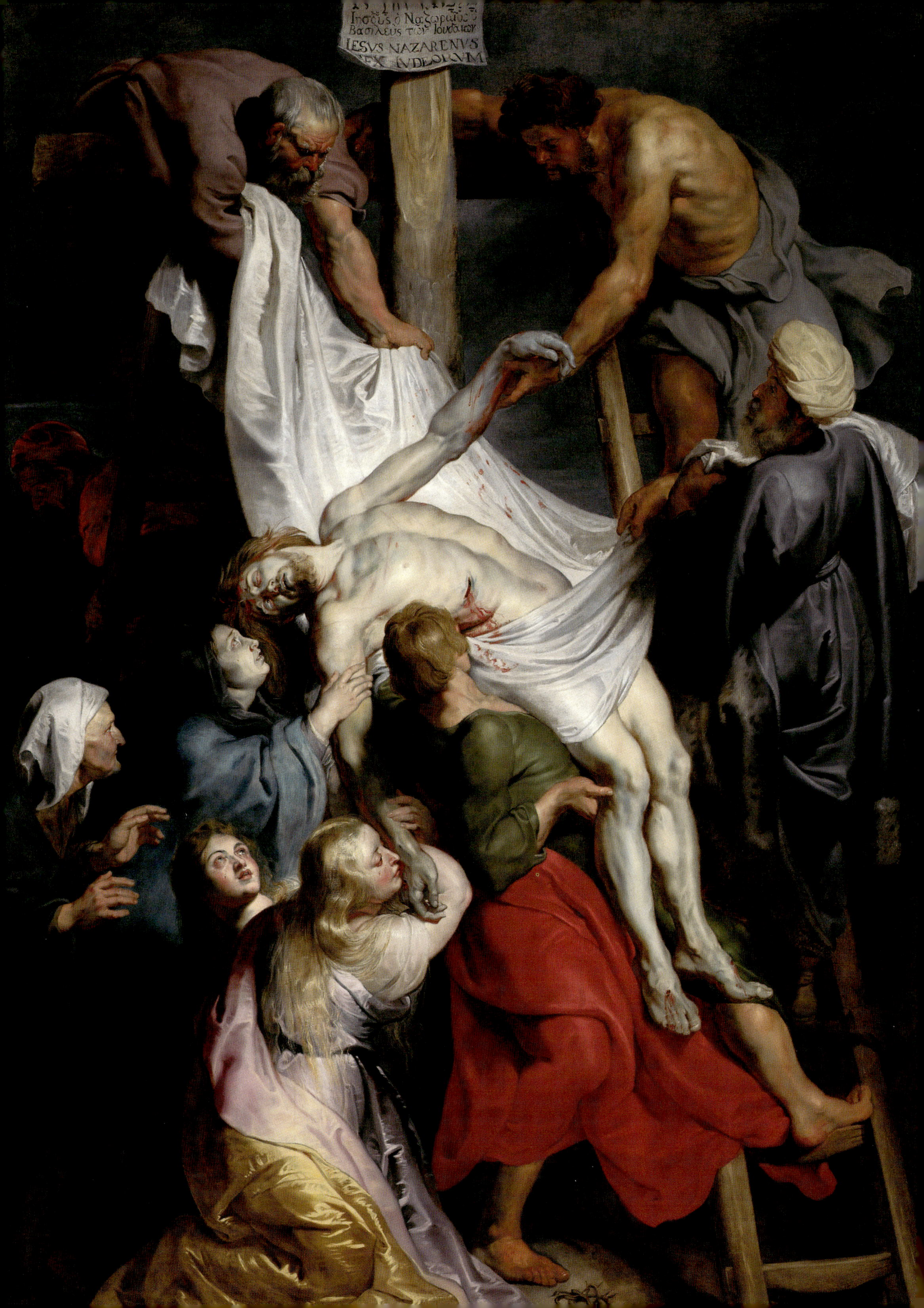
IESVS NAZARENVS

Flemish Painting

In 1792, Louis Watteau proposed opening a museum where paintings from churches in the North could be exhibited. The main providers of these were Rubens, his studio and his pupils. The distance from Antwerp leads one to think that the paintings were not painted on the spot but shipped. This would be true of the *Martyrdom of St Catherine*, for the church of the same name, the 39 *Deposition* and *St Francis Receiving the Stigmata* by Peter Paul Rubens, for the Capuchins of Lille, and the *Christ on the Cross* by Anthony van Dyck, for the high altar of the monastery of Augustinian Recollects of Lille, to name only works now at the Palais des Beaux-Arts, issuing essentially from the Flemish sphere. This choice was confirmed when, in 1807, the state dispatched forty-six works to the Recollects church. One might also have mentioned the *St Michael Vanquishing the Rebel Angels* for the Jesuit church in Lille, had it not been destroyed in a fire at the college in 1740. The treatment of images fostered by the spirit of the Counter-Reformation engendered an art of brilliance and expression beyond the scope of the local studios accustomed to painting processional banners, altar frontals and small works for private devotion. In 1629, the Dominicans of Lille commissioned from Jeremias Mittendorff a *Martyrdom of St Peter of Verona* for their monastery. The painting is a fine combination of the Mannerist aesthetic and the power of realism. Jan Boeckhorst sent a *Martyrdom of St Maurice and His Companions* from Antwerp for the Church of St Maurice in Lille.

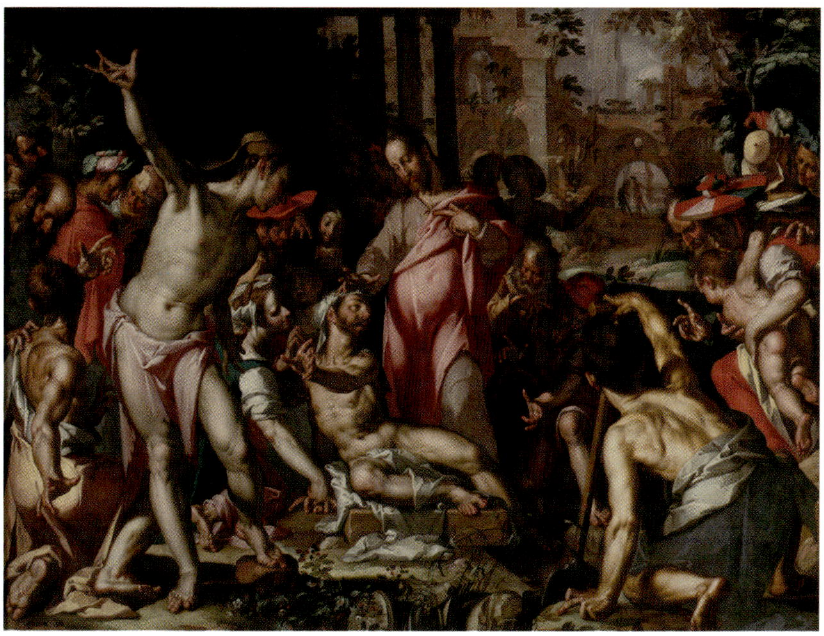

40. Joachim Wtewael 1566–1638
The Raising of Lazarus, *c.* 1600.
Oil on canvas, 158 x 208 cm
Acquired 1900. Inv. P. 150

39. Peter Paul Rubens 1577–1640
The Deposition, 1617. Oil on canvas,
425 x 295 cm
Confiscated under the Revolution. Inv. P. 74

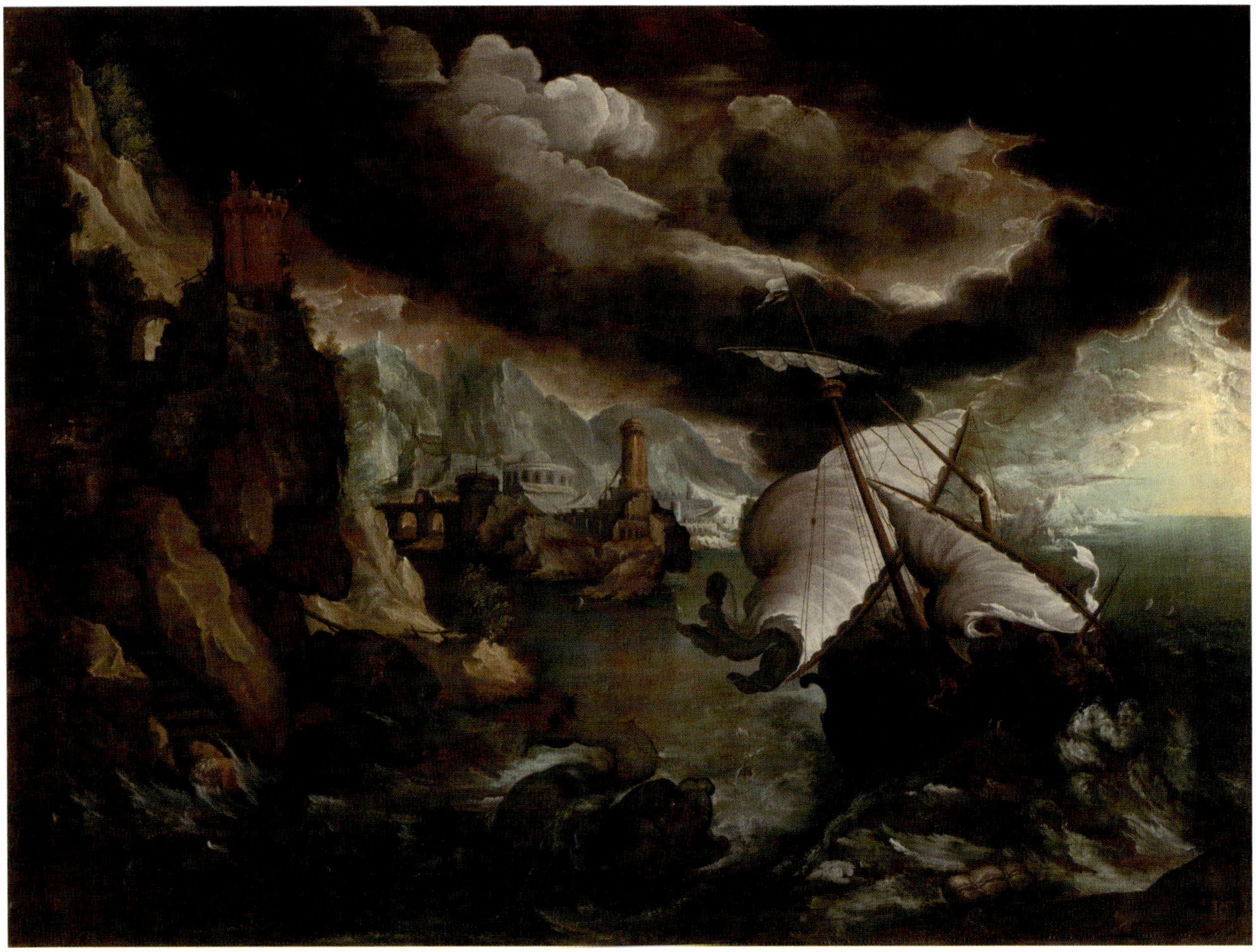

41. Paul Bril 1554–1626
Jonah Cast Ashore, c. 1600.
Oil on canvas, 125 x 169.5 cm
Acquired 1976. Inv. P. 1904

Because of its essentially local origin, the museum's Flemish collection magnificently reconstructs the strength and uniqueness of this culture. If before the Renaissance a sort of equality of territorial expansion in Europe represented both the Flemish and the Italian spirit, the spread of the model of Antiquity obliged artists to go beyond a style forged by the personality and artifices of the trade. From the mid-16th century, before Rubens, what have been called the Antwerp Romanists were also able to absorb this passion for an Antiquity-inspired Italy of generous forms, intimate in expression but extroverted in space, all in all rhetorical. Without denying Raphael's lessons based on the quest for simplicity and the ideal, the Flemish conveyed their innate taste for the spirit of the land by adapting it to figures that had become monumental, filled out and swollen with life, invading the main scene while the backgrounds opened onto the low-horizoned landscapes they painted so well.

The explosion of opulent materials and blazing palettes was made possible by the emergence of the great workshops based on the family ties often instituted among artists: beyond the overt rivalries was the capacity to incorporate the most heterogeneous elements into a common substance, as in a natural laboratory. Even before Rubens, his studio, pupils and followers, one must cite the activity of the Brueghel dynasty. Pieter the Elder (1525–1569), who scoured Germany and Italy to supply himself with images, made the landscape a meditation on the spirituality that emanates from the natural world. His son Pieter the Younger (1564–1637) – nicknamed 'Hell' Brueghel – copied him, with a particular taste for conflagrations. The descriptive skills of his younger brother, Jan Brueghel (1568–1625), whose training as an illuminator conditioned his handling of figures and chiselled treatment of vegetation, qualified him for every type of representation – flowers, fruit, forests, mountains and animals. His joy in painting and taste for beautiful fabrics earned him the nickname 'Velvet' Brueghel.

The Palais des Beaux-Arts possesses a significant group of paintings from the circle of the Brueghels, whose abundant production ensured the domination of the art of the landscape established by Joachim Patinir at the beginning of the 16th century. Landscape is an insistent presence in Flemish altarpieces, such as those of the Master of the Embroidered Foliage, which were already disposed to encompass life in an everyday diversity bearing symbolic messages. A Northern Mannerism spread across these landscapes in the form of *vedute* that were both realistic and bucolic. The emblematic and decorative natural setting won out over the often biblical subjects, which were reduced to miniature description.

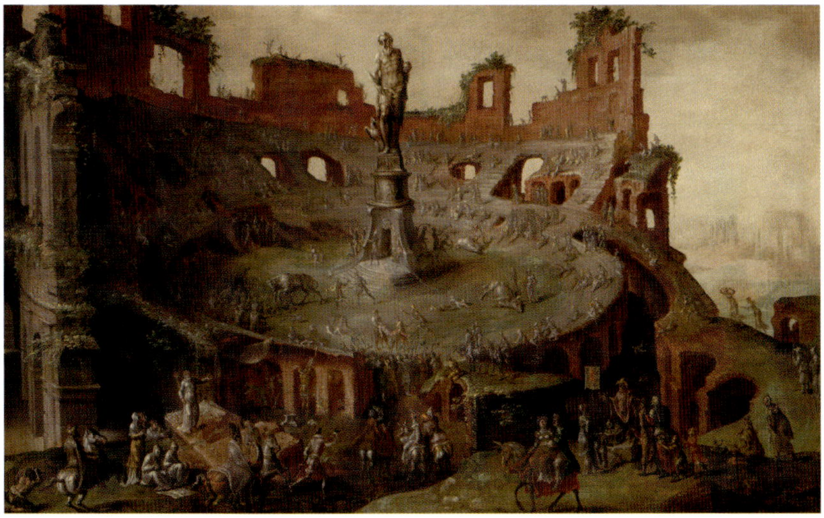

42. Maerten van Heemskerck 1498–1574
Bull Race in the Ruins of the Colosseum, 1552. Oil on panel, 73.5 x 121 cm
Antoine Brasseur donation, 1878. Inv. P. 819

This reversal of priority between landscape and history is the main feature of Northern Mannerism.

The artists inspired by Rome effected this reversal differently. Maerten van Heemskerck and Joachim Wtewael set models of antique-style figures in a pathos-filled, sensual composite theatre, giving pride of place to architectonic motifs and natural phenomena. Heemskerck's 1552 *Bull Race in the Ruins of* 42
the Colosseum is a signal example. The unreal ruins shelter allegorical figures like Bible scenes; iconography and detail overwhelm the composition. In Wtewael's *Raising of Lazarus*, painted about 1600, the very proliferation of 40
bodies and gestures combined with the overflowing modelling of the nudes forms a landscape in its own right. The same physical overflowing characterizes the *Vanitas* of Jan van Hemessen, painted about 1540. Considered one 43
of his most important works, it shows a good knowledge of Tuscan Mannerism. The physically powerful and expressive figure of the angel wears fascinating and extravagant butterfly wings, a reference to the symbolism of the Salvation of the Soul. The figure, in a state of serene yet exhilarated expectation, spontaneously points to the mirror reflection of a skull, perhaps that of someone depicted in a pendant portrait. This configuration suggests the requisite meditation on human destiny. *Jonah Cast Ashore*, painted by Paul 41
Bril about 1600, magnificently summarizes the Flemish contribution to the Mannerist culture. Here, the reversal of the hierarchy between motif and landscape is at its height: Jonah, spewed out by the whale after three days, can just be discerned amid the turbulence of rock and atmosphere, whose Venetian luminism becomes the painting's true subject. Romanticism in the 1830s treated the landscape no differently.

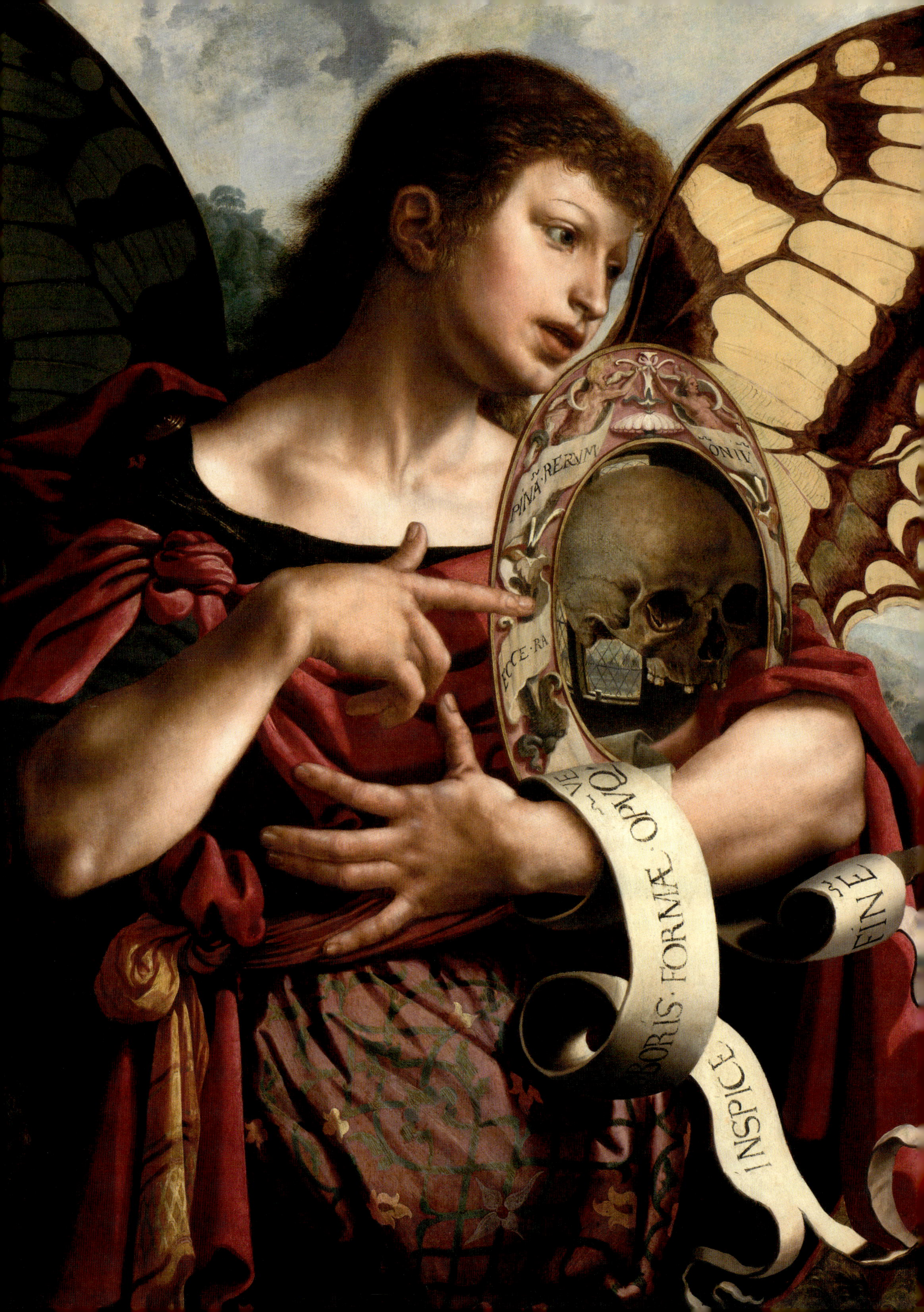
PINA·RERVM
ONIV
ECCE·RA
BORIS·FORMÆ·OPVQ
INSPICE
FINE

As we have seen, the Flemish 17th century fell along the Antwerp-Rubens-Lille axis. The master's works in the museum's collection evoke the richness of his training with the Romanist Otto van Veen, as well as his natural capacity to understand Italian art – not only the figures of Michelangelo, but also the landscapes and compositions of Titian and Tintoretto. Rubens expresses the essence of the Baroque era, for his painting successfully combines every possible contrast: the picturesque and the emotional, popular and luxurious, spiritual and pagan, ample and flamboyant dominate the early decades of his career, especially in the religious works. If the influence of Italian models remains visible, it is nevertheless blurred in a flood of subtle excesses in the modelling as well as a drifting of tones. Thus, Rubens had a complete vocabulary at his disposal. He turned eclecticism into absolute richness. After Venetian painting, he singlehandedly enriched the foundations of realistic painting. 'He made himself by making worlds', Hippolyte Taine said, providing the best definition of the Baroque, which is, as Jules Michelet reminds us, again in regard to Rubens, a vital expression and representation of organic life. The painter's faith and uninterrupted flights of mysticism were fuelled by pagan verve and blunt picturesqueness; ugliness and beauty are swept along together in a concentrated summary of naturalism's modern future.

The *Deposition* painted in 1617 can stand on its own for all the art of Rubens. Close in composition to the Antwerp Cathedral *Deposition*, it shows the artist's 39
awareness of the treatment of the Passion in late Gothic altarpieces, while exploding the boundaries of the image. In this regard, he drew inspiration from the Jesuit vision, which favoured the sensation of continual movement among the figures. The arrangement derives from the Hellenistic *Laocoön* group. The marble-like modelling is at once pained and graceful. The space is occupied in all its verticality, obliging the gaze to delve into the details of the anatomical expressions. The intensity of the blues, reds and yellows infuses the lighting of the flesh tones with the impalpable and sublime character that infects the faces of the Virgin and, above all, Mary Magdalene, through the downward flow of Christ's arm, a privileged connection strengthened by the kiss she bestows upon the blood of Christ's wound.

The predilection for the figure of Mary Magdalene central to the Counter-Reformation did not escape Rubens. In the painting from 1620, from the 44
Augustinian Recollects in Ghent, he refers to the miracle whereby the saint in constant prayer sustained herself solely with heavenly music brought by angels, producing in her an ecstatic abandon. His best pupil, Jacob Jordaens, gives us a strange and complex *Temptation of the Magdalene*, as picturesque as it is full of pathos: another Mary Magdalene, at once Flemish and Venetian, as could occur around 1615, renouncing worldly riches. The exaltation here is optimistic, serene, even sensually ascetic.

As much Flemish painting as Dutch painting was done for private collectors. The various genres intermixed personal devotion, symbolic meditation, visual experience of knowledge of the natural world and delight in nature's riches. The *Temptation of St Anthony* was a favourite subject of David Teniers, 45
who, as Hervé Oursel said, treated the closed space with visual and psychological refinement by heaping up fantastic and at times zoomorphic boulders, thus endowing the traditional struggle between virtue and vice with a new vision. With great formal subtlety and fluid modelling, in the 1630s Jacob Jordaens painted landscapes inspired by Rubens in a format suitable for the collector's cabinet, such as *A Huntsman and His Dogs*. To this he added a breadth 46
of field spread with delicate passages of light that, as in the *Rape of Europa*, 48
almost make one forget the mythological subject.

The Palais des Beaux-Arts' Flemish collection has few symbolic still lifes, but Pieter Boel's large-format *Allegory of the World's Vanities*, a monumental 47

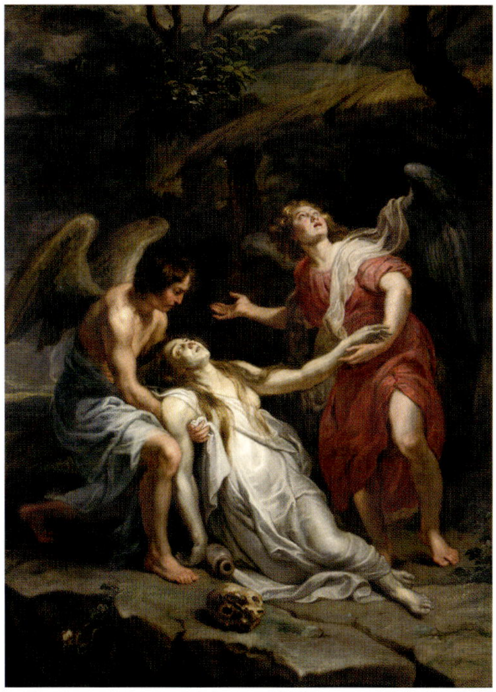

44. Peter Paul Rubens 1577–1640
Mary Magdalene in Ecstasy, 1620.
Oil on canvas, 295 x 220 cm
Church of the Recollects, Ghent, state consignment, 1801. Inv. P. 64

43. Jan van Hemessen *c.* 1500–*c.* 1560
Vanity (detail), *c.* 1540. Oil on panel, 93 x 70 cm
Acquired 1994. Inv. P. 2009

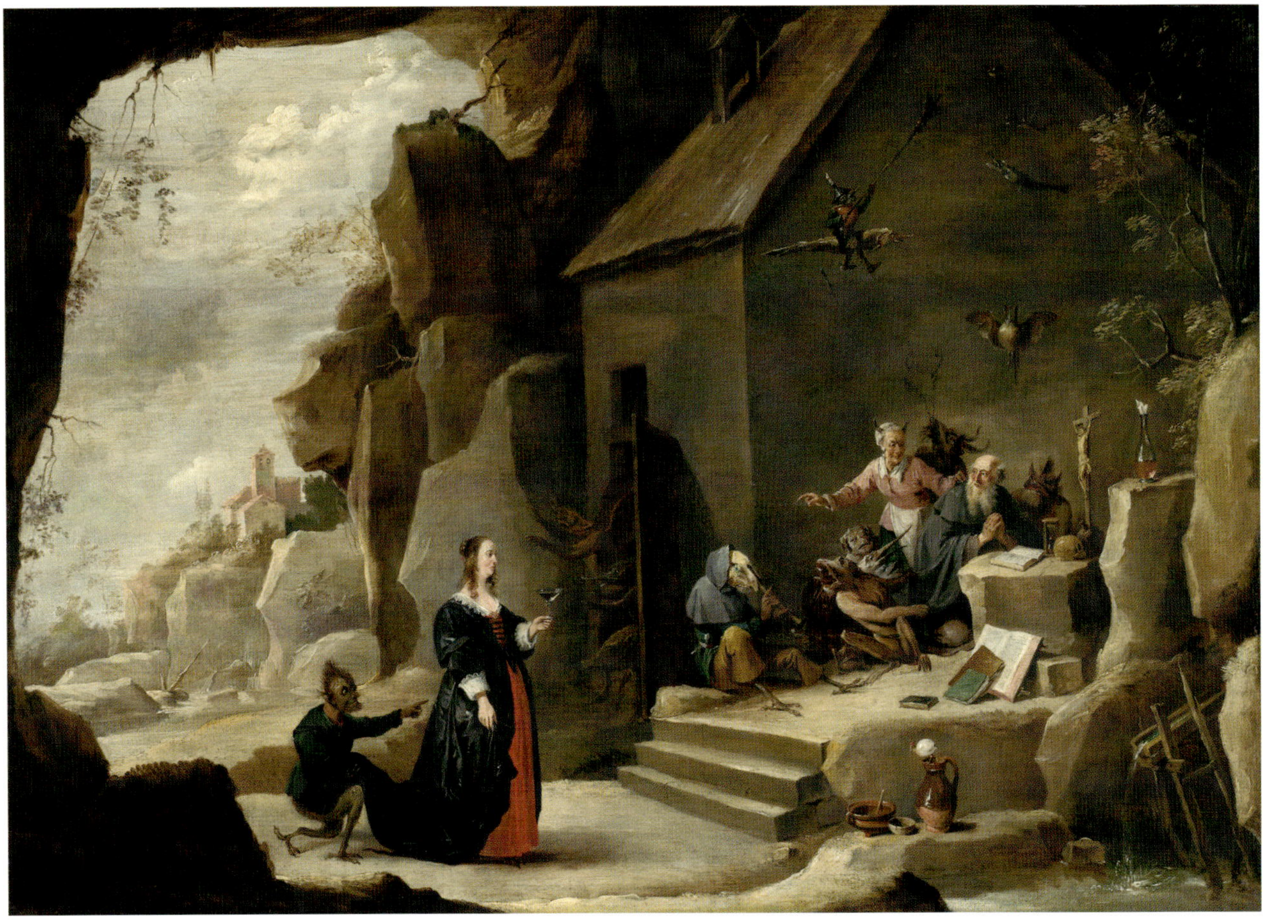

45. David Teniers the Younger
1610–1690
The Temptation of St Anthony.
Oil on panel, 62.8 x 87 cm
Acquired 1861. Inv. P. 95

composition of pure baroque effect painted in 1663, provides the most complete synthesis of the symbols of this predominant theme in 17th-century spirituality. Contrary to the Latin countries' scenes composed of figures of saints and antique-style allegories, the Northern countries, under the influence of the Reformation, favoured arrangements of objects that express the vanity of the world and the hope of Resurrection. The futility of worldly pleasures is illustrated by musical instruments, wine and games. Earthly goods are evoked through jewellery, the gold and silverware, armour and coats of arms, the crown, sceptre and mitre, prompting a meditation on power. True knowledge is underscored by books and the instruments of science and art. The temporary character of life is proclaimed by the skull, watch, hourglass and candle; hope of eternal life is symbolized by wheat and the laurel crown. Boel's masterpiece, a veritable human epic without figures, sets this clutter of symbols amid ruins. The sensuality it emanates curtails any vague desire of the melancholy gaze. AT

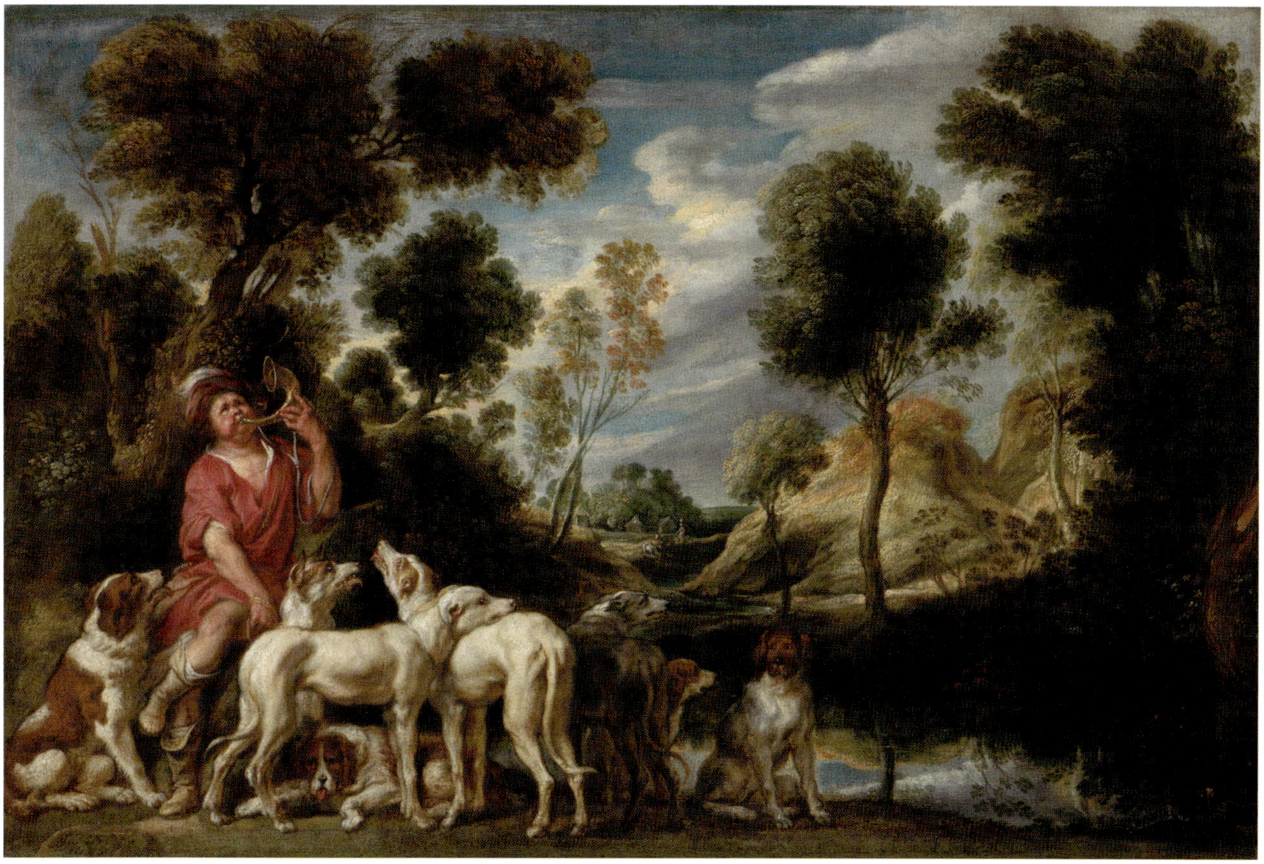

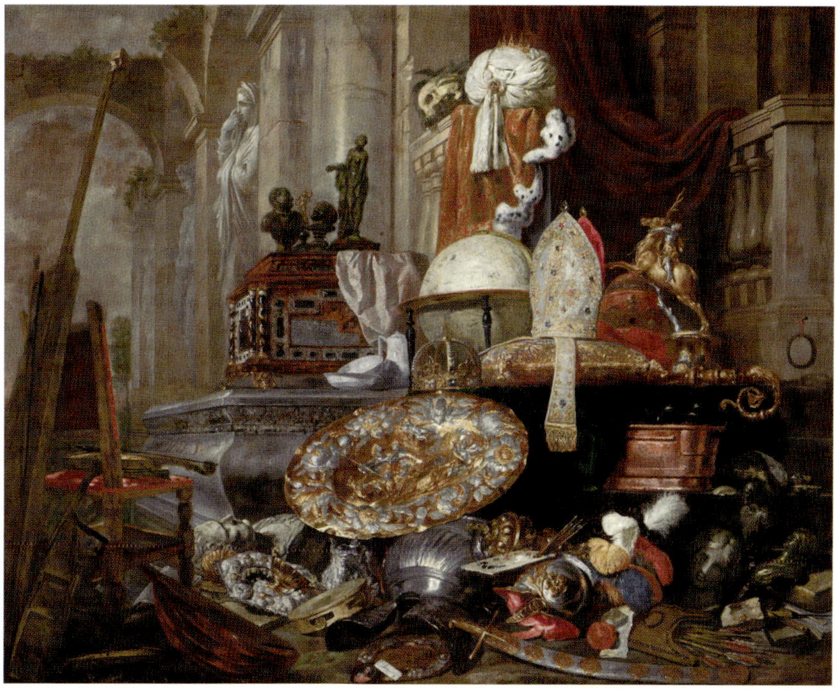

46. Jacob Jordaens 1593–1678
A Huntsman and His Dogs, c. 1630.
Oil on canvas, 79 x 120 cm
Acquired 1881. Inv. P. 60

47. Pieter Boel 1622–1674
Allegory of the World's Vanities, 1663.
Oil on canvas, 207 x 261 cm
Acquired 1878. Inv. P. 78

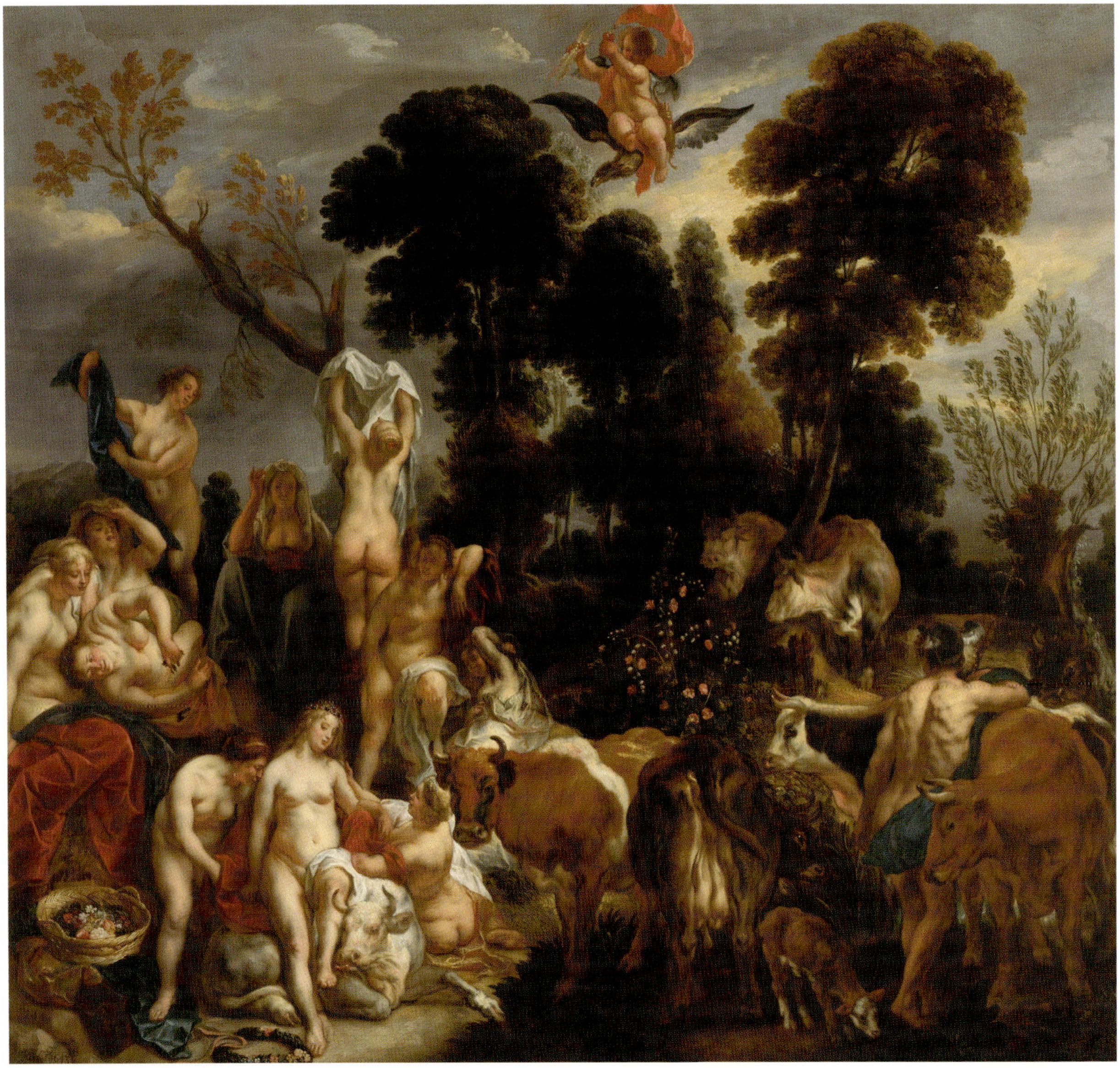

48. Jacob Jordaens 1593–1678
The Rape of Europa, 1643.
Oil on canvas, 172 x 190 cm
Acquired 1908 with funds from the Brasseur foundation. Inv. P.76

49. Jacob Jordaens 1593–1678
The Temptation of the Magdalene (detail), *c.* 1620. Oil on panel, 125.5 x 96.7 cm
Acquired 1890. Inv. P.77

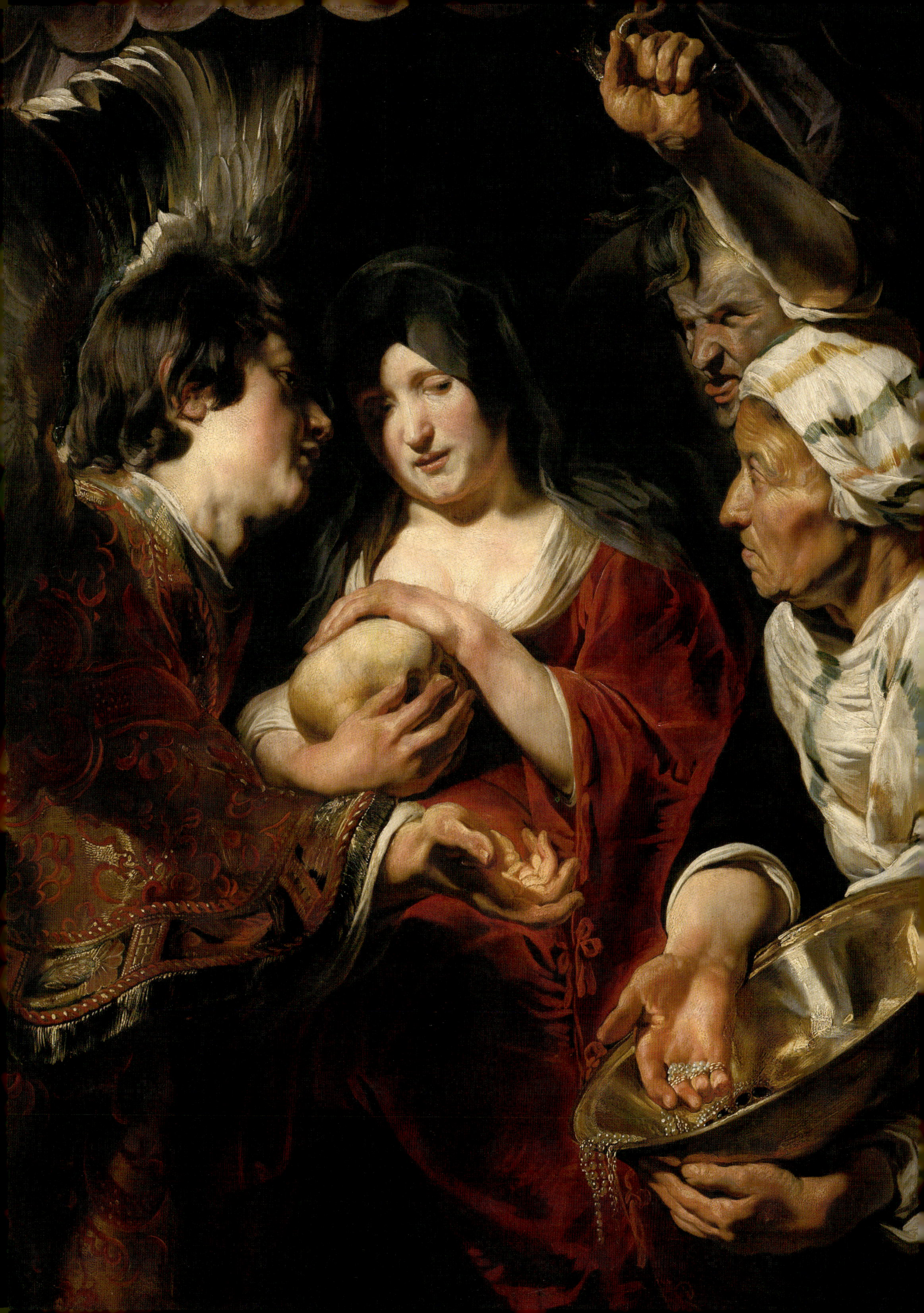

Dutch Painting

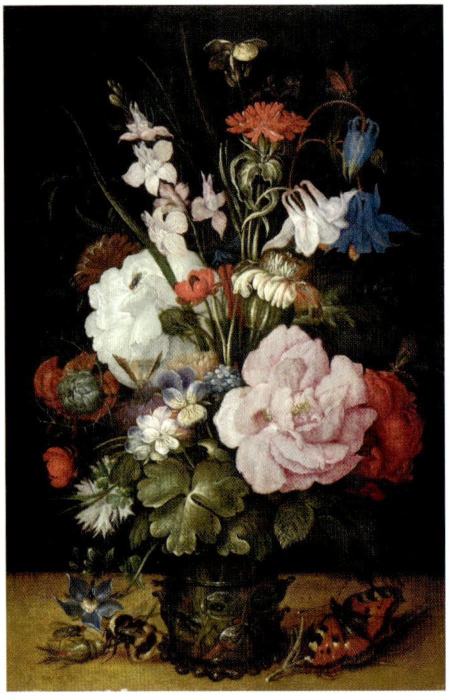

50. Roelandt Savery *c.* 1576/78–1639
Bouquet of Flowers. Oil on panel, 26.6 x 18.4 cm
Alexandre Leleux bequest, 1873. Inv. P. 1036

Lille's Dutch collection is probably the richest in France outside Paris. Unlike the Flemish painting collection, however, which received a good number of its masterpieces early on by way of Revolutionary confiscations, this is not due to some hypothetical geographical determinism. In 1853, Clément de Ris could still write that 'the Dutch School, properly speaking, is very little present at the museum'. The modest original holdings, scarcely a dozen works, reflect 18th-century collectors' taste for certain painters who tend to be forgotten nowadays. Hence the small *Annunciation to the Shepherds* by Adam Colonia (1634–1685), an Italianizing painter from Rotterdam who liked nocturnal effects inspired by the Bassano family.

Things began to change in the 1870s thanks to two great donors. The owner-director of the newspaper *L'Écho du Nord*, Alexandre Leleux (1812–1873), bequeathed his collection of about 120 mainly Dutch paintings. Lille-native Antoine Brasseur (1819–1886) established himself in Cologne as a painting dealer and restorer. Best known for works by artists of his adopted city, his collection also included a not negligible number of Dutch paintings. In addition, the income from the foundation set up under the terms of his will fuelled acquisitions in the 1880s and 1890s, in which the Northern schools had a large share. Though purchases slowed somewhat thereafter, the curators made an effort to expand the collection by diversifying it.

Perhaps to a greater extent than Brasseur, Leleux had the taste of his times. His collection reflects the vision of Dutch painting that was taking hold in the mid-19th century, bringing landscape, portrait, still life and genre painting to their peak under the banner of realism. Several paintings acquired in the 20th century escaped this firmly entrenched canon. We have already seen Wte-
40 wael's *Raising of Lazarus*, a magnificent example of the Mannerist explorations of Utrecht painters around 1600. One of the masters of this trend, Cornelis Cornelisz van Haarlem, is represented in Lille only by a somewhat subdued
51 but none the less greatly refined late work, *Venus, Cupid, Bacchus and Ceres*. Of Flemish origin, Roelandt Savery spent the last twenty years of his life in
50 Utrecht. The precious and delicate *Bouquet of Flowers* probably dates from his stay at the court of Emperor Rudolf II in Prague from 1603 to about 1613.

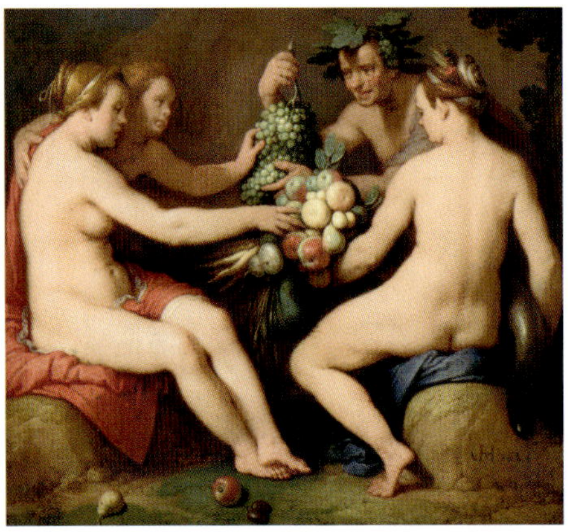

51. Cornelis Cornelisz van Haarlem 1562–1638
Venus, Cupid, Bacchus and Ceres, 1624. Oil on copper, 21.5 x 24.1 cm
G. Herlin donation, 1928. Inv. P. 1680

Pieter Lastman, too, is among the Dutch artists little represented in French public collections. The passage of the young Rembrandt through his studio earned the trend of which he was the leading light the name of 'pre-Rem-
53 brandtesque'. The discovery and acquisition of Lastman's *Entombment* in the early 1960s coincided with a reassessment of these artists. Largely inspired by the Italian masters whose works he saw during his sojourn on the peninsula, he gives a strongly personal interpretation of them, combining the lessons of the High Renaissance masters, Raphael at the head, with the assimilation of Caravaggesque chiaroscuro.

In the absence of works by Rembrandt himself, the group of Rembrandtesque paintings in Lille offers a fascinating glimpse of his influence on his contemporaries. No doubt few of the painters of this current were his students, and some of them adopted his manner only sporadically, concurrently with other styles. It is striking to see how Gerbrand van den Eeckhout, faithful to Rembrandt in the *Tribute Money*, diverges from him noticeably in the
55 minutely detailed technique of the *Continence of Scipio*, where only the two old men in the background recall the broad brushwork associated with the master. And his *Portrait of a Young Boy* has nothing Rembrandtesque about it.

52. Balthasar van der Ast 1593/94–1657
Fruit and Shells (detail, see also p. 3), 1623.
Oil on panel, 37 x 65 cm
Purchased 1977. Inv. P. 1937

Jeroboam's Wife and the Prophet Ahijah (dated 1671), by Frans van Mieris I (1635–1681), shows the variety of treatment of religious subjects in Dutch painting. A 'painter of the fine manner' (*fijnschilder*), Mieris was renowned for

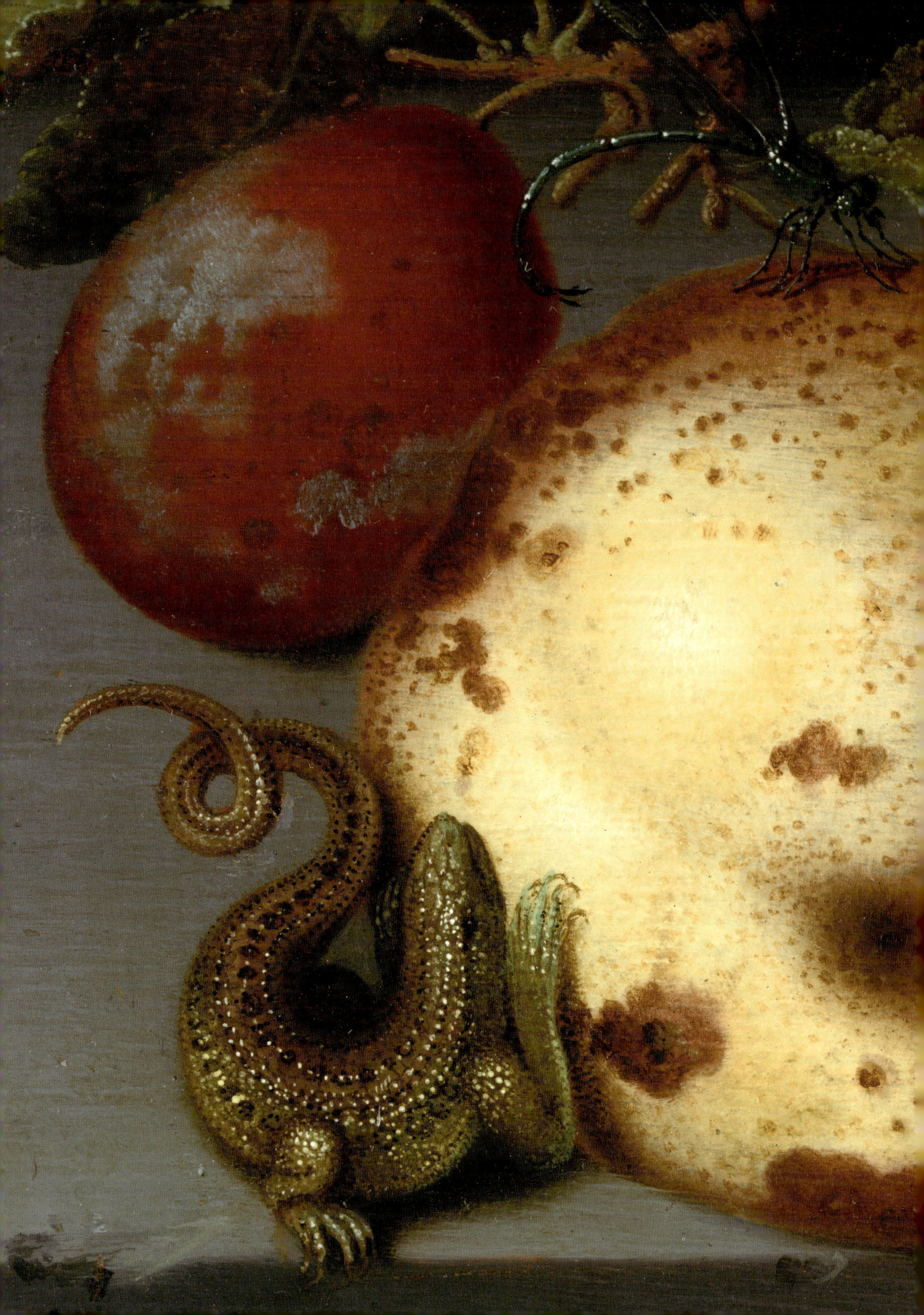

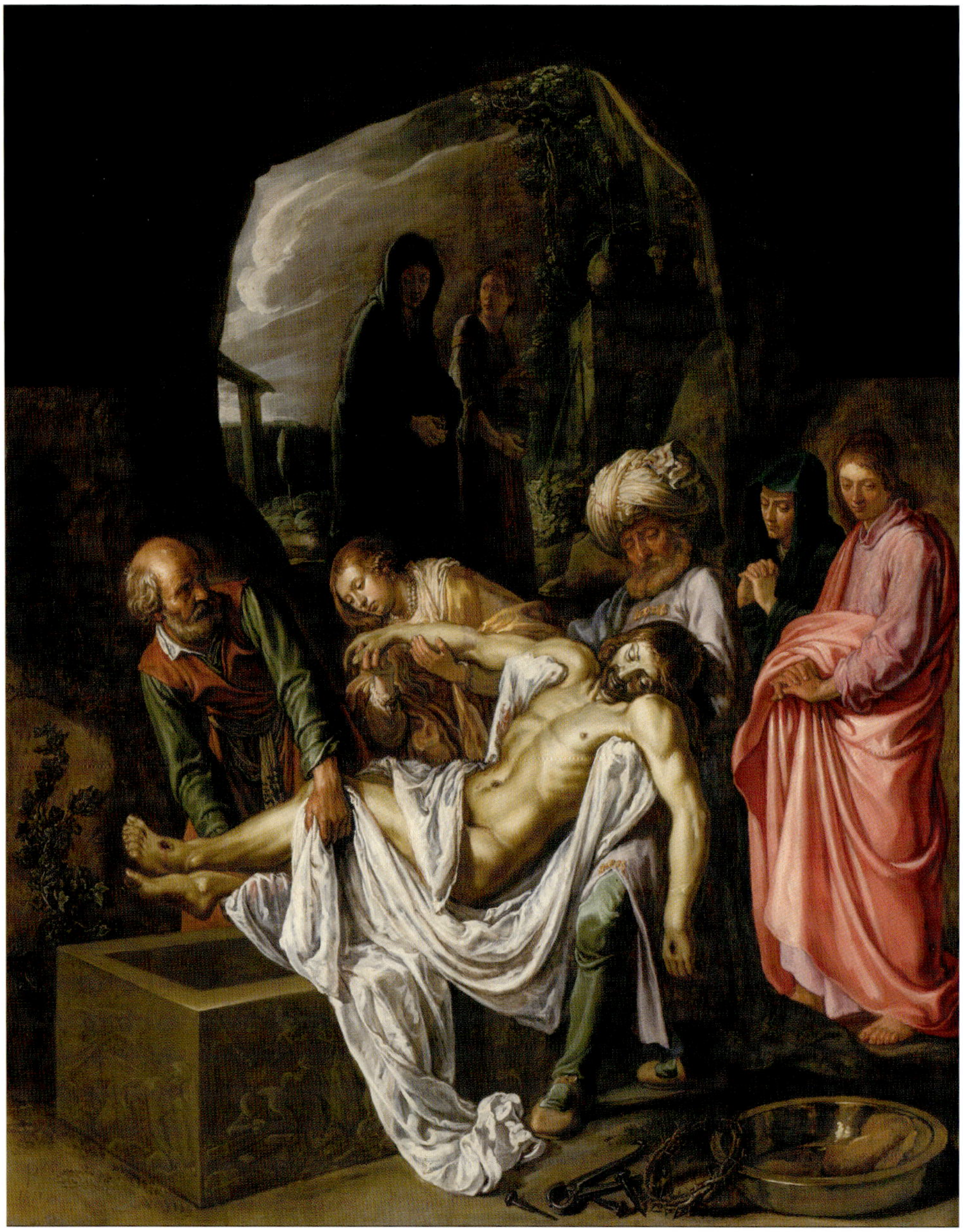

53–54. Pieter Lastman *c.* 1583–1633
The Entombment, 1612. Oil on panel,
123 x 101.5 cm
Purchased 1962. Inv. P. 1819

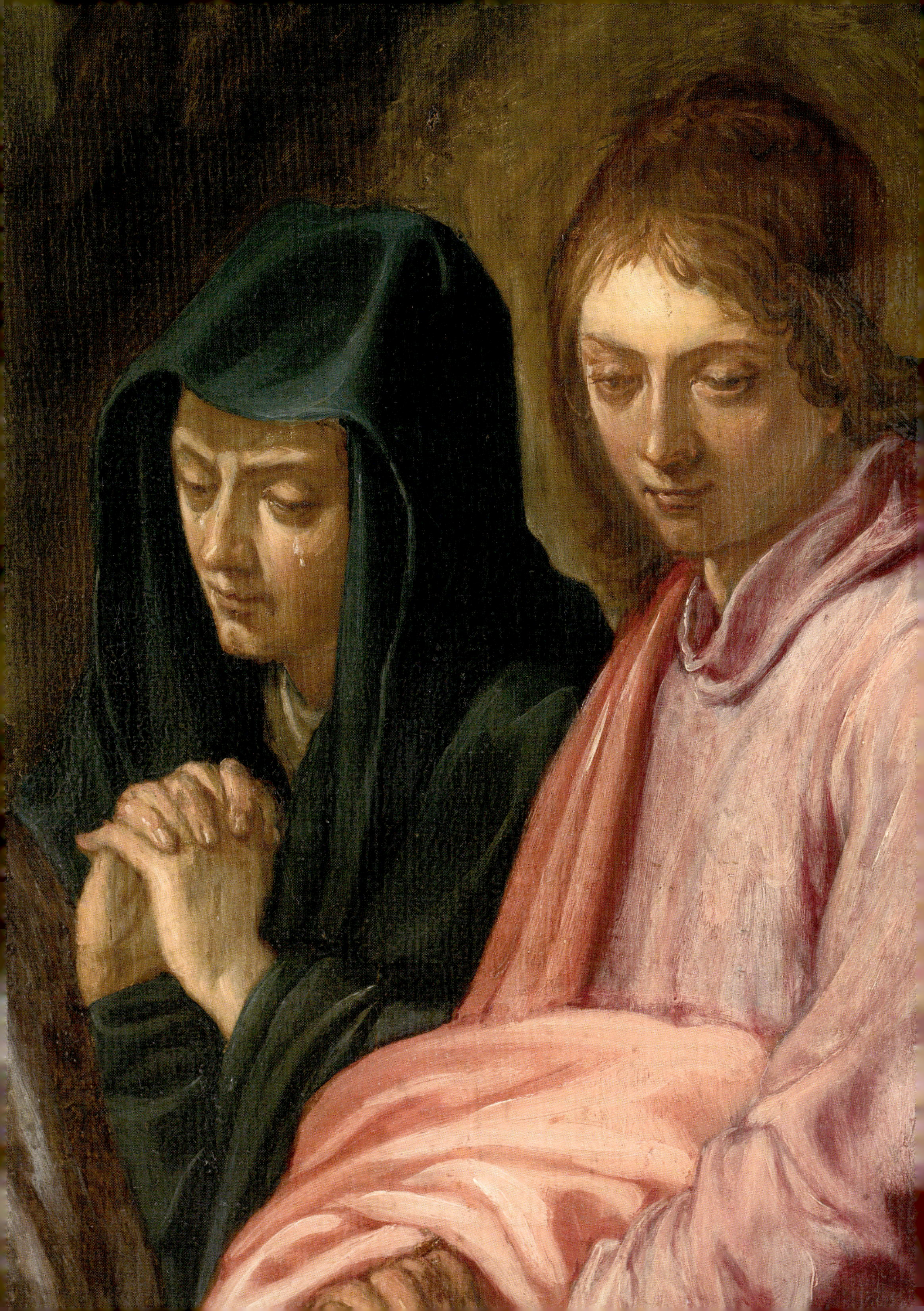

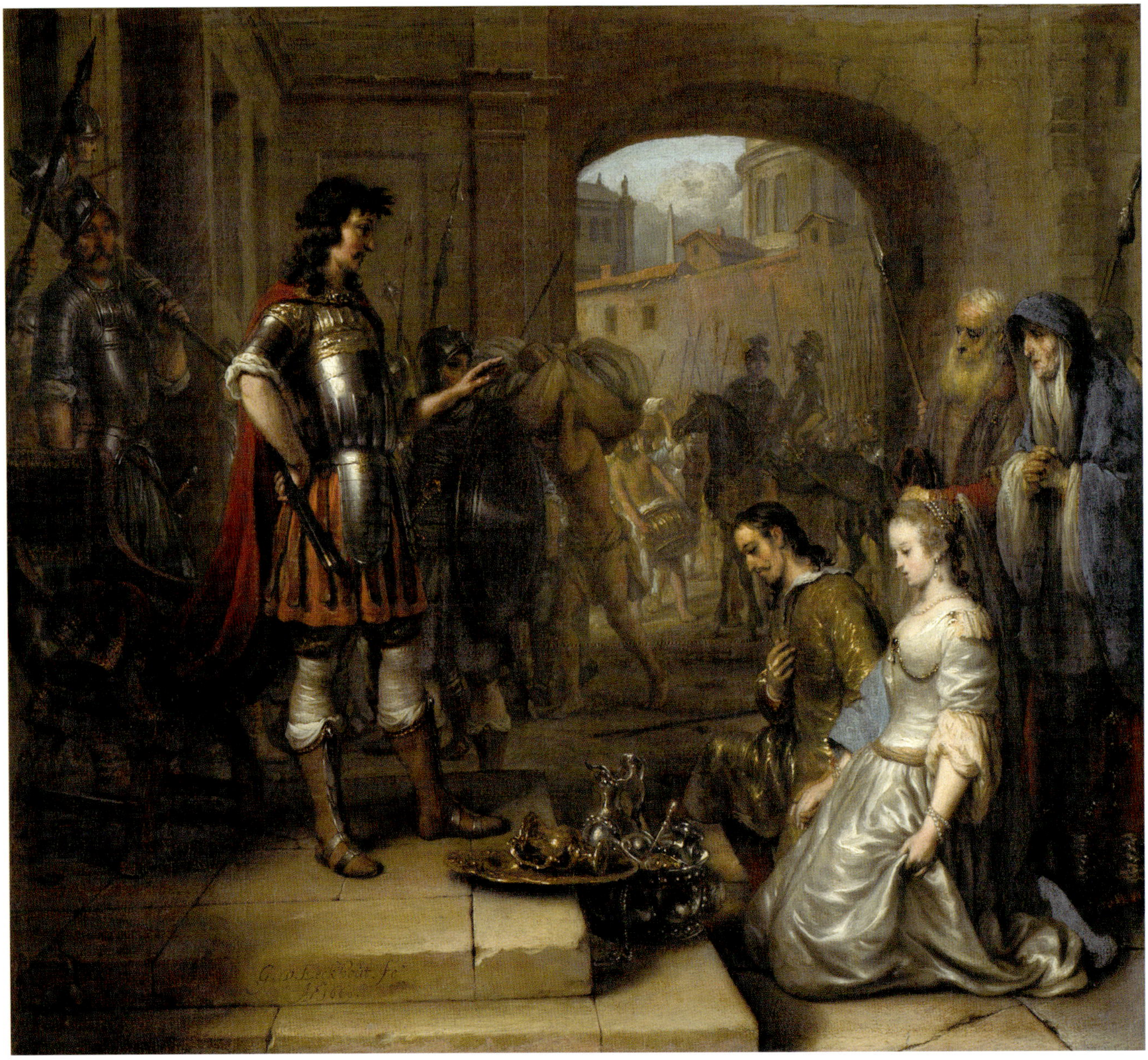

55. Gerbrand van den Eeckhout 1621–1674
The Continence of Scipio, 1669. Oil on canvas, 44.7 x 50.2 cm
Alexandre Leleux bequest, 1873. Inv. P. 291

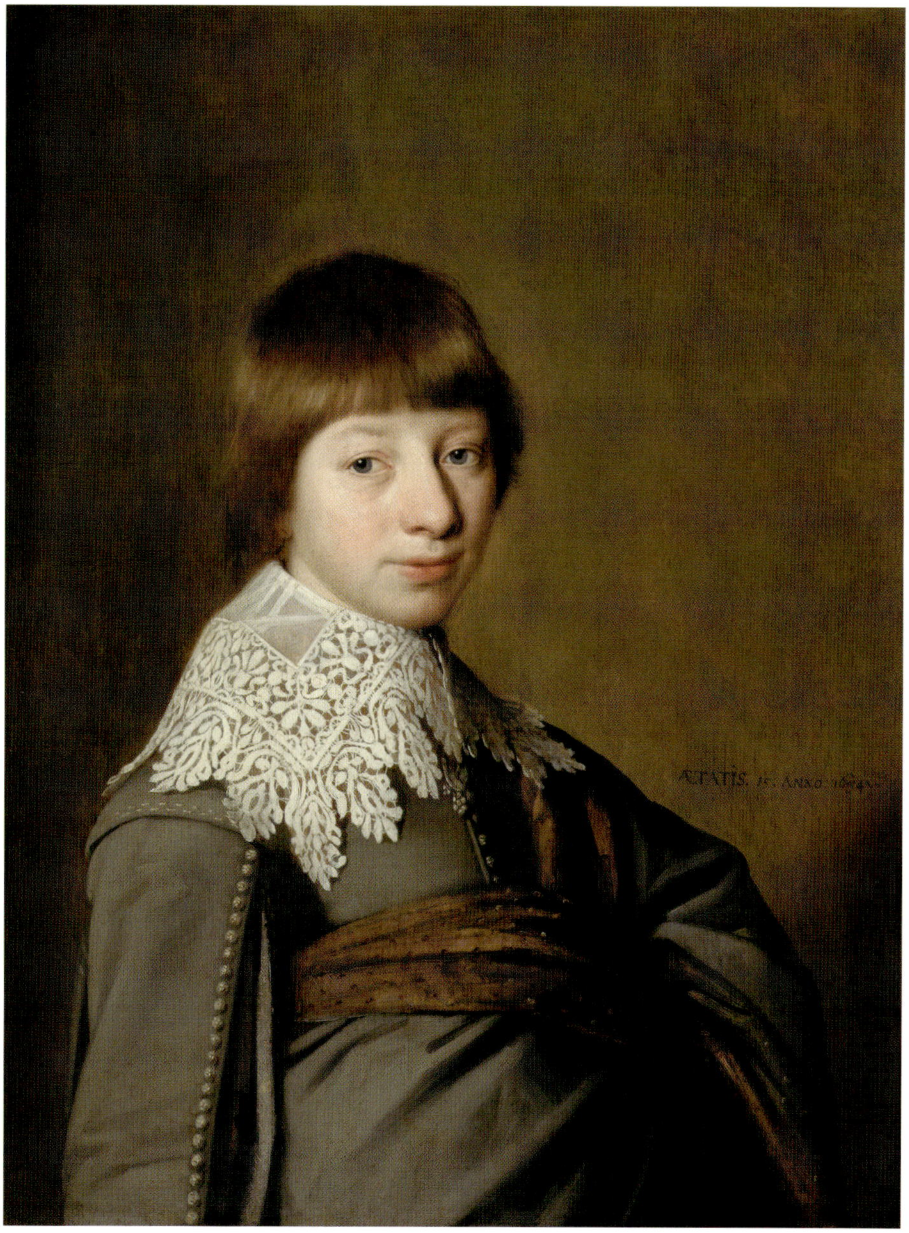

56. Johannes Cornelisz Verspronck 1606/09–1662
Portrait of a Young Man, 1634.
Oil on panel, 71 x 54 cm
Purchased 1888. Inv. P. 300

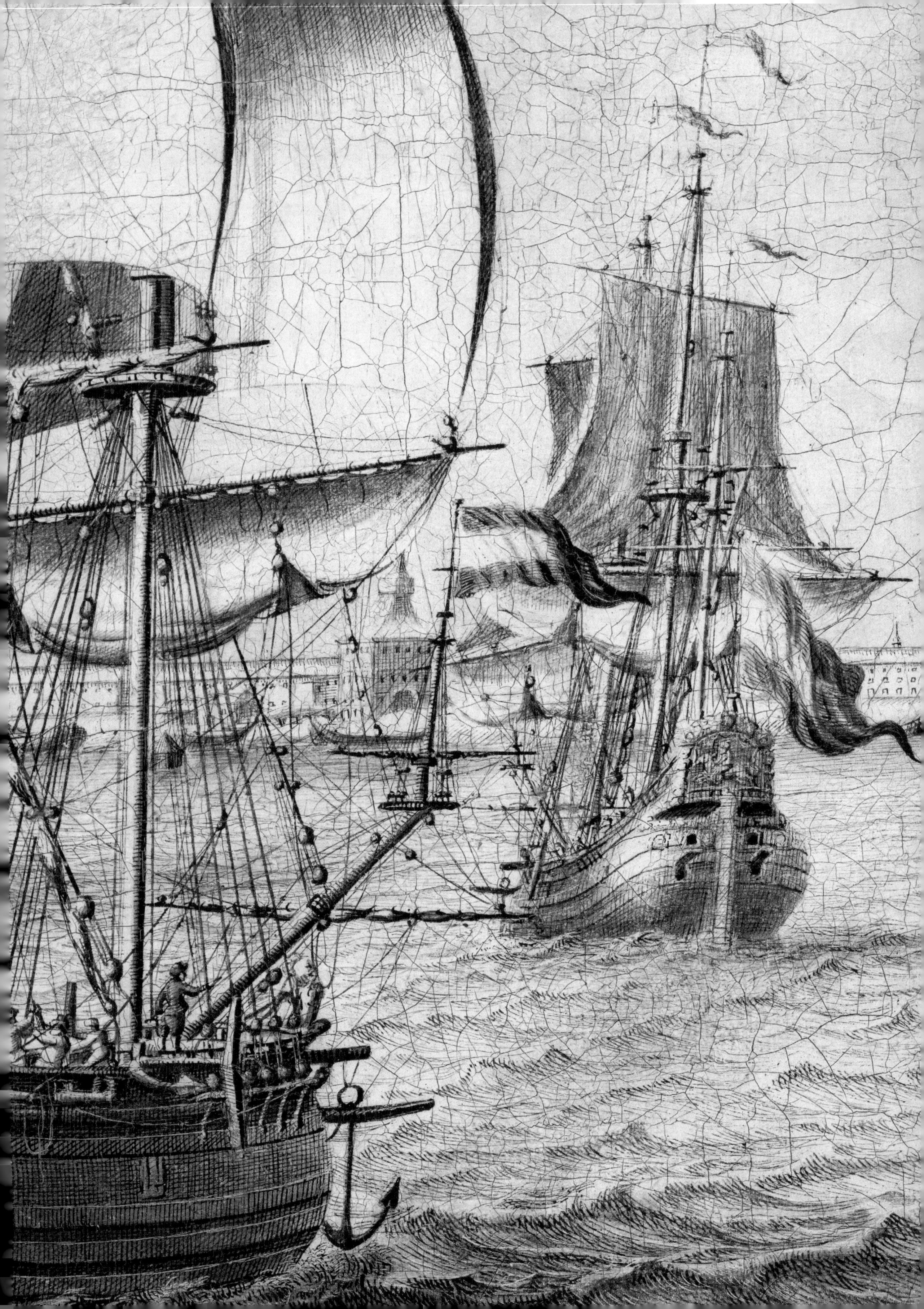

his virtuosity in rendering fabric. Here, he puts this skill in the service of a particularly dramatic subject: the prophet, wearing a coarse sackcloth, announces to the satin-draped queen who has come to visit him that her son is going to die as punishment for the idolatry of his father, King Jeroboam.

There are relatively few still lifes in Lille's Dutch collection. The magnifi-
cent panel by Balthasar van der Ast helps fill this gap. With its crystalline, 52
mineral-like brushstroke, it brilliantly represents the School of Middelburg
as well.

Noteworthy among the portraits is the *Portrait of a Young Boy* by Johannes Cornelisz Verspronck. This alleged pupil of Hals, whose delicate paint handling moves away from the broad touch of his master, sensitively portrays a fifteen-year-old boy whose still-childish features contrast with the adult demeanour he endeavours to adopt.

The most influential landscape is probably Jacob van Ruisdael's *Wheat* 60
Field. Though less impressive than many others by this artist, it is luminous
and in an exceptional state of preservation. A disciple of Frans Hals like his
elder brother Adriaen, Isack van Ostade was a painter of genre scenes and
landscapes. His landscapes often recall Salomon van Ruysdael, but his *Skaters* 59
makes one think more of Jan van Goyen, for example his *Landscape with the*
Pellekussenpoort, also in the Lille collection. It was composed in the studio, as
was Van Goyen's custom, by assembling motifs drawn from nature.

Church interiors, as they are depicted in several paintings, exemplify the
Dutch interest in perspective. The *Interior of the Church of St Lawrence, Rotter-*
dam by Anthonie de Lorme (*c.* 1600/05–1673) is the work of a respectable artist
from Rotterdam who specialized in views of that city's large church. The *Inte-*
rior of the Nieuwe Kerk, Delft by Emanuel de Witte shows an entirely different 58
ambition. Unconcerned with accurate perspective, the artist uses light admira-
bly. The figures mark out the space and lead the eye toward the focus of the
composition: the tomb of William of Orange.

Seascapes reflect an essential aspect of life in the Dutch Republic. Lille has
several 'painted in pen', executed in ink on a white ground, imitating the ap-
pearance of an engraving. A late minor master, Adriaen Cornelisz Salm was 57
so successful with this technique that he practised it exclusively, simplifying it
somewhat by replacing the fine hatches of a Van de Velde with washes.

The most famous work in Lille's Dutch collection is undoubtedly the small panel by Pieter Codde, a delicate monochrome of ochres and browns, that to a certain extent lies on the boundary between genre scene and allegory. The wealth and ambiguity of its iconography account for its success: is this young man satisfied with his austere life of study, or has he suddenly become aware of the vanity of knowledge? The energetic brushstroke, exceptional for Codde, has sometimes led art historians to evoke the influence of the young Rembrandt, to whom it has even recently been suggested to reattribute this work.

AD

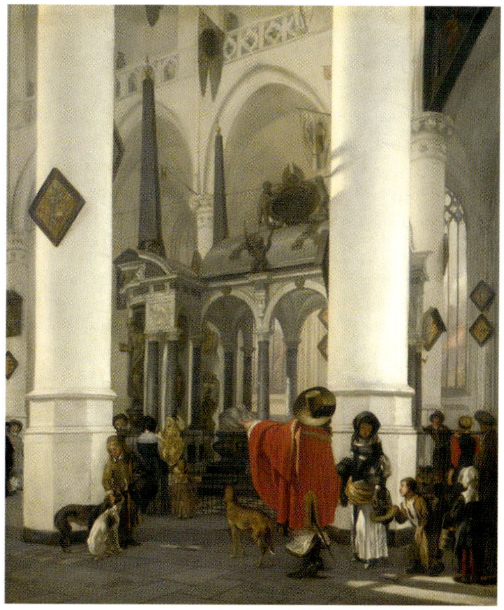

58. Emanuel de Witte *c.* 1616/18–1691/92
Interior of the Nieuwe Kerk, Delft, 1656.
Oil on canvas, 97 x 85 cm
Purchased 1890. Inv. P. 236

57. Adriaen Cornelisz Salm 1657–1720
Calm Sea. Pen and wash on canvas,
78 x 110 cm
Purchased by the city, 1860. Inv. P. 1605

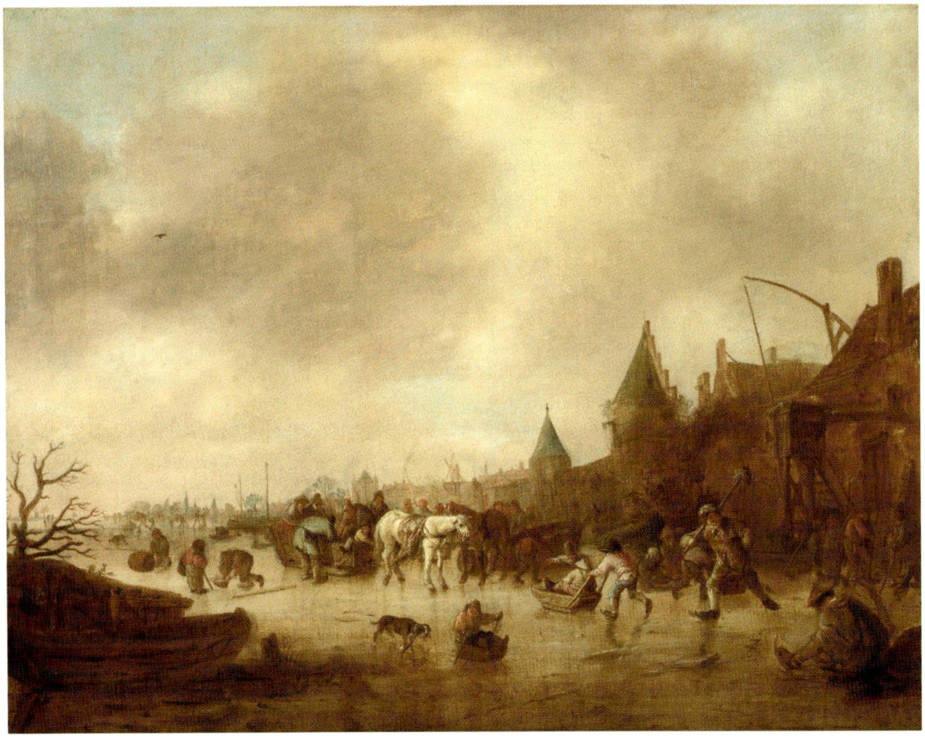

59, 61. Isack van Ostade 1621–1649
Skaters, 1641. Oil on canvas,
85 x 110 cm

Antoine Brasseur donation, 1885. Inv. P. 275

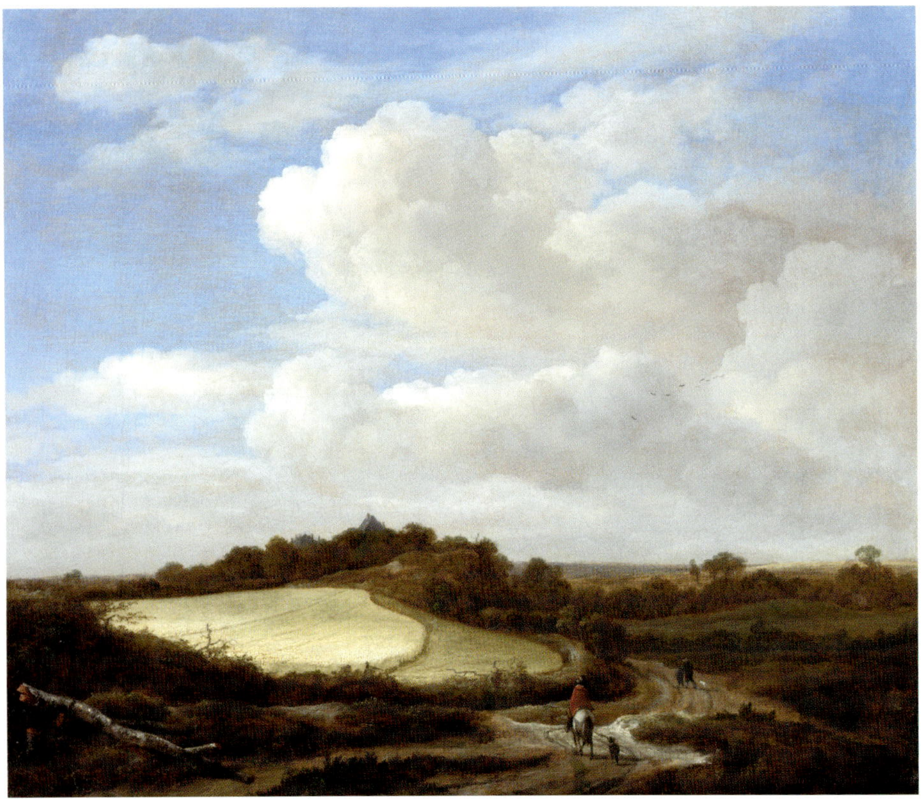

60. Jacob van Ruisdael *c.* 1628/29–1682
Wheat Field, *c.* 1660. Oil on canvas,
46 x 56 cm

Alexandre Leleux bequest, 1873. Inv. P. 224

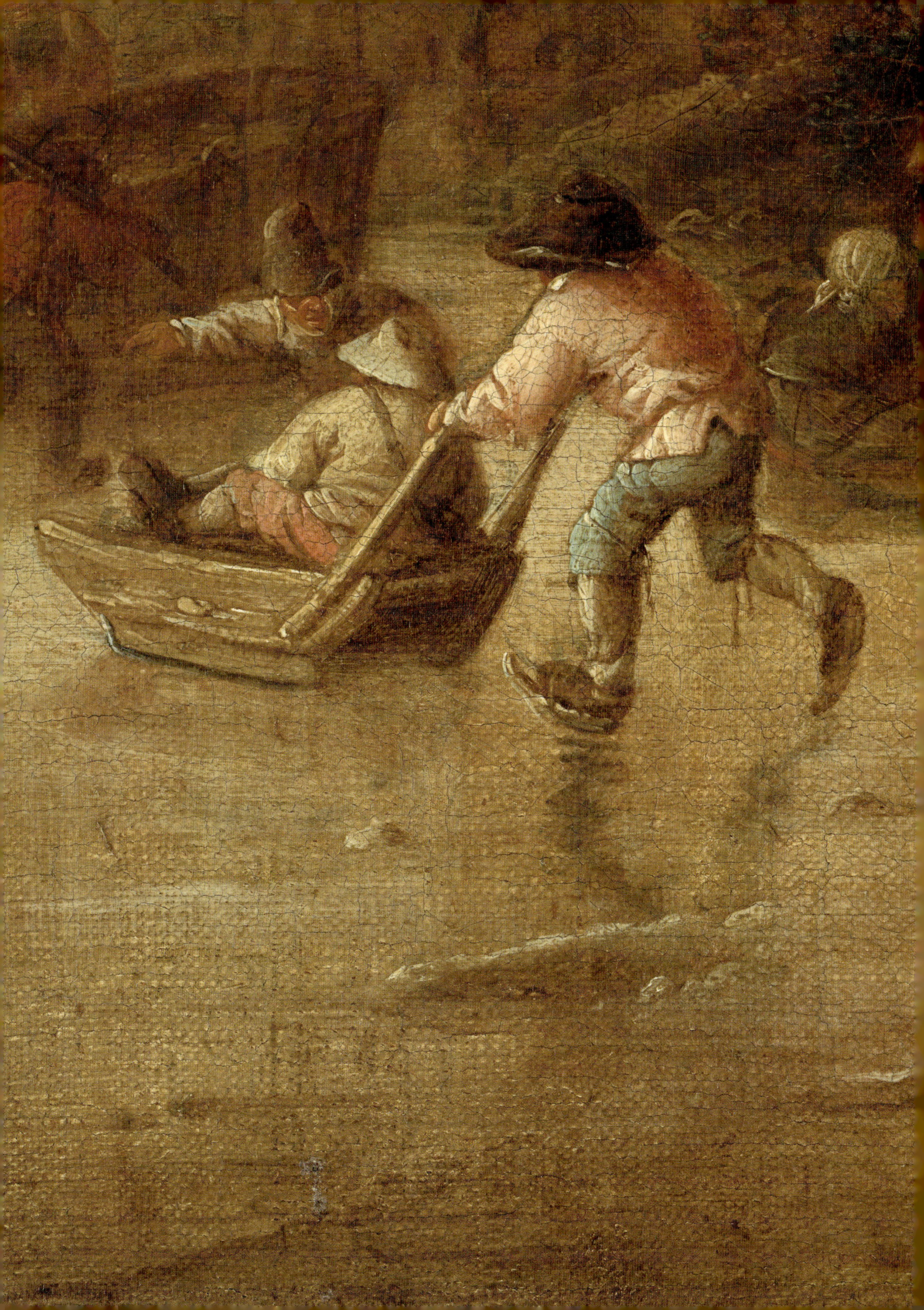

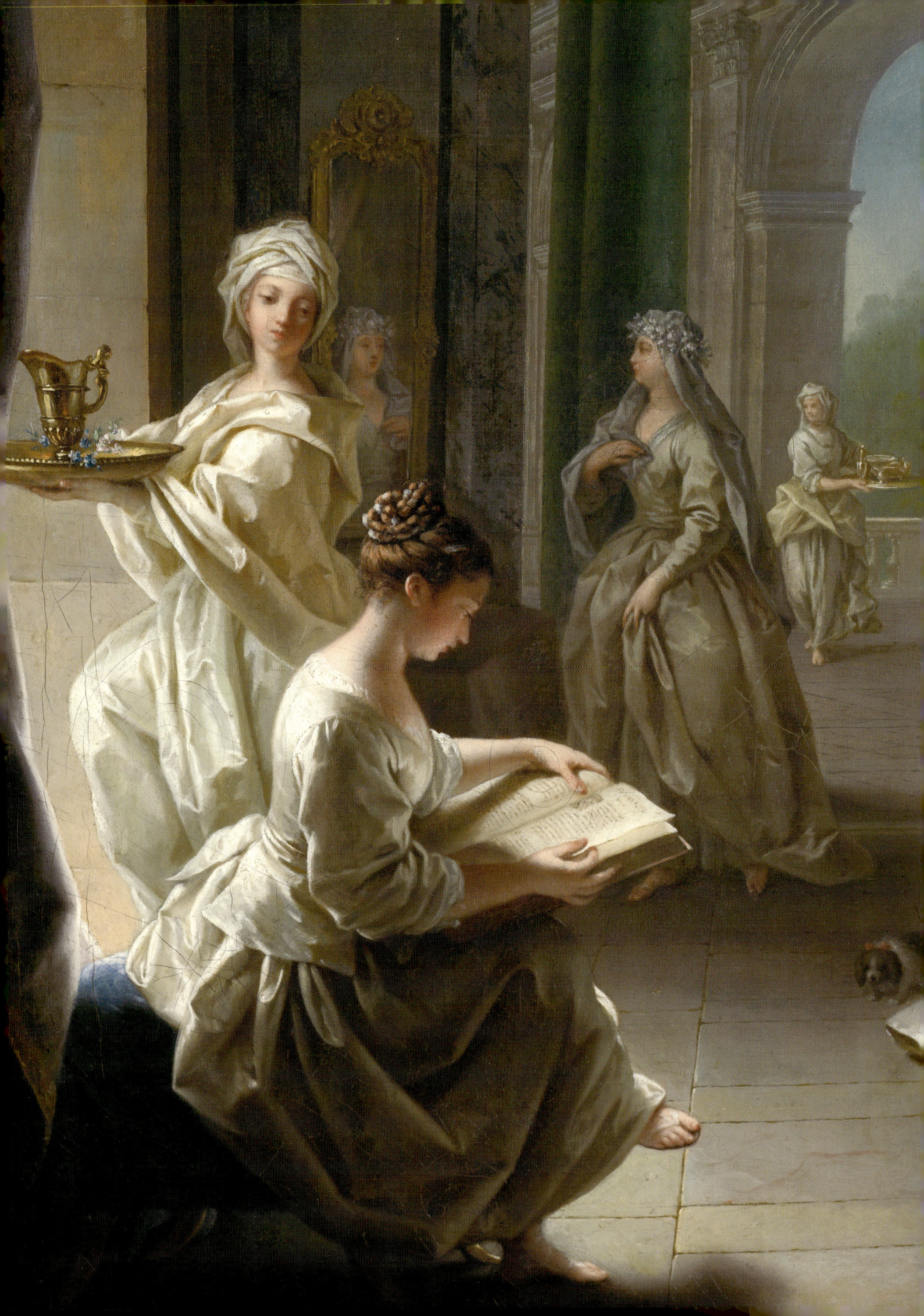

French Painting in the Seventeenth and Eighteenth Centuries

The Seventeenth Century

The collection of 17th-century French painting reflects the particular relationship that Lille maintained with the central power after its reattachment to France in 1667 and through its participation in the Chaptal decree, when state consignments favoured painters from the Flemish cultural sphere, to the detriment of those who had spent time in Rome. Thus, the absence of Simon Vouet, Claude Lorrain and Nicolas Poussin is noticeable, which highlights all the more the presence of Philippe de Champaigne and Georges Lallemant. Lallemant's studio, where Philippe de Champaigne studied, was an eclectic forum of various influences mingled with recollections of the late Gothic style. This is the case with Lille's *Adoration of the Magi*, in the arrangement of *64* the figures – a Flemish-style naturalism that does not mask the Mannerist character seen in the angularity of the drapery, the vibrancy of the colour and the ornamental richness.

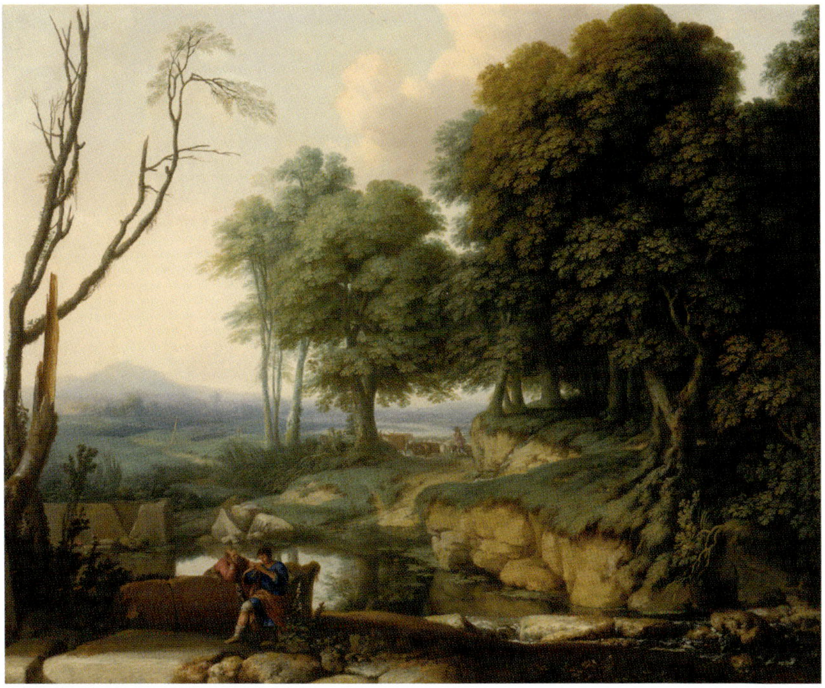

63. Laurent de La Hyre 1606–1656
Landscape with Flute-Playing Shepherd.
Oil on canvas, 106.5 x 131.5 cm
Acquired 1973. Inv. P. 1877

Another of Lallemant's students, Laurent de La Hyre, having entered the collection in 1973, introduces the artistic consideration of the landscape. The *Landscape with Flute-Playing Shepherd* at first appears to be a personal medita- *63* tion suffused with a sober melancholy that ties Arcadian happiness to a reflection on time and death. To implement his philosophical proposition, La Hyre calls upon the double experience of linear perspective, required for history

62. Jean Raoux 1677–1734
Modern Maidens (detail), 1728.
Oil on canvas, 92 x 72 cm
Acquired 1979. Inv. P. 1948

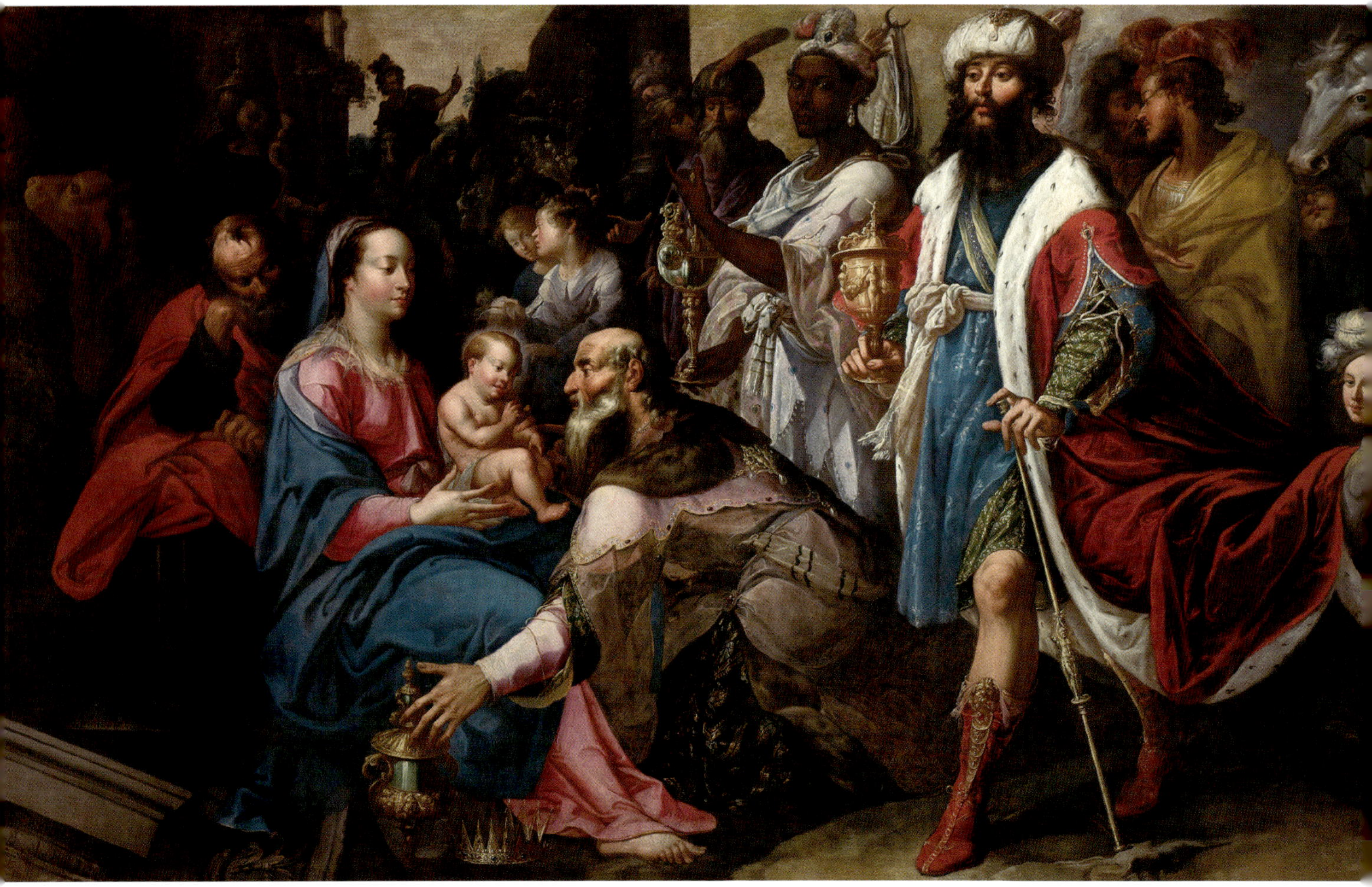

64. Georges Lallemant *c.* 1575–1636
The Adoration of the Magi. Oil on canvas, 189 x 315.5 cm
From a church in Paris, state consignment, 1804.
Inv. P. 322

painting, and Flemish-style aerial perspective based on the play of tonal values, recalling the manner of Paul Bril. The dark green masses of the clumps of trees stand on rock embankments in chiaroscuro, prolonged by the reflection in a spring that follows the composition's diagonal axis.

66 *The Nativity* by Philippe de Champaigne, from the high altar of the Tubœuf family chapel in the Church of the Oratory in Paris, dates from 1643. Flemish sensibility shows through in the fullness of the drapery and the warm shading of the faces. Still, the almost implacably precise use of line is already there. It marks the quest for an inner identity in the painter's spiritual aesthetics.

We must not forget the great Lille painter Arnould de Vuez, whose *St Cecilia*
65 *with Three Angel Musicians* is one of many commissions he executed for the religious buildings of his city. In it, he skilfully arranges the lessons of a classicism inspired by Charles Le Brun with remnants of Rubens. Also an offshoot from Charles Le Brun is Charles de La Fosse. *Jesus Delivering the Keys to St Peter*, completed in 1700, is from the high altar of the collegiate church of Saint-Pierre in Lille. Eustache Le Sueur, of the classical current and a student of Simon
67 Vouet, painted a *Mary Magdalene in Prayer*, perhaps for an individual Carmelite. The spiritual function of the cult of Mary Magdalene was the exhortation to penitence. She is exemplary in her turning away from a life encumbered with ephemeral wealth and pleasures and towards a sparing, solitary life.

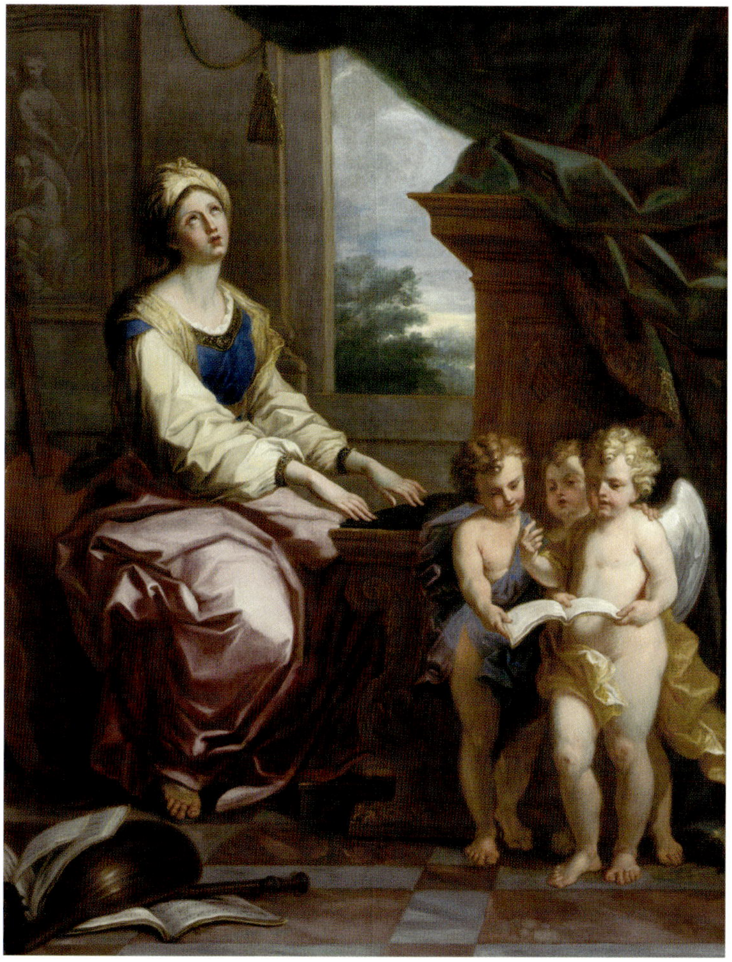

65. Arnould de Vuez 1644–1720
St Cecilia with Three Angel Musicians.
Oil on canvas, 270.5 x 212 cm

Executed for the collegiate church of Saint-Pierre, Lille. Inv. P. 359

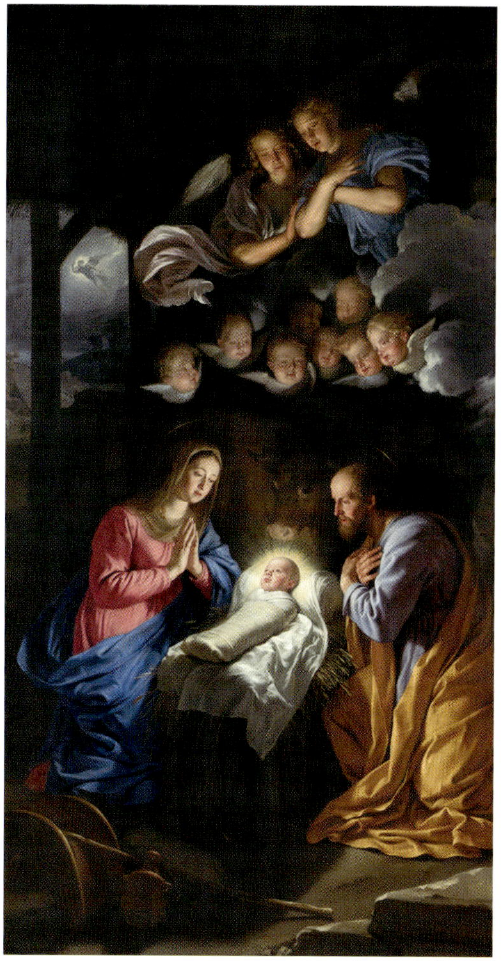

66. Philippe de Champaigne 1602–1674
Nativity, 1643. Oil on canvas, 207 x 116 cm

Church of the Oratory, Paris, state consignment, 1804. Inv. P. 162

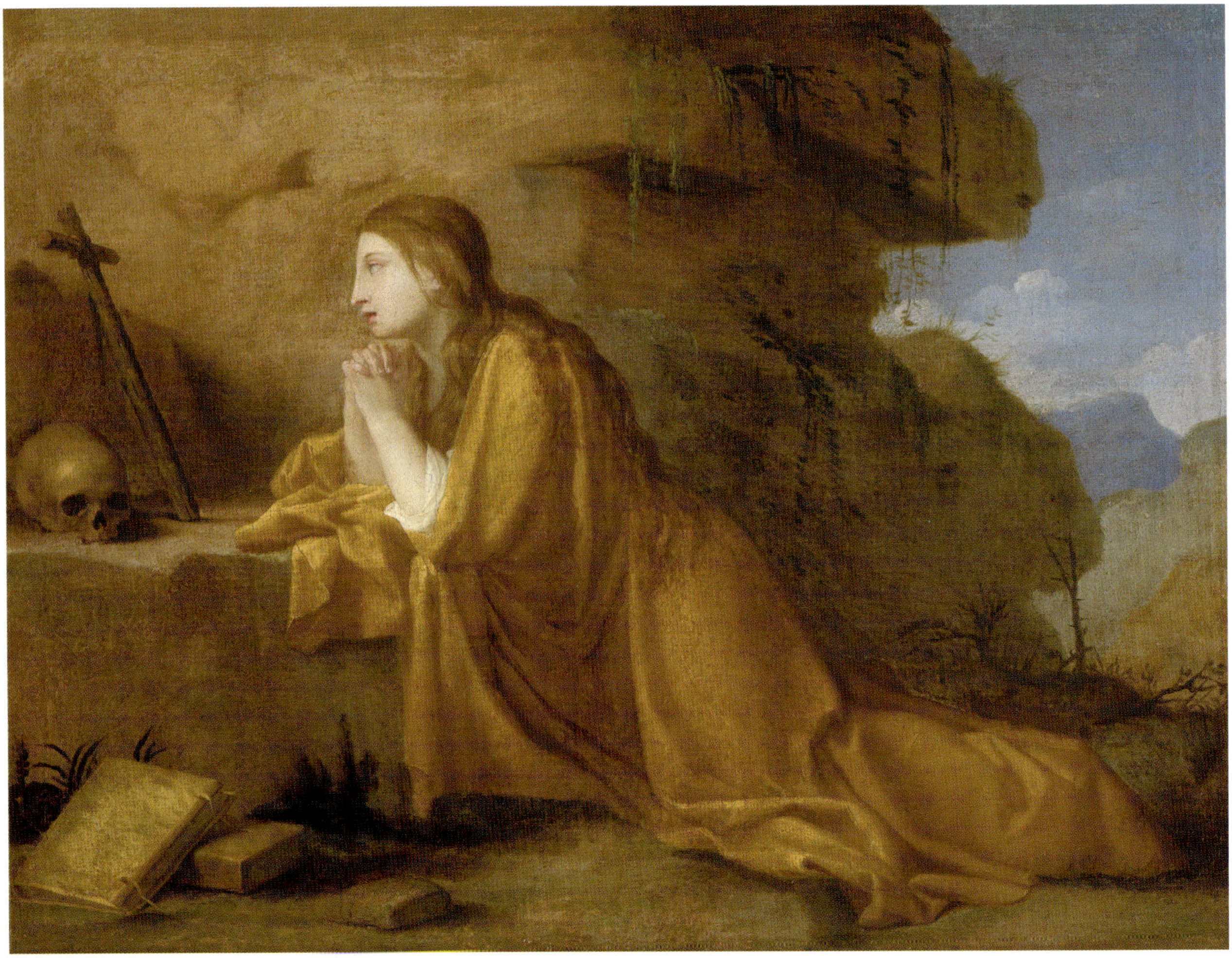

67. Eustache Le Sueur 1617–1665
Mary Magdalene in Prayer.
Oil on canvas, 48.5 x 64 cm
Gift of Jules Maciet, 1888. Inv. P. 951

Recently, to highlight the Atticist current so powerful in the Paris milieu of the 1640s, the museum acquired the *Birth of the Virgin* by Jacques Stella. The official painter to Richelieu, Stella falls under the grand tradition of Raphael. This painting is a major addition to the collection for both its quality and its origin: it was commissioned by Anne of Austria for her private oratory when she was settling into the Palais Royal (at the time, the Palais Cardinal). Anne of Austria wanted to make this oratory her crowning achievement. It housed a group of paintings by the most famous Parisian painters of the day, like Philippe de Champaigne, Simon Vouet, Sébastien Bourdon and Laurent de La Hyre, all of whom painted compositions on the life and attributes of the Virgin.

The Eighteenth Century

There are not many 18th-century French paintings in Lille, and at times their thread is discontinuous. However, the collection saw a number of additions between 1975 and 1985, crowned by the acquisition of Chardin's *Silver Beaker* in
72 1990. This acquisition makes it possible to evoke the vitality of 18th-century painting. The previous century's dispute between Poussinistes and Rubénistes underscored 18th-century French painting's debt to the Flemish for their rich and supple craft and taste for colour. By extension, the palette of the Venetians and Italian baroque art would exert its fascination before rococo painting unfurled its swirling splendours under the aegis of Boucher and Fragonard.

1700–1750: 'The Grand Manner'

Jean Jouvenet's *The Last Rites* marks the passage from the 17th to the 18th century: prolonging the classicism of Poussin, it contains the breath of life that would animate the century's entire production. Implicitly, it foretells the reaction of David, eighty years later. 68

Mindful of the Flemish masters, Nicolas de Largillière, the great portraitist of his time, painted the famous likeness of his father-in-law, the painter Jean-Baptiste Forest, with authority and an obvious sense of psychology. The sitter poses with his palette and brushes in a soldierly way, his right hand resting on 71

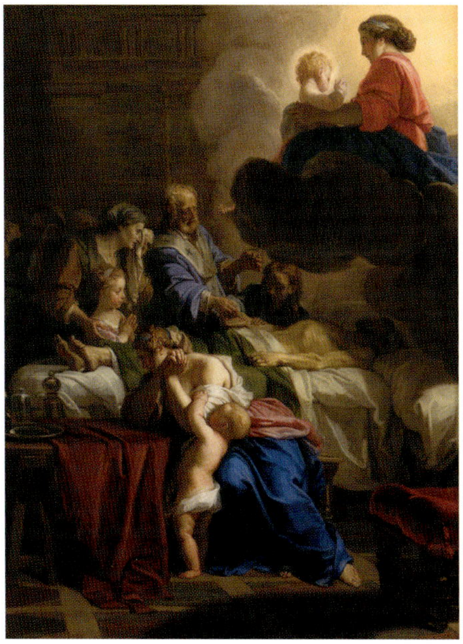

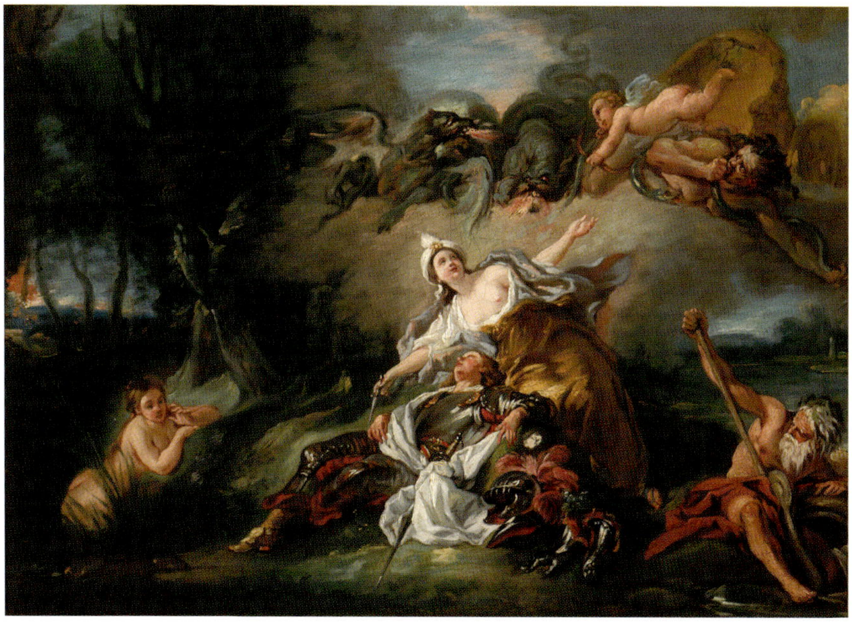

68. Jean-Baptiste Jouvenet 1644–1717
The Last Rites. Oil on canvas,
232 x 172 cm
Deposit from the Musée du Louvre in 1998. Inv. D. 98.1.1

69. Jean-François de Troy 1669–1752
Armida about to Stab Rinaldo, 1725?.
Oil on canvas, 53.8 x 76.6 cm
Acquired 1970. Inv. P. 1860

his hip. The figure is full of energy, the colouring warm. A surprising portrait by a little-known painter, Robert de Séri, depicts the face of a young woman who is indifferent to our gaze. The firm, colourful execution in a familiar and spirited mode anticipates the art of Renoir by a century and a half. Before preferring still life, Jean-Baptiste Oudry tried his hand at the portrait for a time: his *'Contrôleur des guerres'*, caressed by a pearly light, is more on the order of the official ceremonial portraits in favour at the time. Oudry derived the virtuoso effects of texture and light from his master, Largillière.

If Alexandre Desportes, a still-life and animal painter, left us canvases executed in a high key, Jean-Baptiste Chardin can embody the genre of still life in France all on his own, so exceptionally wide is his work's influence. Skilfully ordered and bathed in the golden glow of the 17th-century Dutch, *The Silver Beaker* expresses a serious and well thought-out personal approach 72
to the real world.

The Rembrandtesque *Old Woman Eating*, formerly attributed to Chardin, has been reassigned to Jean-François de Troy. The other side of this talented painter features gallant history subjects such as *Armida about to Stab Rinaldo*, 69
a sketch that attests to the liveliness of the genre in that century, exalting the colouring of the 16th-century Venetians. Henri de Favanne illustrates the art of decoration in a preparatory sketch for a ceiling at the Château de Chanteloup, *The Kingdoms of Valencia and Aragon Surrendering to Philip V of Spain*.

Jean Raoux was fond of genre scenes, skilfully making use of a theatre-like decorative interplay. In *Antique Maidens* and *Modern Maidens*, he contrasts two 62
worlds, where young women illustrate the severe vocation of ancient priestesses on the one hand and the frivolous life under Louis XV on the other hand.

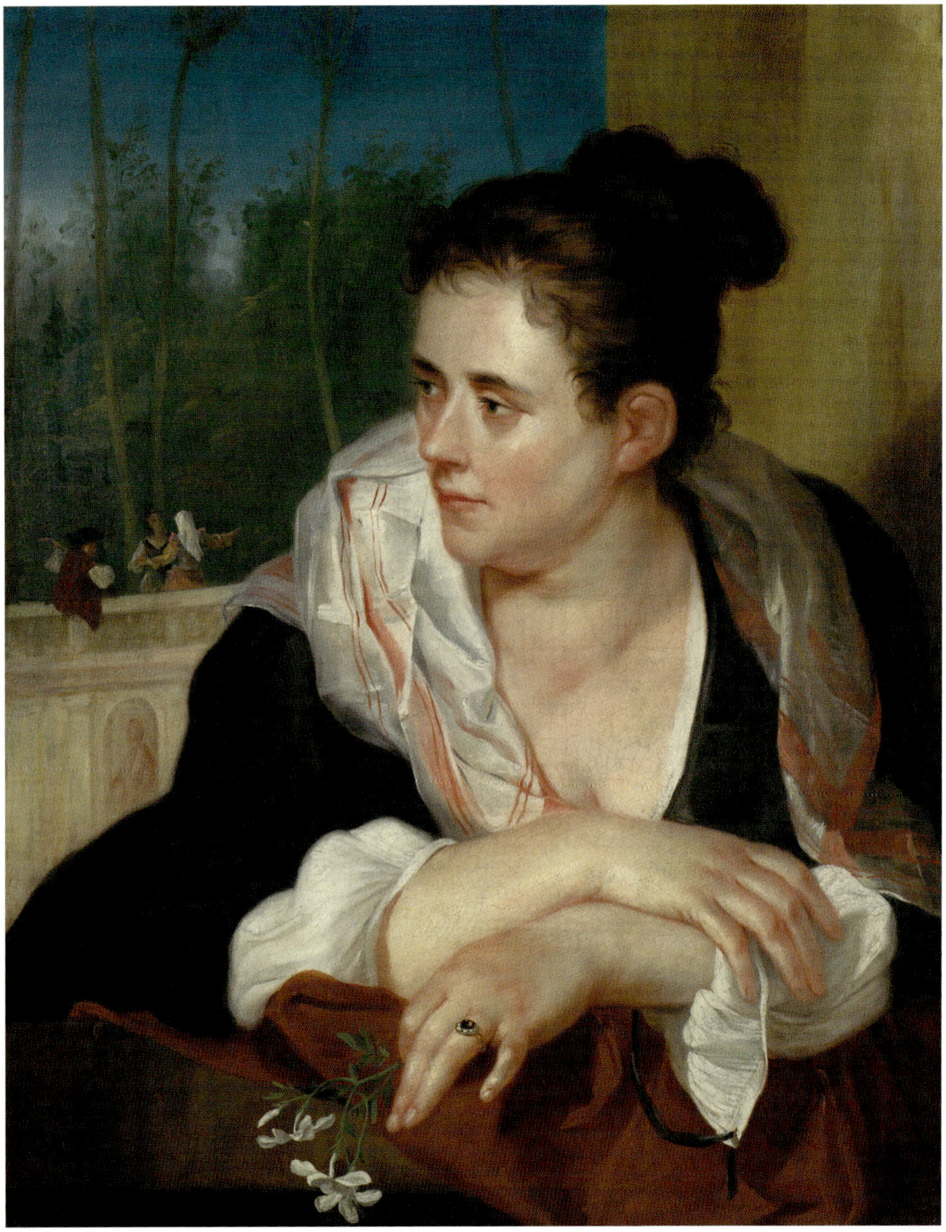

70. Robert de Séri (Paul-Ponce Robert) 1686–1733
Portrait of a Woman, 1722.
Oil on canvas, 71 x 58 cm
Gift of Paul Leroi, 1883. Inv. P. 347

71. Nicolas de Largillière 1656–1746
The Painter Jean-Baptiste Forest (1636–1712), Salon of 1704.
Oil on canvas, 128.5 x 96 cm
Gift of Jules Brame (deputy of the Département du Nord), 1861. Inv. P. 328

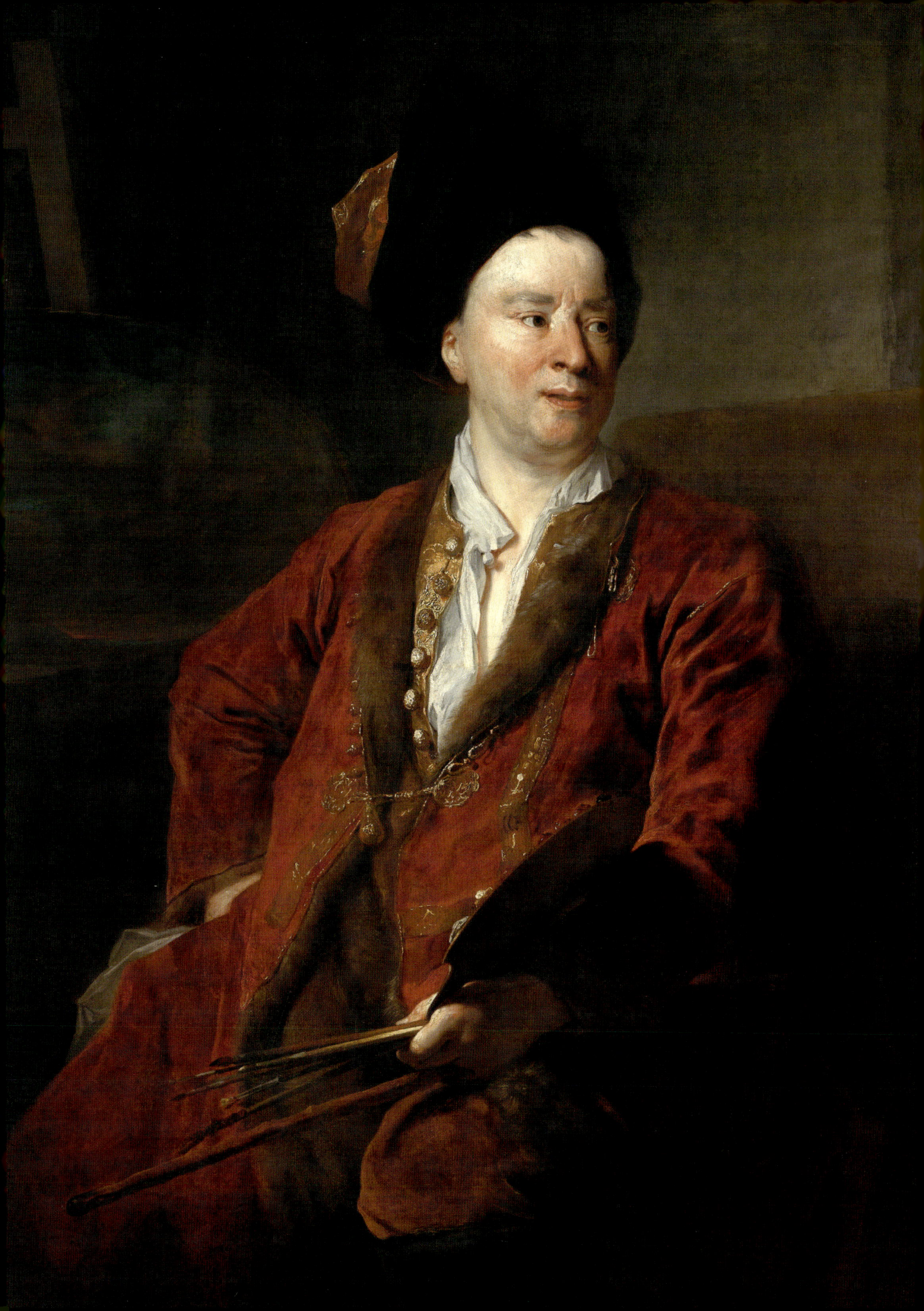

Jean Restout, a nephew of Jouvenet, would contribute to giving ecclesiastical history painting a baroque impulse, as seen in his famous *Journey to Emmaus* (1735). The later oil sketch of the *Assumption of the Virgin* by Noël Hallé follows the same current.

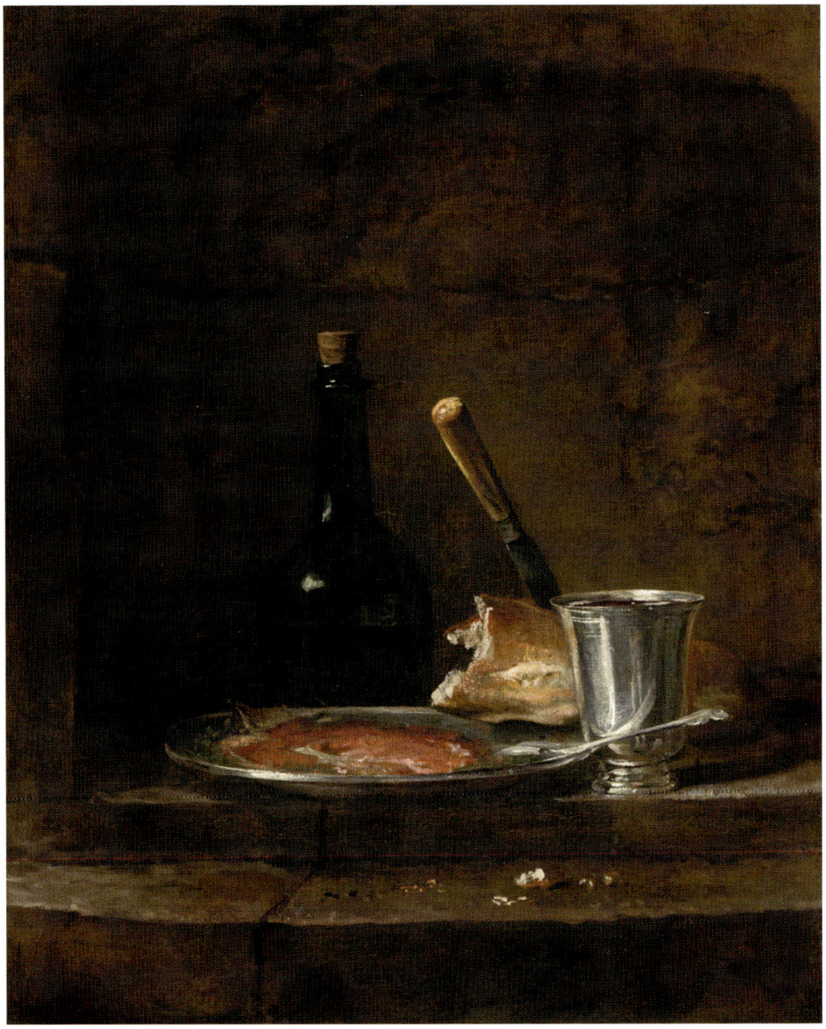

72. Jean-Siméon Chardin 1699–1779
The Silver Beaker, c. 1730. Oil on canvas, 81 x 64.5 cm
Acquired with the assistance of FRAM, the state (Fonds national du Patrimoine) and White Public Relations, 1990. Inv. P. 1998

1760–1800: Rococo and Neoclassicism

The oil sketch became an autonomous work of art in its own right. This is epitomized by the *Adoration of the Shepherds*, a lively interpretation by Fragonard after Rubens. François Boucher's graceful and sensual art shines in the fluid touch and myriad nuances of his grisailles, a genre in which he excelled. As the frontispiece of a book, he produced a satire on the reign of Louis
73 XV: *France Groans with the Troubles That Divide Her; Fidelity Consoles Her and Presents Her with Zealous Subjects*.

Painters introduced light-heartedness and seduction, favouring gallant mythology, such as Noël Hallé in *Aegleis and Silenus* (1771). On the other hand, Nicolas Lépicié with *The Courage of Porcia* (Salon of 1777) and Lagrenée the Elder with *Popilius and Antiochus* (Salon of 1779) created calm and dignified scenes glorifying ancient history. Hubert Robert arranged imaginary views based on ancient Rome. Though attracted by this modernity, Joseph-Marie Vien and Jean-Baptiste Greuze kept the memory of Boucher's
75 grace in *Psyche Recognizing Cupid Asleep* (1761) and *Psyche Crowning Cupid* (c. 1790).

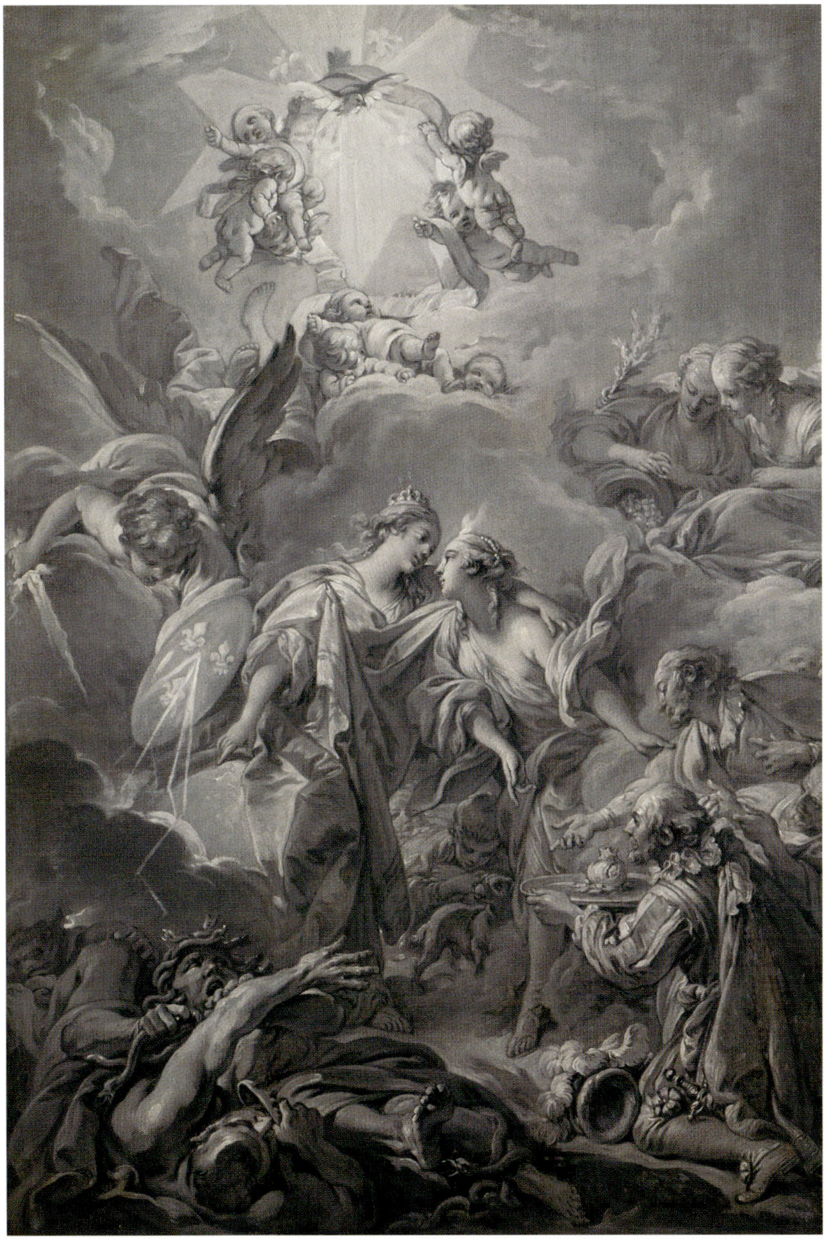

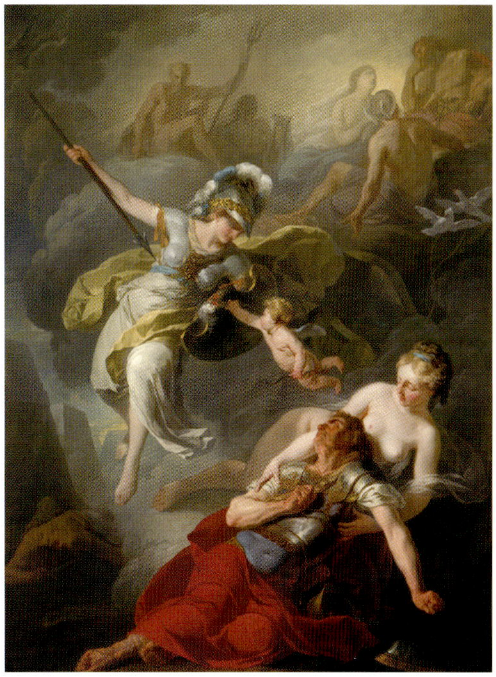

74. Joseph-Benoît Suvée 1743–1807
The Combat of Minerva and Mars, 1771.
Oil on canvas, 142 x 108 cm
Deposit from the Musée du Louvre, 1872. Inv. P. 1957

73. François Boucher 1703–1770
France Groans with the Troubles That Divide Her, 1760?. Oil on canvas, 63.2 x 42.3 cm
Acquired 1882. Inv. P. 338

In 1771, Joseph-Benoît Suvée won the Prix de Rome over David with his
painting on the theme of the Combat of Minerva and Mars. He made skilful
use of antique vocabulary to paint the scene from the *Iliad* in which Venus 74
attempts to shield the wounded Mars from the wrath of Minerva. A small
painting, today considered to be an autograph replica, reconstructs David's
mannered and cluttered composition.

Despite a hard-won Prix de Rome (1774), upon his return from Rome Jacques-
Louis David conceived the painting that first signals Neoclassicism, *Belisarius
Begging for Alms*, which caused a sensation at the Salon of 1781. Make way for 80
heroic and virtuous subject-matter for the edification of citizens: the unjust
downfall of the victorious Byzantine general, who, now blind, is reduced to
begging, to the utter astonishment of an old soldier. The sketch for a portrait of
Napoleon dressed for his coronation attests to the glorious career of David until
his exile to Brussels in 1816, at the fall of the Empire. *Apelles Painting Campaspe*,
an unfinished work from this period, recalls the painter's taste for love themes
of Antiquity. Alexander magnanimously gives his mistress Campaspe to the
painter Apelles, who has fallen under the spell of the young woman's charms.

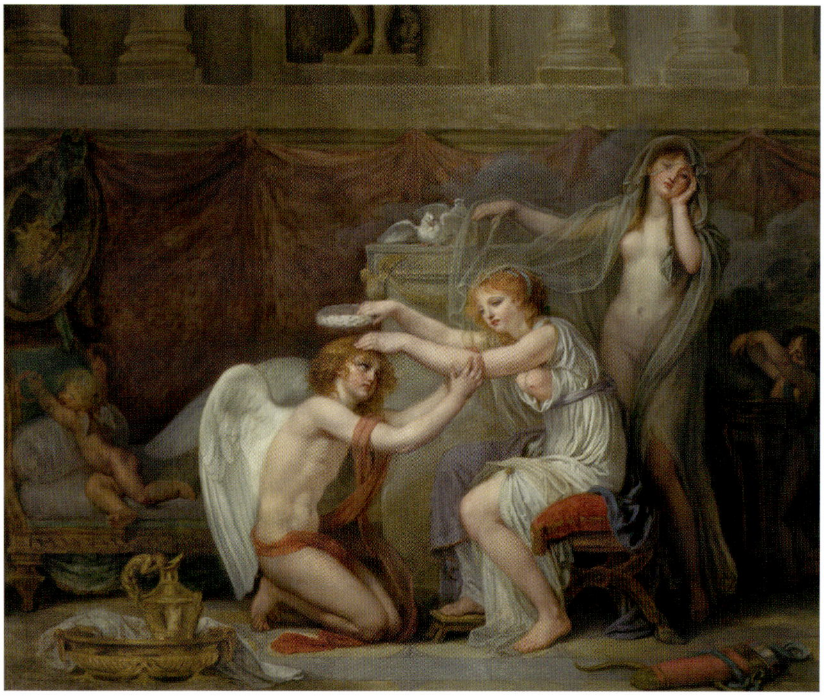

75. Jean-Baptiste Greuze 1725–1805
Psyche Crowning Cupid, c. 1790.
Oil on canvas, 147 x 180 cm
Caroline Greuze sale, 1843. Alexandre Leleux bequest, 1873. Inv. P. 389

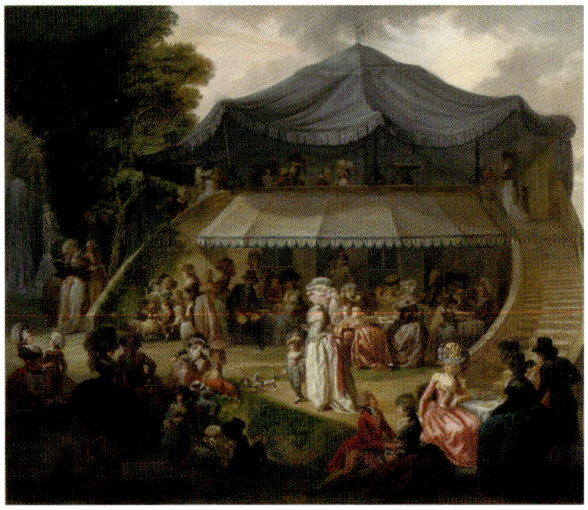

76–77. François-Louis-Joseph Watteau
1758–1823
A Festival at the Colosseum, c. 1789–92.
Oil on canvas, 76.5 x 92.3 cm
Gift of A. and J. Delannoy, 1861. Inv. P. 352

David's studio trained a host of artists. A follower of Neoclassical princi-
5 ples, Jean-Baptiste Wicar eventually opted for an Italian career under the seal
of Raphael, as is shown by the ambitious *Raising of the Widow's Son of Nain*
(1816). Despite promising talent, François Watteau restricted his career to Lille,
where, at the dawn of the Revolution, he created the masterpiece *A Festival at*
76 *the Colosseum*, an elegant evocation of the last glimmer of Lille's genteel soci-
ety under the *ancien régime*. His father, Louis Watteau, nephew of the great
Antoine, displayed a pictorial verve, tinged with poetry, to depict an embellish-
ment of country life in the framework of *The Fiddlers* and of its pendant *The
Wafer Vendor*.

Finally, let us mention Louis Boilly, who looks forward to the 19th century.
Heir to 17th-century Northern painting but none the less admired by David,
he forged a solid reputation under the Restoration and the Empire. The mu-
79 seum has a series of strong works, among them *The Triumph of Marat*, related
to the cult of the hero extolled by the Revolution: the painting describes the
popular rejoicing at the acquittal of Marat, 'the friend of the people', who was
suspected of hostility toward the Girondins. The famous *Studio of Isabey*, from
1798, assembles the greatest artists of the time – painters, sculptors and archi-
tects – around Isabey. The museum owns twenty-six preparatory studies, in-
81-85 cluding *Corbet, Drölling, Duplessis-Bertaux, Bourgeois, Lethière and Carle Vernet*,
true masterpieces where the psychological quality vies with the minutely de-
tailed virtuosity of the brushwork in treating light and material. Less common
than his many small head-and-shoulders portraits, the full-length portraits re-
veal Boilly's fine pre-Romantic sensitivity. He ascribes the sitter's mood to the
78 landscape. Thus, the melancholy of *Mme d'Aucourt de Saint-Just* is captured in
the dark cave and the water flowing, like life. ADW

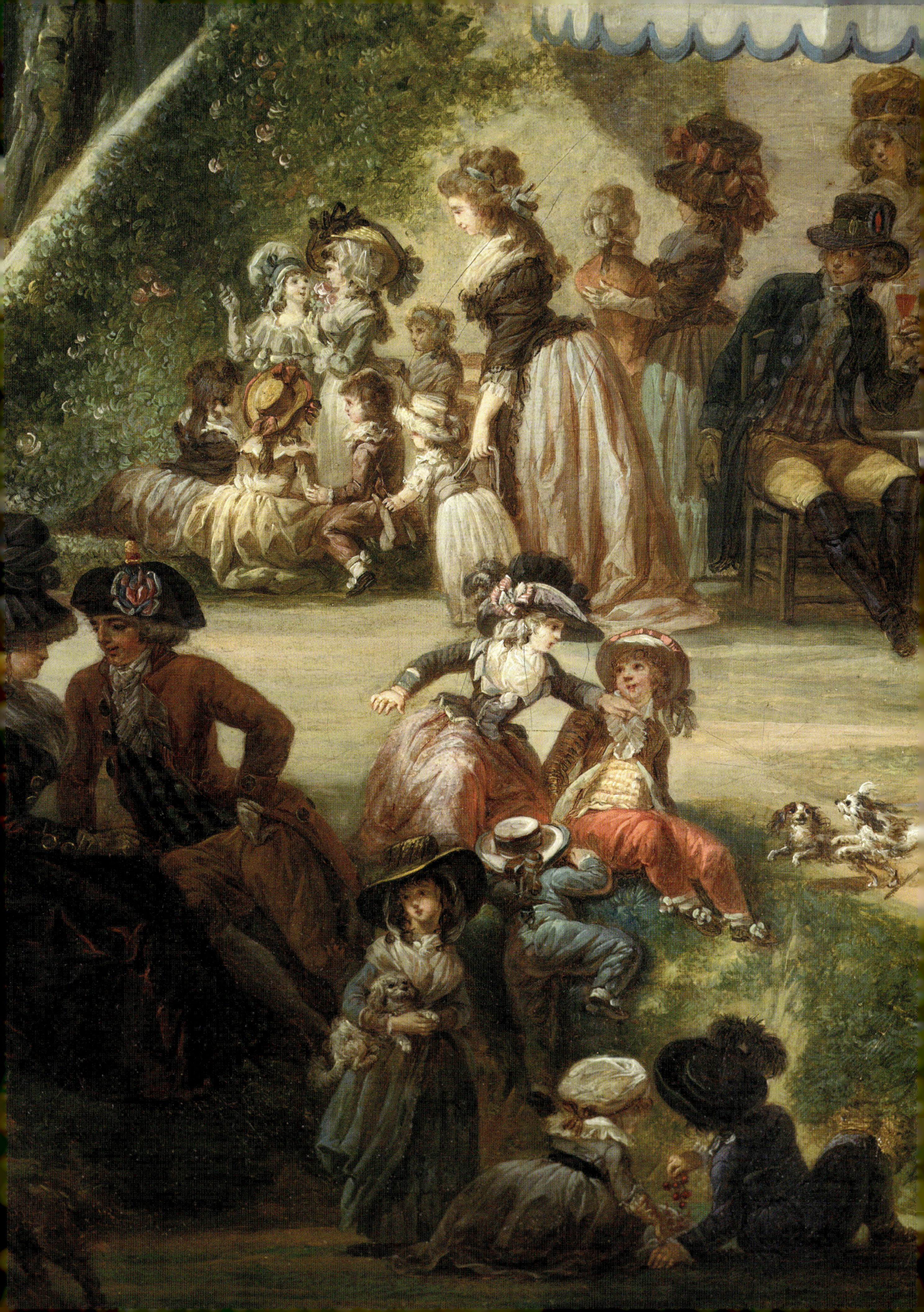

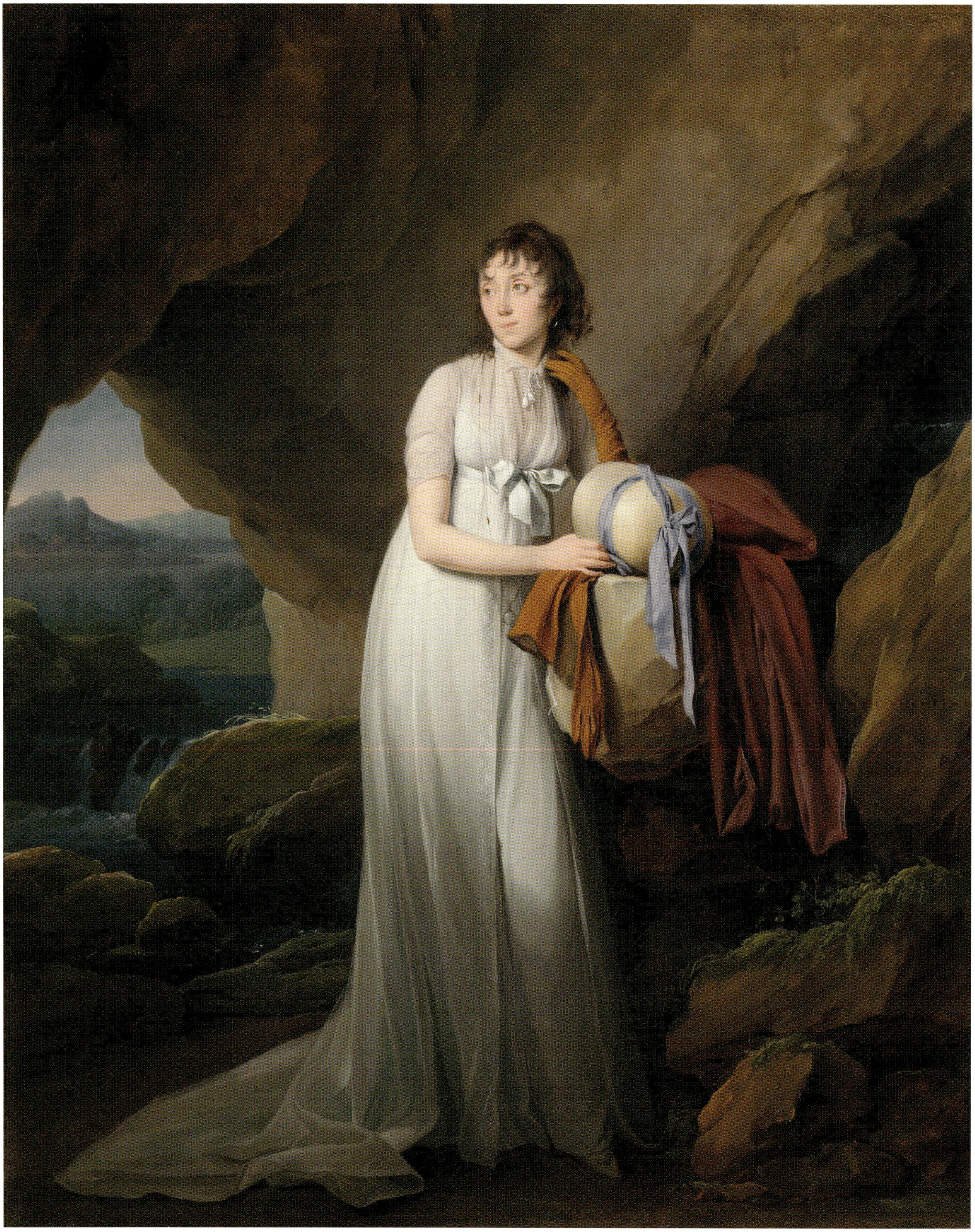

78. Louis-Léopold Boilly 1761–1845
Madame d'Aucourt de Saint-Just,
c. 1800. Oil on canvas, 56 x 46 cm
Acquired 1980. Inv. P. 1950

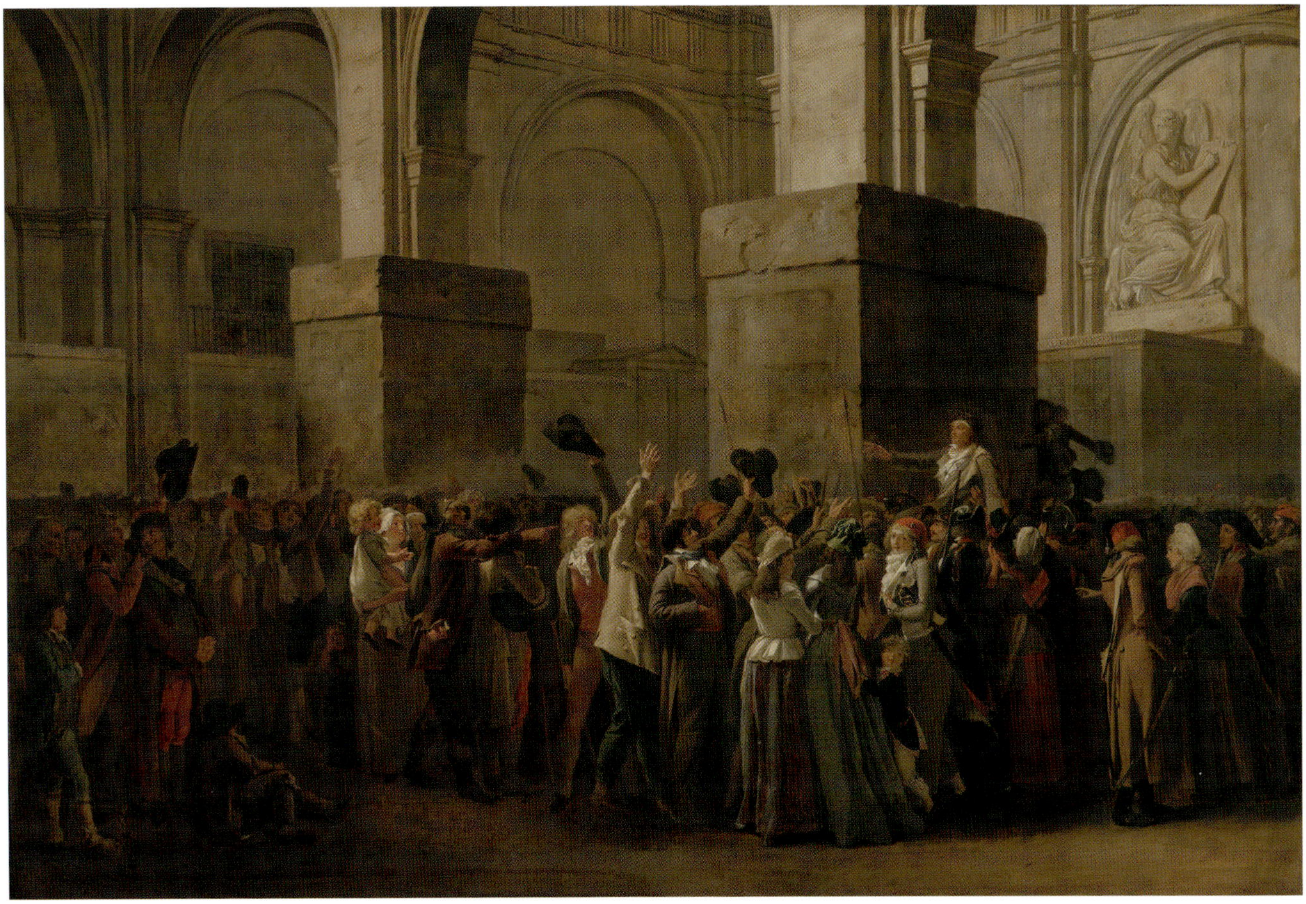

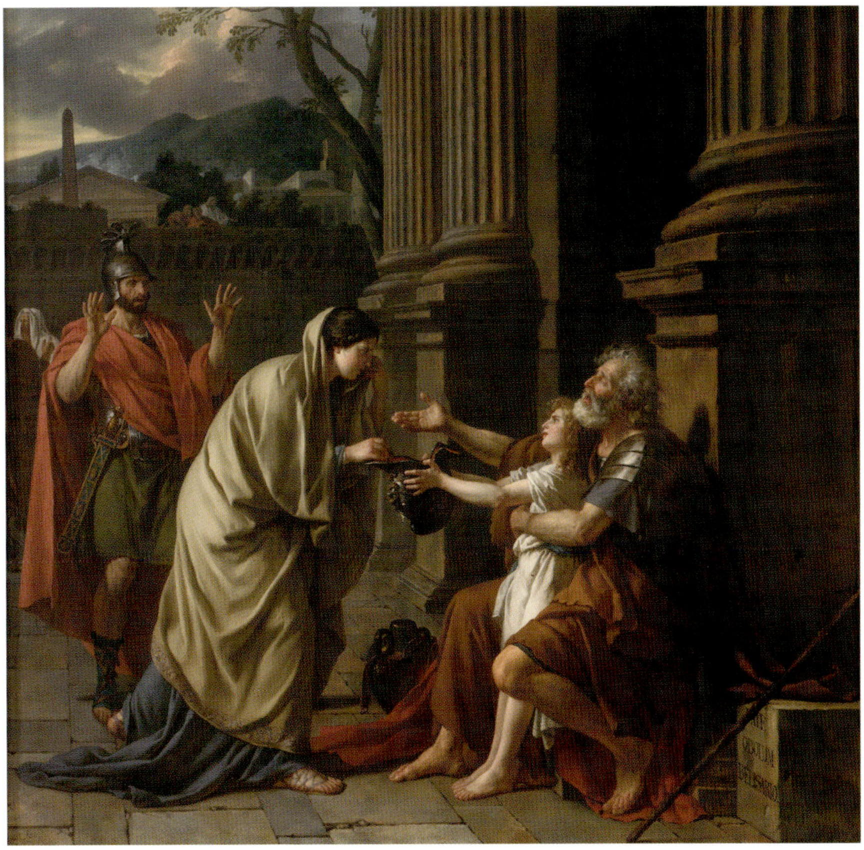

79. Louis-Léopold Boilly 1761–1845
The Triumph of Marat, 1794.
Oil on paper (7 sheets) on canvas,
80 x 120 cm

Acquired from Julien Boilly, the artist's son, 1865.
Inv. P. 395

80. Jacques-Louis David 1748–1825
Belisarius Begging for Alms, Salon
of 1781. Oil on canvas, 288 x 312 cm

Acquired from M. Meffre, 1863. Inv. P. 436

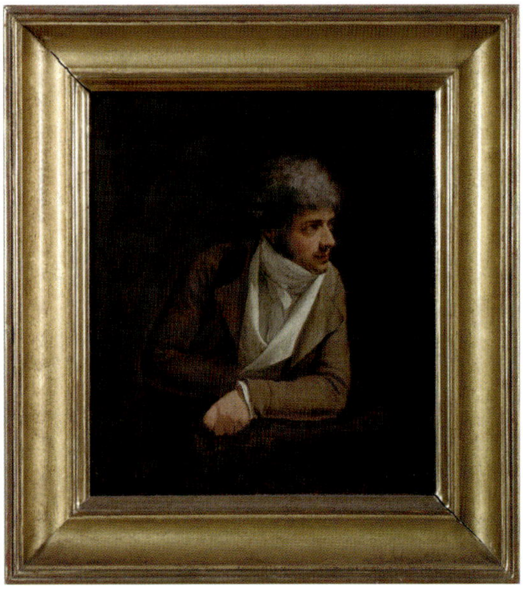
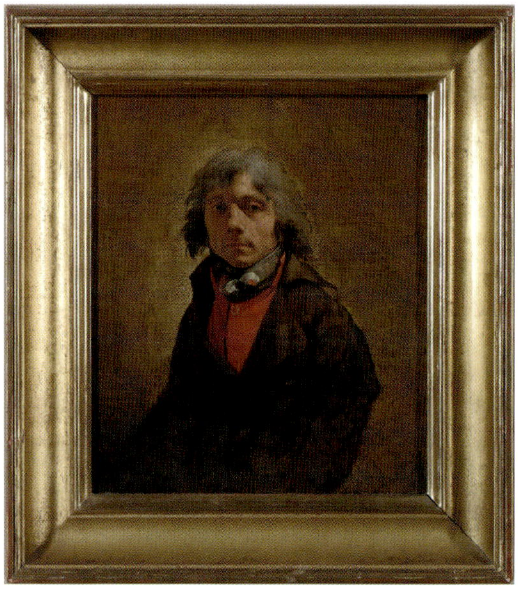
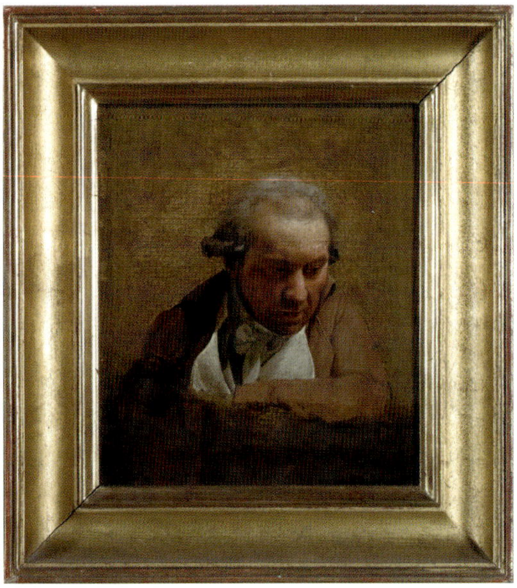
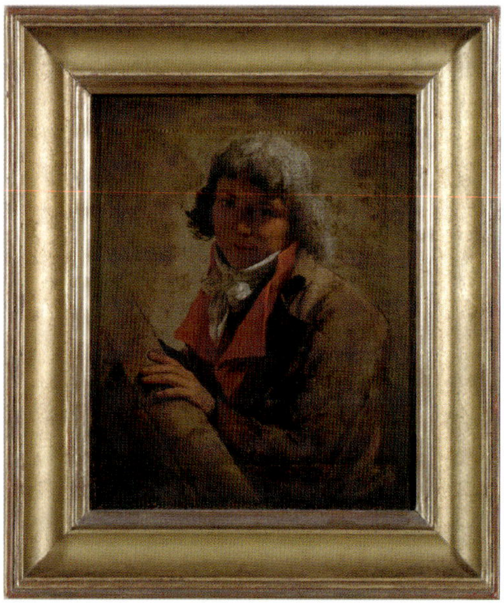

81–85. Louis-Léopold Boilly 1761–1845
Corbet (1758–1808), Drölling (1752–1817), Duplessis-Bertaux (1747–1820), Bourgeois (1759-1832), Lethière (1760–1832) and Carle Vernet (1758-1836). Oil on paper on canvas, 20 x 18 cm, 21 x 17 cm, 17 x 15 cm, 21 x 17 cm, 43 x 37 cm

Acquired from Julien Boilly, the artist's son, 1863.
Inv. P. 379, 378, 366, 369, 387

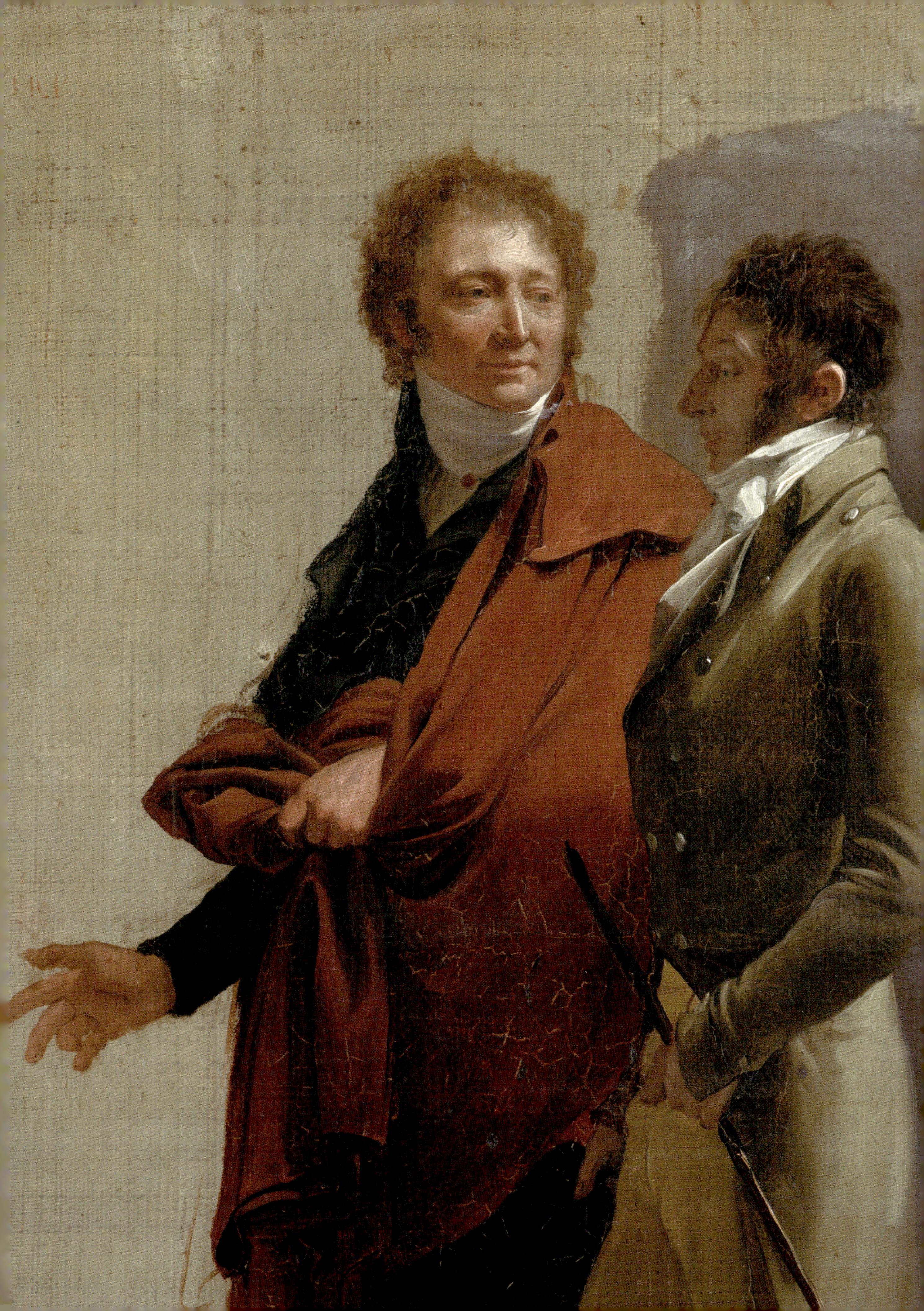

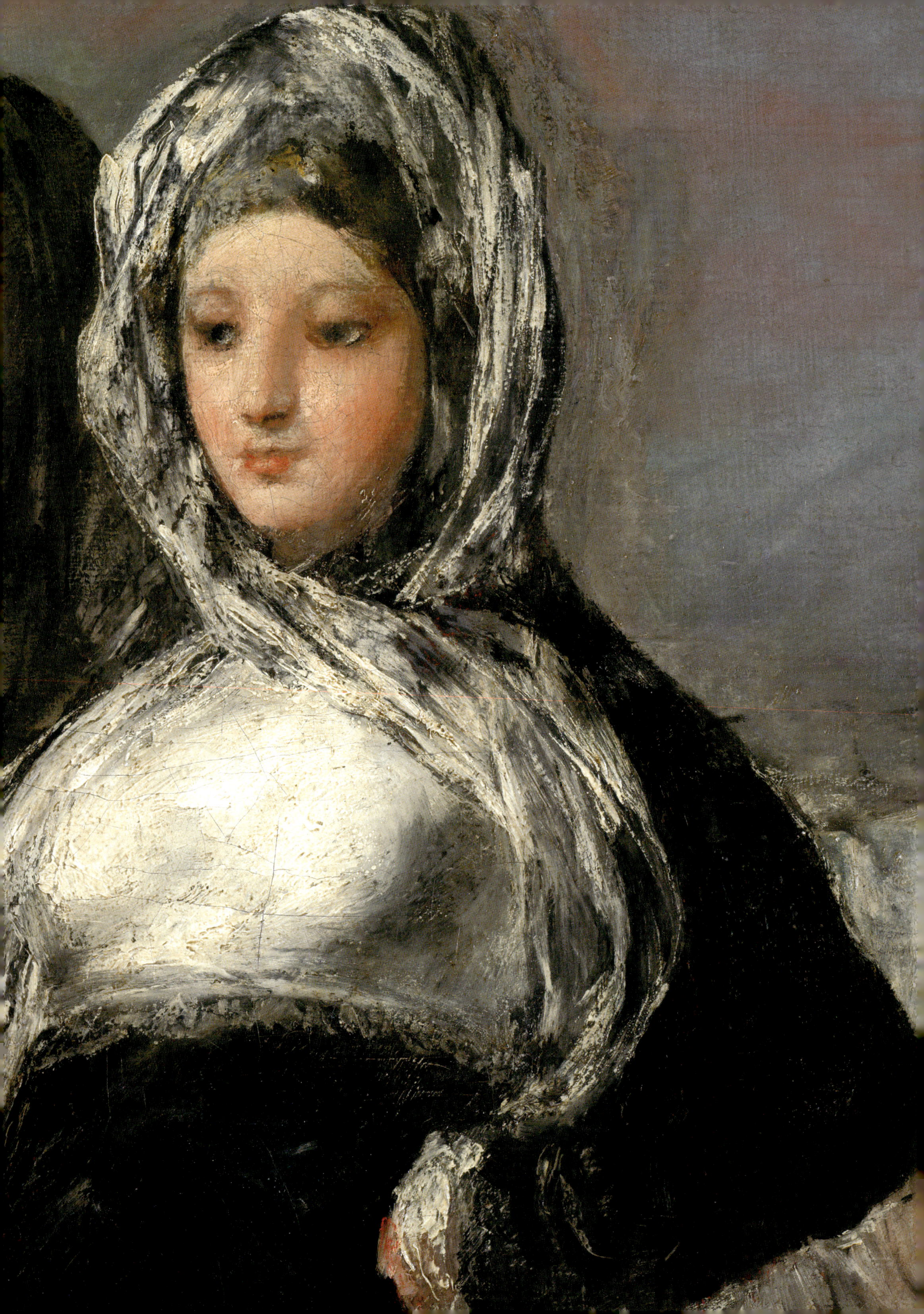

Italy and Spain

Italian Painting

Limited but diversified, the Italian gallery shows a clear preponderance of the Venetian School from the 16th to the 18th century, illustrating the tendency that guided the growth of the collection, mainly through purchases, deposits and gifts in the second half of the 19th century.

The second generation of Venetian painters in the 16th century was dominated by three great masters: Jacopo Bassano, Tintoretto and Veronese, who
in turn were thoroughly marked by Titian's mature style. In the *Portrait of a* 87
Venetian Senator, Tintoretto isolates the sitter's features in the light. The neutral background and more summary treatment of the hands and senatorial robes contribute to the expressive power of the likeness, strengthened by a point of view from above. Veronese's *Paradise*, a preparatory sketch for the decoration of the Hall of the Great Council at the Ducal Palace in Venice, is one of the major works in the collection. The expressive touch, the beauty of the shading and the coloured shadows illustrate the artist's virtuosity and creative freedom. The death of Veronese left this project in the sketch stage. The fresco was executed on site by Tintoretto. Although born in Amsterdam, Lambert Sustris, too, was influenced by Titian, whose studio he frequented. His *Judith Holding the Head of Holofernes* and *Noli me tangere*, two paintings from the collection of Louis XIV, attest to this heritage.

The Bassano dynasty is represented by two of the great Jacopo's sons. *The Story of Anne and Joachim* illustrates the production of domestic Bible scenes by the studio of Francesco Bassano, in the luminist style inherited from Jacopo.
Jesus Driving the Money Changers from the Temple, after Leandro Bassano, is one 89
of many versions of this theme by the artist, who distinguished himself mainly as a portraitist. *Bastiano Gardalino* is one of his most beautiful works in this genre, and the only one in France.

Along with Domenico Fetti, whose vibrant brush in *St Gregory the Great* heralds the 18th century, the German-born Johann Liss was one of the initiators of the renewal of the Venetian School. His training brought Venice a breath from the North in the early 17th century. One of the artist's master-
pieces, *Moses Rescued from the Water* is a fine example of the brightly lit, sensual 88
manner he developed, combining Flemish opulence and Venetian light. This subject, dear to the Venetian School, gave him the opportunity to represent a group of full-figured women arrayed in sumptuous fabric. The composition's strong diagonals and the bright palette make this work a preamble to baroque painting.

The *veduta* was a genre highly appreciated by a large private clientele in 18th-century Venice. If the *View of the Piazza San Marco, Venice*, from the studio of Canaletto, adheres to a strict and precise style, in the second half of the
century, Francesco Guardi introduced lightness and fantasy. His *Architectural* 90
Capriccio illustrates the freedom he gave this genre when his imagination developed the simple city view into an architecture of unreal charm.

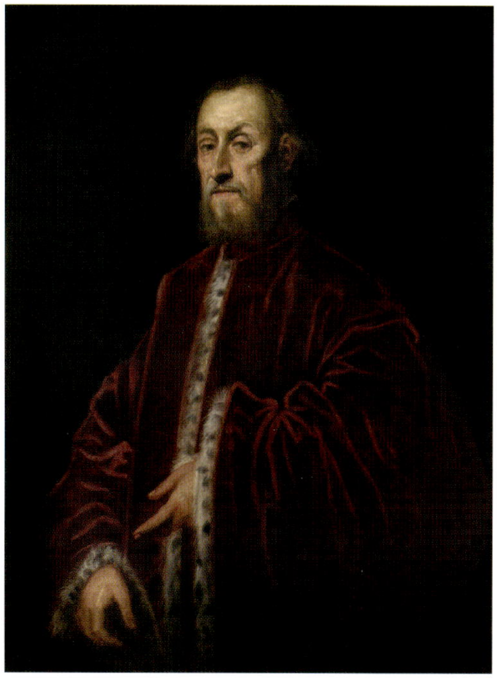

87. Tintoretto (Jacopo Robusti)
1518–1594
Portrait of a Venetian Senator.
Oil on canvas, 110 x 84.5 cm
State consignment, 1803. Inv. P. 43

86. Francisco de Goya y Lucientes
1746–1828
The Young Women (The Letter).
Detail of ill. 93

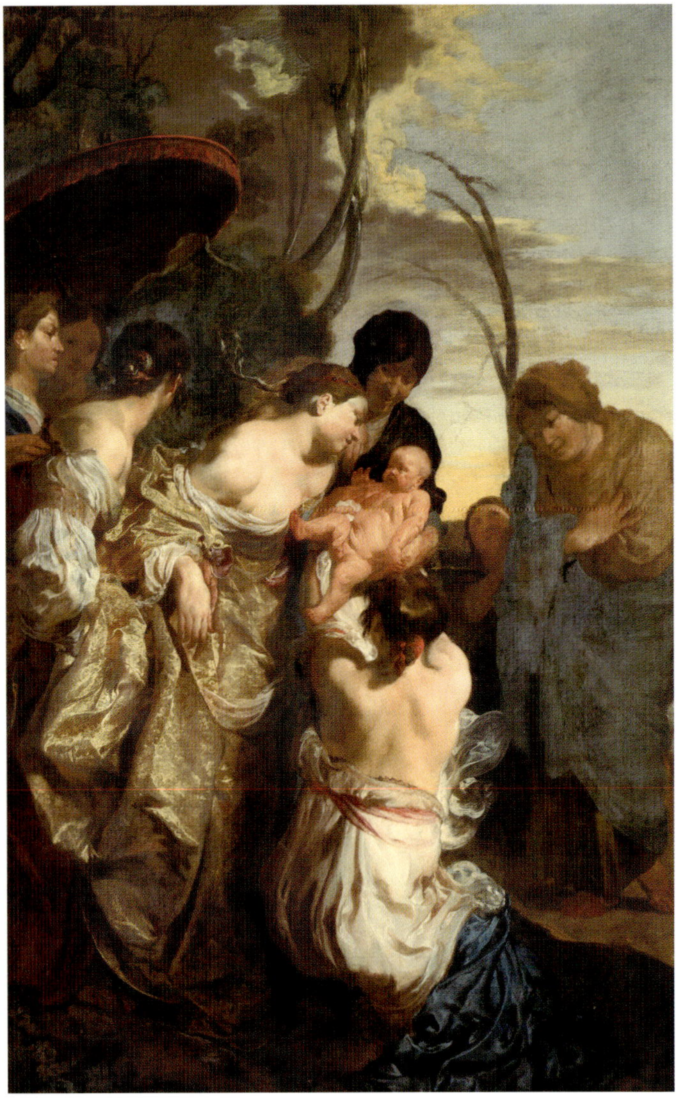

88. Johann Liss 1595/97–1629
Moses Rescued from the Water.
Oil on canvas, 155 x 106 cm
Acquired 1896. Inv. P. 22

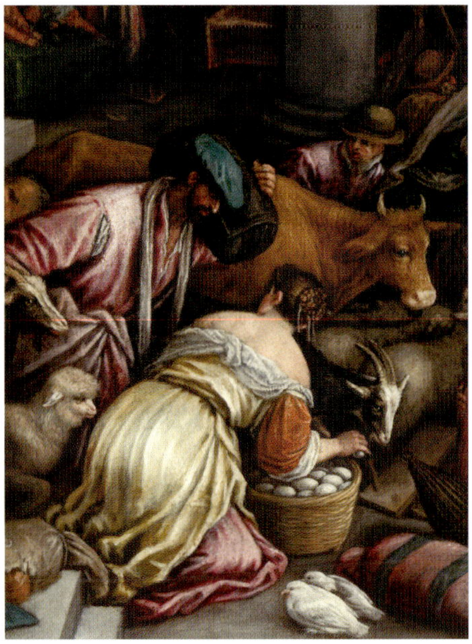

89. After Leandro Bassano 1557–1622
Jesus Driving the Money Changers from the Temple (detail). Oil on canvas, 120 x 134 cm
State consignment, 1803. Inv. P. 18

90. Francesco Guardi 1712–1793
Architectural Capriccio.
Oil on canvas, 17 x 13 cm
Acquired 1896. Inv. P. 24

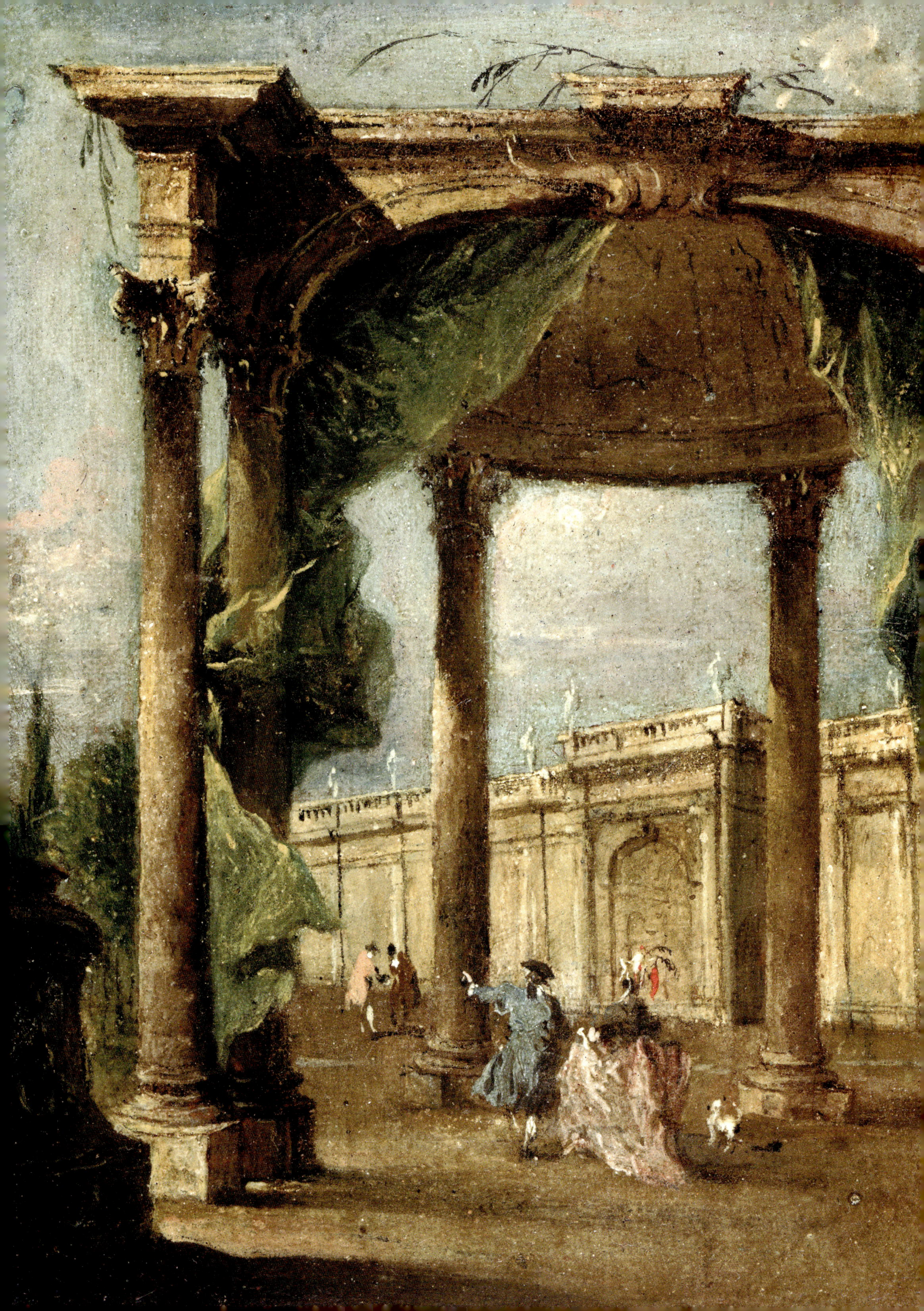

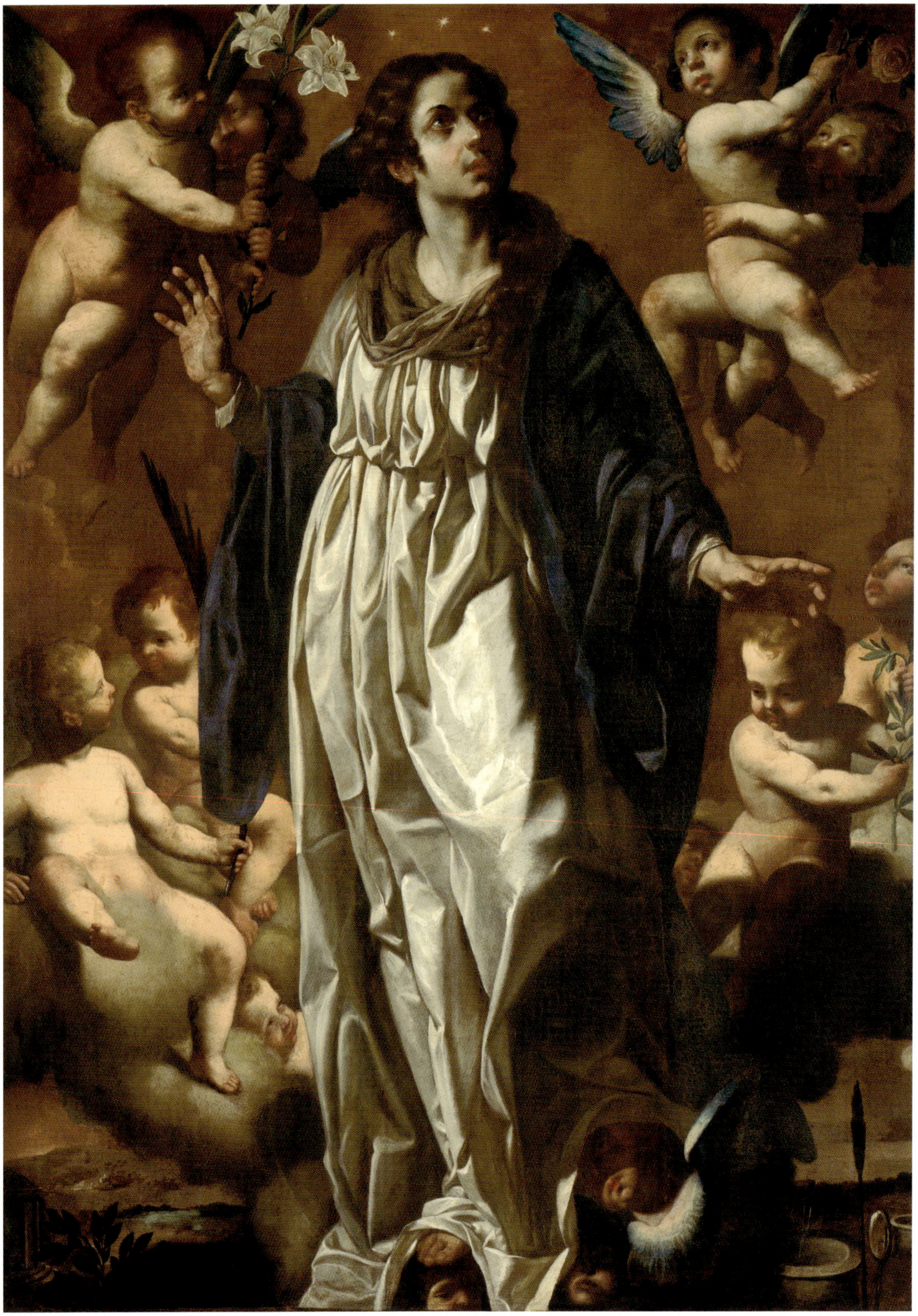

91. Paolo Domenico Finoglia 1590–1645
The Immaculate Conception. Oil on
canvas, 194.5 x 140 cm
Acquired 1892. Inv. P. 47

Some 17th-century painters from Naples, Bologna, Genoa and Rome also contribute to this panorama. The *Immaculate Conception* of Paolo Domenico Finoglia, influenced by a Caravaggism tinged with academicism, attests to the success of this theme in Naples and all Europe after the Council of Trent. Andrea di Lione, another Neapolitan, participated in the renewal of this school beginning in 1635–40. The *Rape of Europa* illustrates this bright new way of painting, rich in colour and material, under the mixed influence of Castiglione and Poussin. If the 17th century is the golden age of the Neapolitan School, Emilian painting, from Bologna in particular, prospered following the pictorial tradition initiated by the Carraccis. In the pendants *Joseph and Potiphar's Wife* by Spada and *Rinaldo and Armida* by Tiarini, the artists succeed in depicting two episodes that correspond admirably in a single spirit of composition, style and drapery effects. The swirling rhythm of the one and the pomposity of the other give these biblical and legendary figures a theatrical dimension. 91

In Genoa, Asseretto borrowed the dramatic vision, eerie light, rich impasto and muted palette of the Lombardians. The expressive and unreal vein of the *Apotheosis of St Thomas Aquinas* is characteristic of the artist. Reconciling the classicist and baroque styles, Carlo Maratta was one of the foremost painters in Rome at the end of the 17th century. *The Emperor Augustus Closing the Doors of the Temple of Janus* (or *The Peace of Augustus*), painted in 1661 for the decorative cycle of the Hôtel de La Vrillière, belongs to the period when the artist became more open to baroque influence, particularly that of Pietro da Cortona.

DD

Spanish Painting

With few works – two El Grecos, two Goyas, one Ribera and one Valdés Leal – the Spanish gallery, a veritable jewel of Spanish painting, establishes a mood of pure meditation. In their intense realism, objects and figures bring the enquiry into human destiny to fever pitch, in both the wisdom of detachment and the demonstrative rejoicing of character. The pose in *St Francis in Prayer before the Crucifix* by El Greco, of an almost rocklike solidity that is sustained by the heavy sackcloth monk's robe, allows a mystic tension to pervade the burning gaze. Like *Agony in the Garden*, the work is among the outstanding 92
19th-century acquisitions, which also include the two masterpieces by Goya.

In 1874 Edouard Reynart, the then curator, acquired a painting entitled 'The Letter' for the museum, an allegory of seduction later called *The Young* 93
Women. One of the young women, her face and bodice bathed in sunshine, is reading a letter. The work is composed like a genre scene, with the little dog serving as an attribute of lust. The feeling of idleness and pleasure emanating from the two young women is contrasted with the toiling washerwomen, distant accomplices of the scene, in the image of amorous licence they often project. The chromatic atmosphere and the vigour of the brushstroke in this painting dating from between 1814 and 1819 anticipate the radicalism of Manet.

The same year, Reynart proposed the acquisition of *Time*, also called *The* 94
Old Women. In response to the city's refusal, he himself donated the painting to the museum with the support of two friends. The similarity of format and the interplay of the titles have long made these paintings *de facto* pendants; however, *The Old Women* was painted between 1808 and 1812. By revealing the truth, the light that catches the two women from behind functions symbolically. In fact, Goya employs the medium of allegory. He depicts a melancholy meditation on the passing of time but without really believing in it, preferring to give free rein to the violent mockery that seems to concern Queen Marie-Louise and offer us a ravaged and allegorical view of a singularly dissolute life.

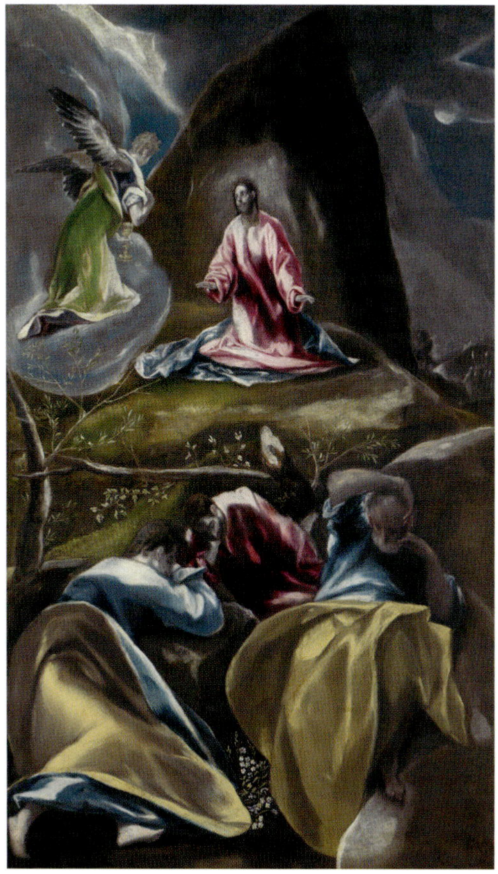

92. El Greco (Domenikos Theotokopoulos) 1541–1614
Agony in the Garden. Oil on canvas, 138 x 92 cm
Gift of Mlles Cottini, 1879. Inv. P. 10

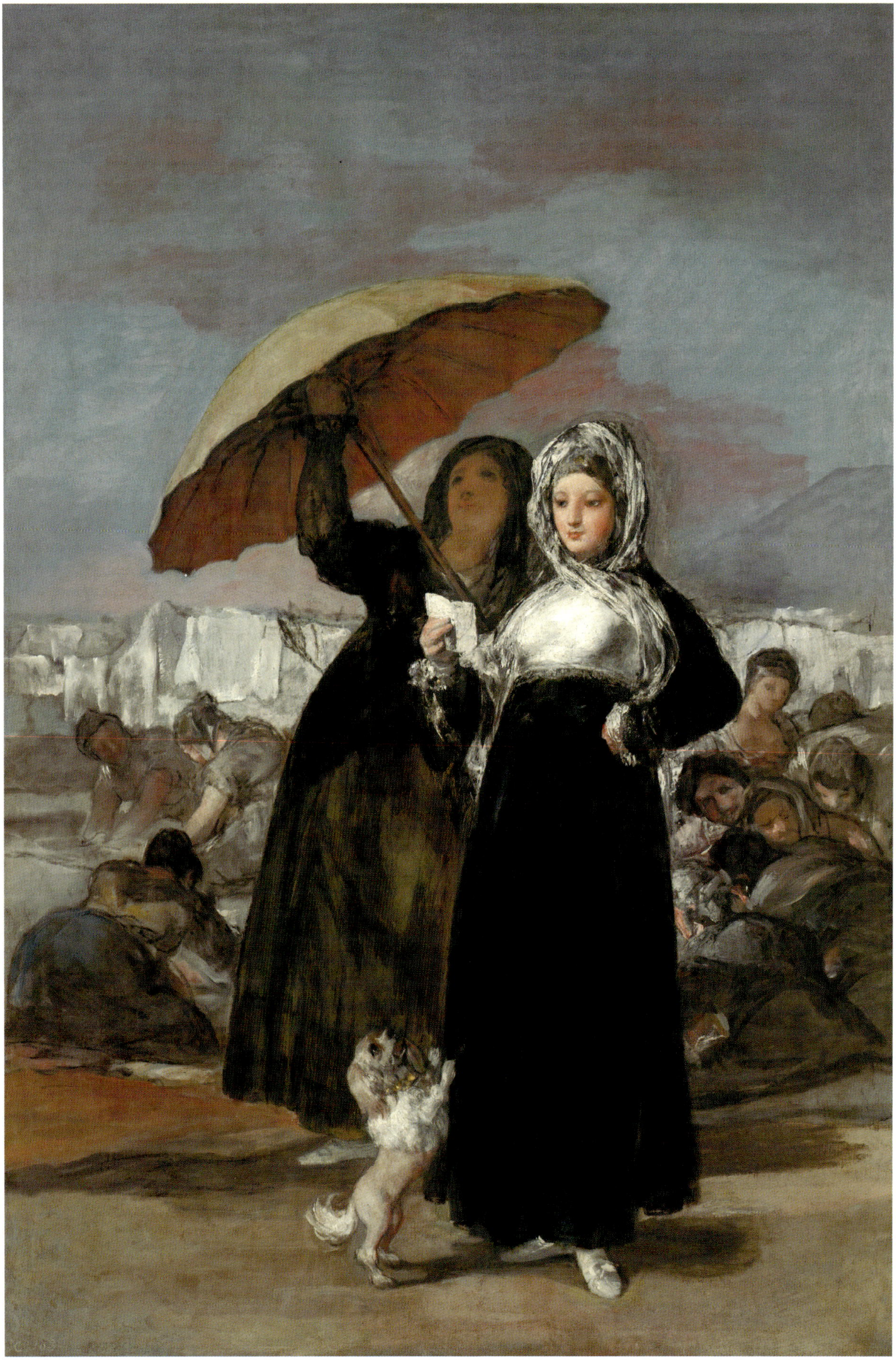

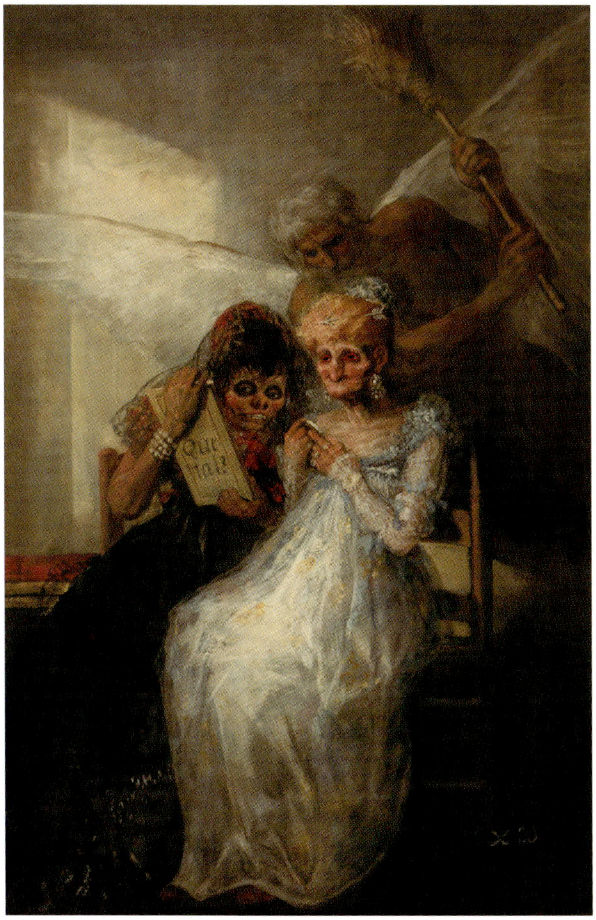

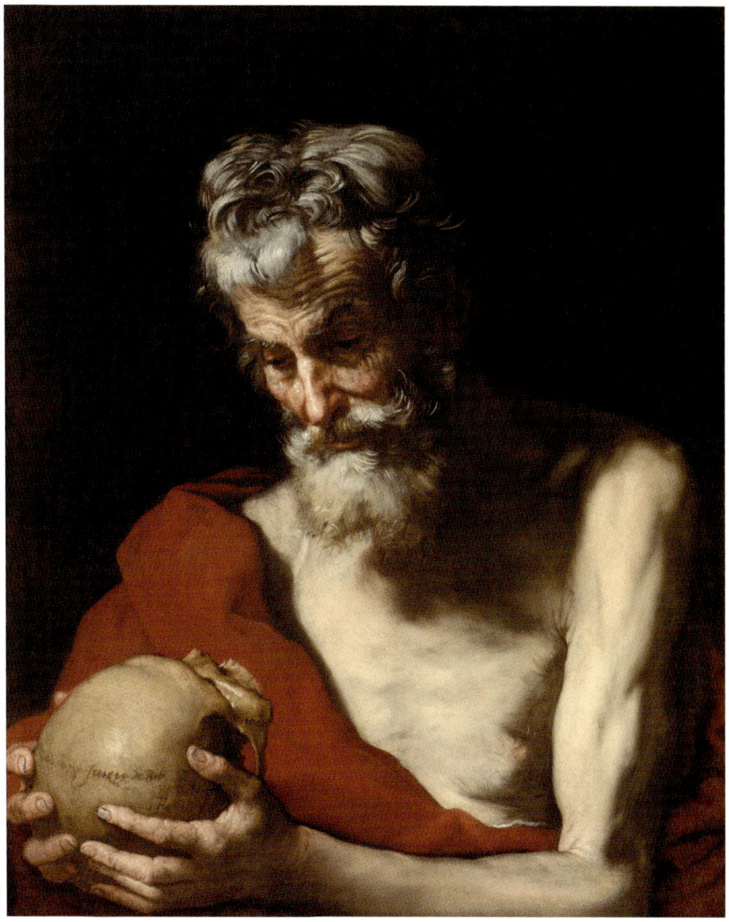

The jewel worn by the old woman is that offered to the queen by her lover, Manuel Godoy. Father Time readies his broom to sweep the queen from the scene. In an atmosphere of witchcraft that characterizes a society's last gasp, the meditation on the passing of time is actually the punishment of a premature old age, the lot of those who indulge in every abuse. It manifests itself here in the immediate sensation, rather than in philosophical depth.

Presiding over this fine group is one of Jusepe de Ribera's many representations of *St Jerome* meditating on a skull. The ghosts of ancient philosophers, 95
penitent saints and pathetic beggars – all visions of Man in the face of destiny – steal into this spare atmosphere. The interrogation goes far beyond the promotion of the cult of penitence. The *Vanitas* probably by Juan de Valdés Leal accompanies the image of St Jerome in the form of a predella. It almost seems that the saint has temporarily left the table with the book on it, encouraging meditation on the wisdom of the Holy Scriptures. The cup, porringer and broken jug reinforce the sensations arising from asceticism and destitution. The often poor colour is counterbalanced by the spirited fluidity of touch, apt for expressing the mute power of passion. AT

95. Jusepe de Ribera *c.* 1590–1652
St Jerome, 1643. Oil on canvas, 78 x 65 cm
Acquired 1880. Inv. P. 42

94. Francisco de Goya y Lucientes 1746–1828
Time (The Old Women). Oil on canvas, 181 x 125 cm
Gift of Messrs Gentil, Reynart and Sauvaige, 1874. Inv. P. 50

93. Francisco de Goya y Lucientes 1746–1828
The Young Women (The Letter).
Oil on canvas, 181 x 125 cm
Acquired 1874. Inv. P. 9

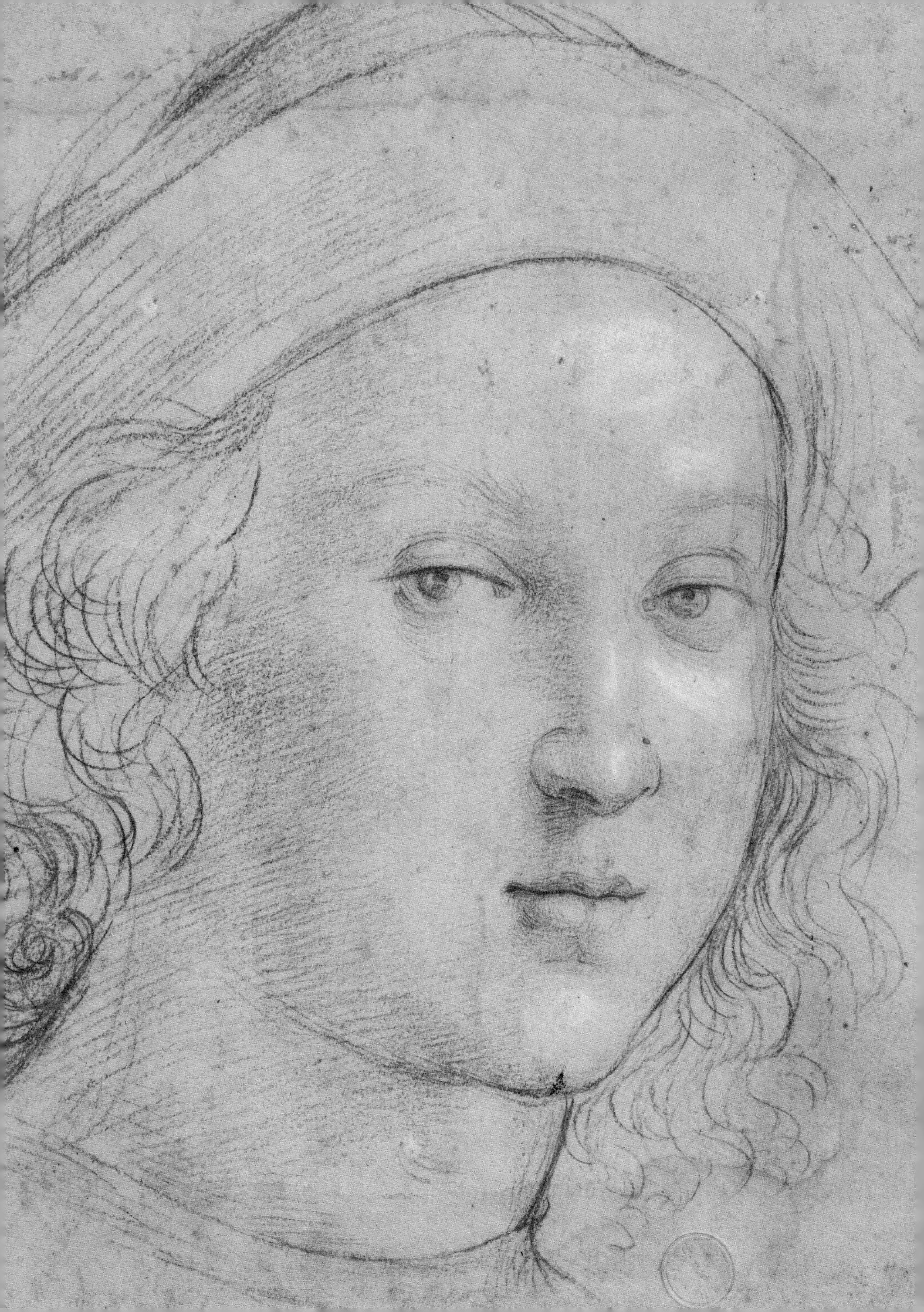

The Prints and Drawings Department

The drawing department at Lille's Palais des Beaux-Arts was created thanks to the Lille painter Jean-Baptiste Wicar (1762–1834), who at his death bequeathed the celebrated Donatello marble relief and the troubling *Wax Head* to the 1 museum, and his prestigious collection of drawings to the Société des Sciences et des Arts. The drawings came to our museum in 1864.

Trained starting in 1772 in the studio of Guéret and Watteau in Lille, Wicar settled in Paris in 1779 and became a student of David in 1781. When David left for Rome to paint *The Oath of the Horatii*, of which the museum possesses the 97 preparatory drawing, he brought with him his pupil, who, won over by the beauty and charm of the peninsula, never left it except for brief stays in France. Celebrated for his portraits and history paintings, Wicar pursued his career mainly in Italy – Florence and Naples, but mostly Rome, where he lived until the end of his life. Protected by the Bonapartist milieu, in 1797 he was named associate curator in charge of requisitioning works of art in the Italian cities for the Musée Napoléon in Paris (today the Musée du Louvre).

Because of his new duties and knowledge of the Italian art market, this enlightened amateur had the opportunity to assemble three collections of drawings for himself. The first was stolen in Florence in 1799, he sold the second to the London dealer Samuel Woodburn in 1823, and he bequeathed the third to the Société des Sciences et des Arts in Lille. Consisting of about 1300 sheets, the bequest includes fine drawings from the German, English, French, Dutch and Flemish Schools. But it is best known for the outstanding group of 15th- to 18th-century Italian drawings, essentially Florentine.

It is in particular the forty sheets by Raphael, covering his career from his beginnings in Umbria to the Florentine and Roman periods, that account for the international renown of this Italian collection and our Lille holdings. In addition to the preparatory drawings for larger projects such as the *St Nicholas of Tolentino Altarpiece*, for the Church of Sant'Agostino in Città di Castello, and the *Coronation of the Virgin* and the *School of Athens* for the Vatican, there are head studies of men on green-prepared paper and a series of *Madonnas*, a favourite theme of the artist, on pink-prepared paper that demonstrate Raphael's extraordinary virtuosity with various techniques – black and red chalk, metalpoint. In another genre, the *Head of a Youth Wearing a Cap* confirms the 96 master's talent for portraiture. His meeting with the two great masters of the Italian Renaissance – Leonardo and Michelangelo – would incontestably have important repercussions on his work. Thus, the spirit of Leonardo appears in the representations of the Virgin and Child, particularly the masterful *Alba Madonna*. The scene – a circular composition similar to Leonardo's *Virgin and* 98 *Child with St Anne* at the Louvre – conveys a deep feeling of fullness and harmony. Works by Fra Filippo Lippi, Fra Bartolommeo, Andrea del Sarto, Pontormo (*Standing Male Nudes*), Titian, Parmigianino and Mantegna, not to 99 mention the *Study for the Dome of St Peter's, Rome* by Michelangelo, admirably complete this collection.

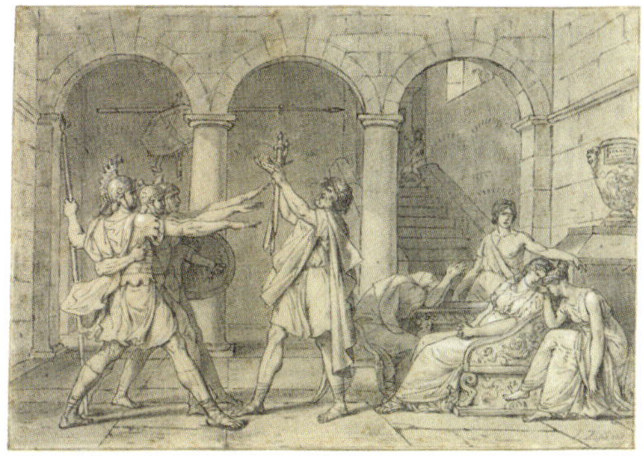

97. Jacques-Louis David 1748–1825
The Oath of the Horatii. Pencil, pen and ink, grey wash with white chalk highlights on ochre-prepared paper, 22 x 33.3 cm
Inv. PL. 1194

96. Raphael (Raffaello Sanzio) 1483–1520
Head of a Youth Wearing a Cap. Black chalk, heightened with white, on grey-brown paper, 21.2 x 18.6 cm
Wicar bequest, 1834. Inv. PL. 461

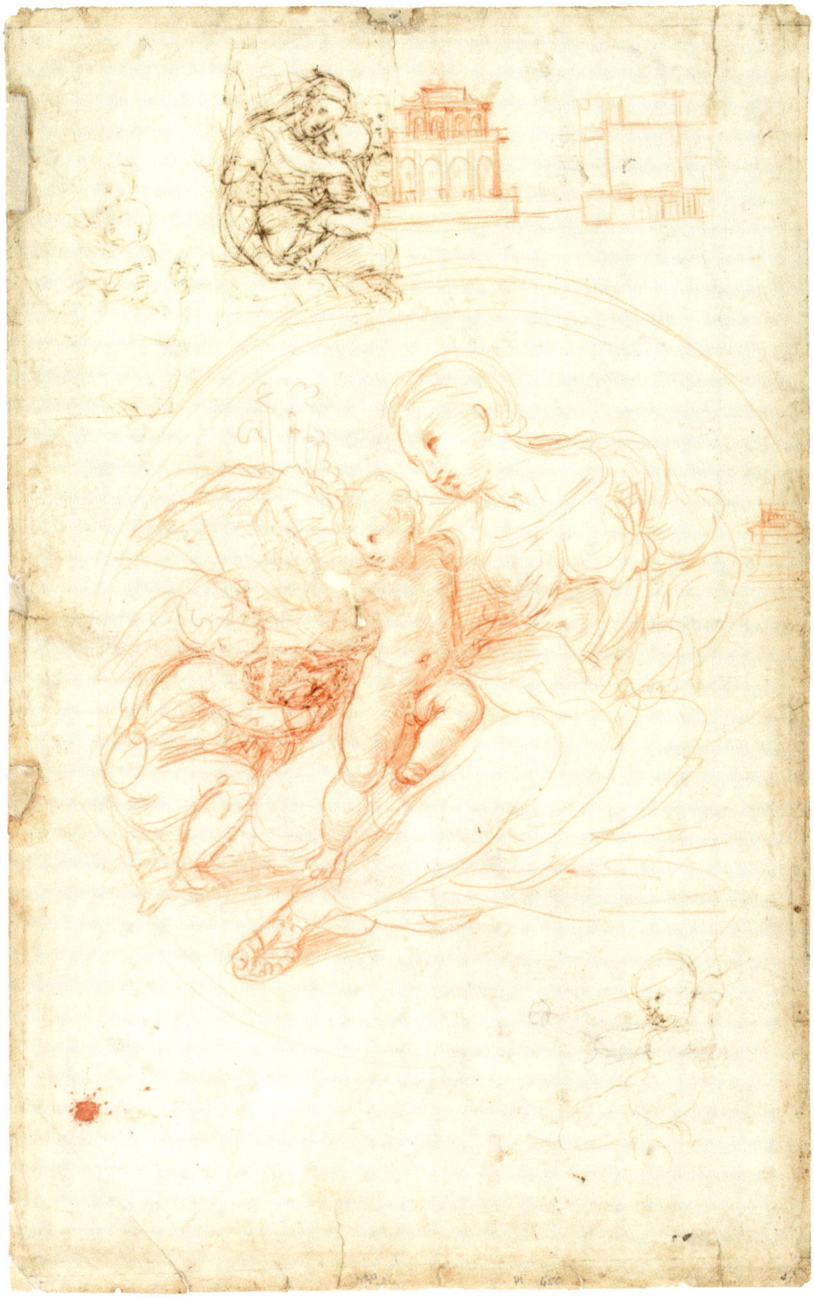

98. Raphael (Raffaello Sanzio) 1483–1520
The Virgin and Child with St John the Baptist and various sketches (*Study for the 'Alba Madonna'*). Red chalk, pen and brown ink, 42.2 x 27.3 cm
Wicar bequest, 1834. Inv. PL. 456, PL. 457

99. Jacopo Pontormo (Jacopo Carucci) 1494–1556
Study for 'Standing Male Nudes'. Red chalk, 39.7 x 26.5 cm
Inv. PL. 162

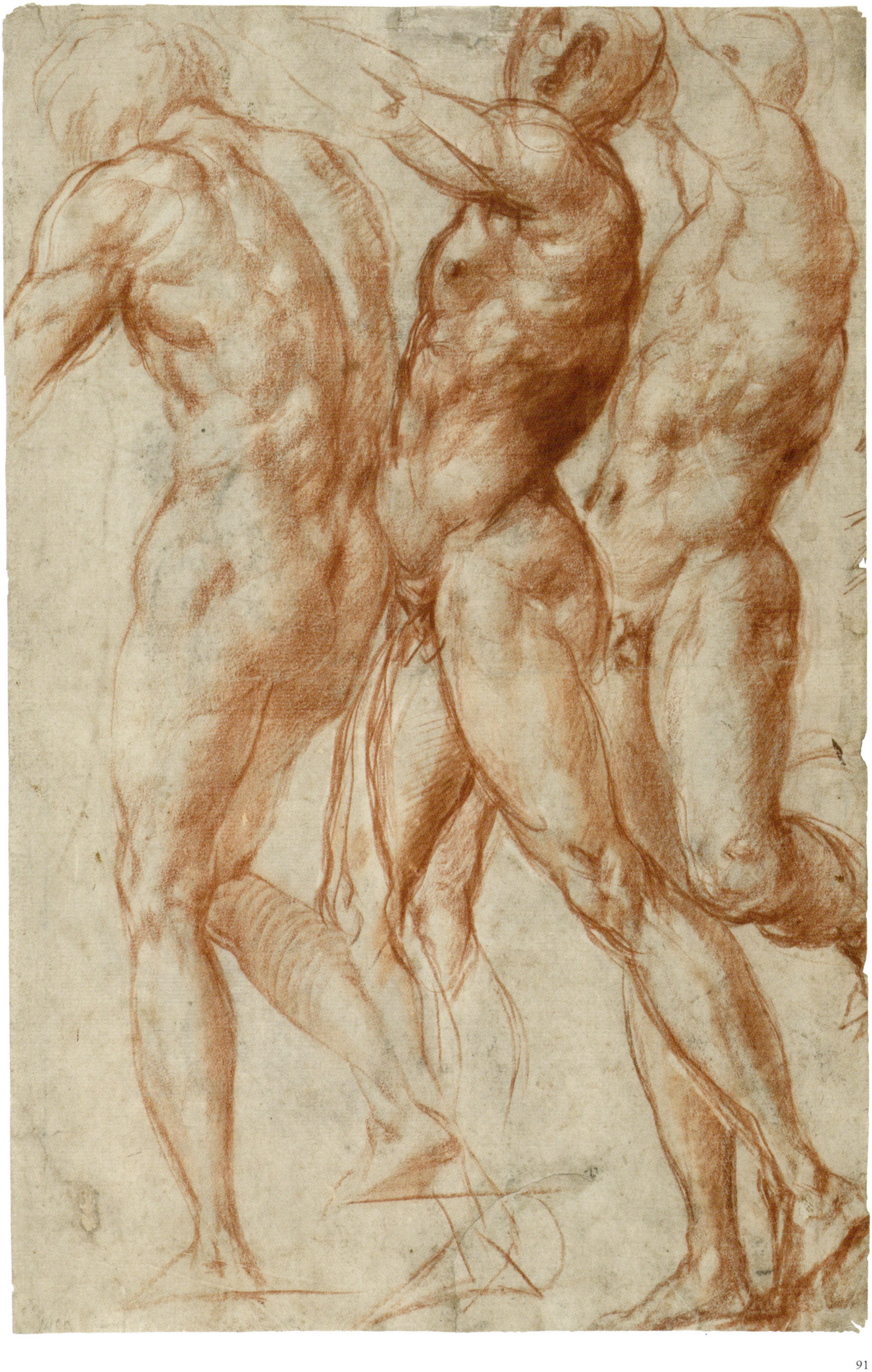

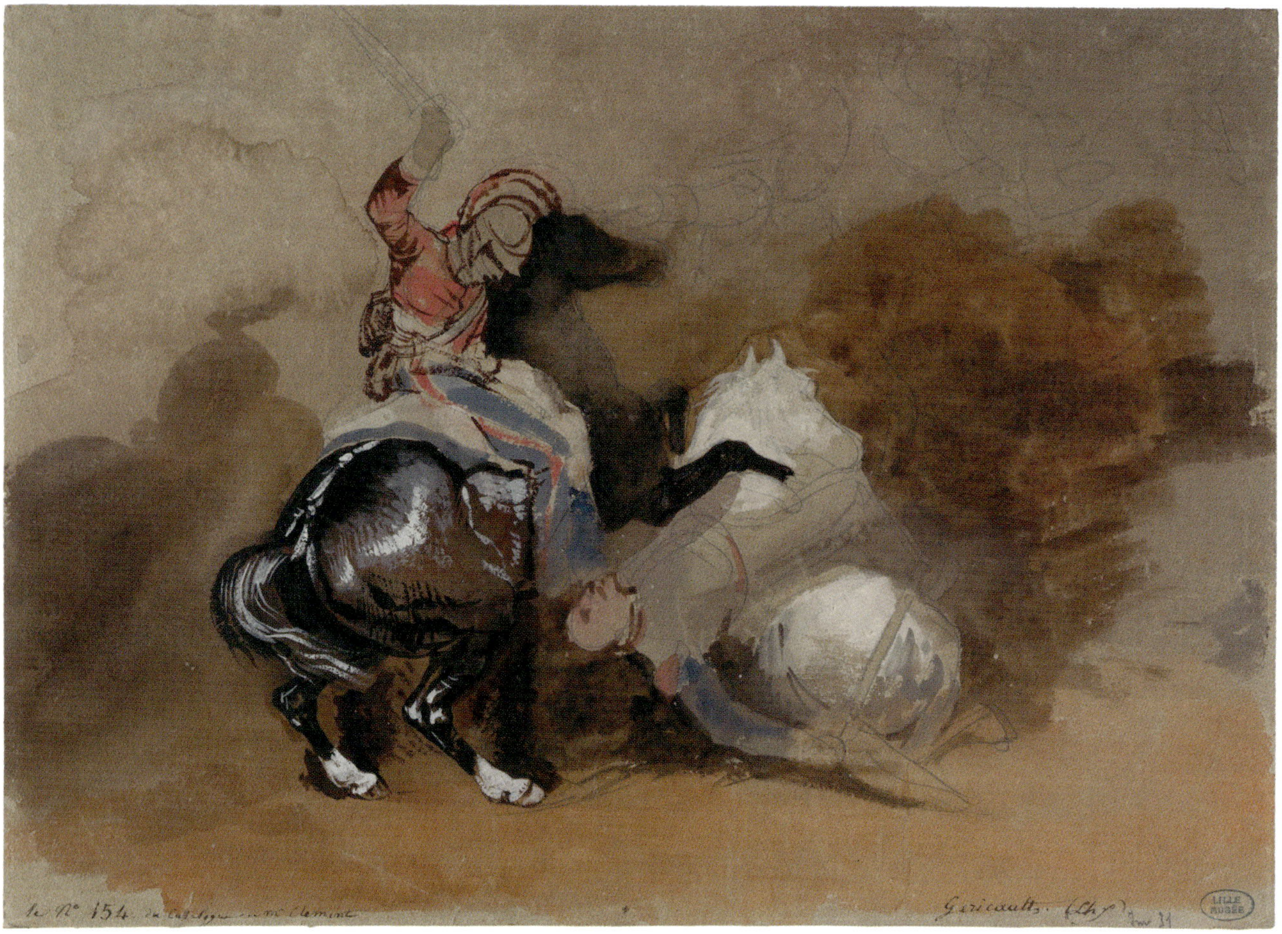

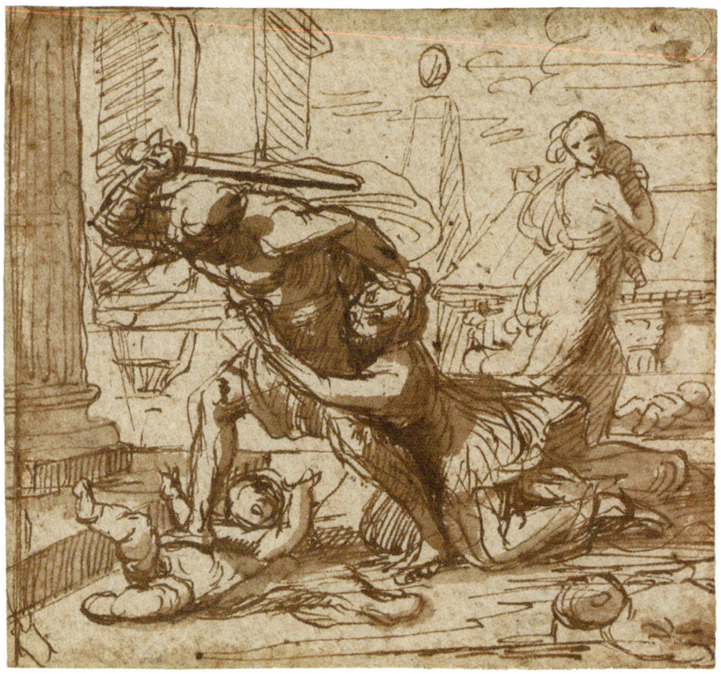

100. Théodore Géricault 1791–1824
Two Horsemen in Combat. Graphite, gouache and watercolour on grey paper, 26.7 x 38 cm
Inv. PL. 1394

101. Nicolas Poussin 1594–1665
Massacre of the Innocents.
Pen and brown ink, brown wash, 14.8 x 16.9 cm
Wicar bequest, 1834. Inv. PL. 1613

Today the Lille collection has grown remarkably to include nearly five thousand sheets, and if the French and Italian Schools are particularly well represented, the museum also has fine pieces from the German, Flemish and Dutch Schools from the 15th to the 20th century, holdings in prints including the *Caprichos* of Goya, about thirty engravings after Rubens and illuminated manuscripts, including one by Jean Bourdichon after Fouquet. Another masterpiece in the collection is the silverpoint portrait of *Lucas van Leyden* by 102
Dürer, executed during his meeting with the famous printmaker in Antwerp in 1521. The accuracy of line and precision of the modelling scrupulously reveal the psychological character of the sitter. A *St John the Baptist* by Lucas Cranach, *Death and the Maiden* by Hans Baldung and some fine studies of saints executed by Hans Holbein further illustrate the German School. Besides a *Raising of Lazarus* by Joachim Wtewael, a highly finished preparatory drawing for the large Mannerist painting kept at the museum, drawings of Van Dyck, Jordaens 40
and Van Goyen represent the Flemish and Dutch collection.

The dynamism and remarkable acquisition policy of curators like Edouard Reynart and Henry Pluchart contributed to practically doubling Lille's holdings of works on paper. At important public sales in Paris, they acquired fine French drawings from the 17th, 18th and 19th centuries, with, among other things, the *Massacre of the Innocents* by Nicolas Poussin, all the preparatory 101
studies for Delacroix's *Medea*, *The Apotheosis of Homer* by Ingres, drawings by Boucher and Lancret, the delicate pastel portrait of *Madame Pelerin* by Quentin La Tour, drawings by Fragonard, Louis and François Watteau, Boilly and Hubert Robert, and the study for *The Raft of 'The Medusa'* by Géricault.

Important gifts have quite obviously contributed to the brilliance of the collection. Among them, *The Father's Curse: The Punished Son* by Jean-Baptiste Greuze and the exceptional drawing heightened with gouache and watercolour by Théodore Géricault, *Two Horsemen in Combat*. Donations were also 100
made by the artists themselves, including Ingres, Corot and Amaury-Duval, and by their descendants – the families of Puvis de Chavannes (with the important series of preparatory drawings for the painting *Sleep*), Fantin-Latour and Bourdelle – as well as the sketchbook of David bequeathed to the museum by his student, the Lille painter François Souchon, to whom we also owe the gift of the superb *Head Study of a Young Boy* by Greuze.

Nineteenth-century landscape by members of the Barbizon School is represented by the painters Harpignies, Huet, Chintreuil and Millet, to name but a few. Camille Corot, known for his forest interiors, gives us in another style the alluring portrait *Girl in Beret*. Auguste Renoir charms us with a delightful pastel, *Young Woman Wearing a Black Hat*, one of the most prestigious gifts made to the department of drawings by Miss Denise Masson in 1974.

Nearer to our time, let us mention the classic beauty of *Olga with a Crown of Flowers* by Picasso, *Woman at Her Toilet* by Matisse, an indian ink *Portrait of a Woman* by Picabia and *Quimper* by Signac, as well as the Dufy bequest, the lithographs and watercolours of Estève, and a pastel by Hartung.

The 'Wicar Museum' lives on. Acquisitions and the publication of theses and catalogues confirm the undeniable interest of such a collection and contribute greatly to its reputation. EDJ

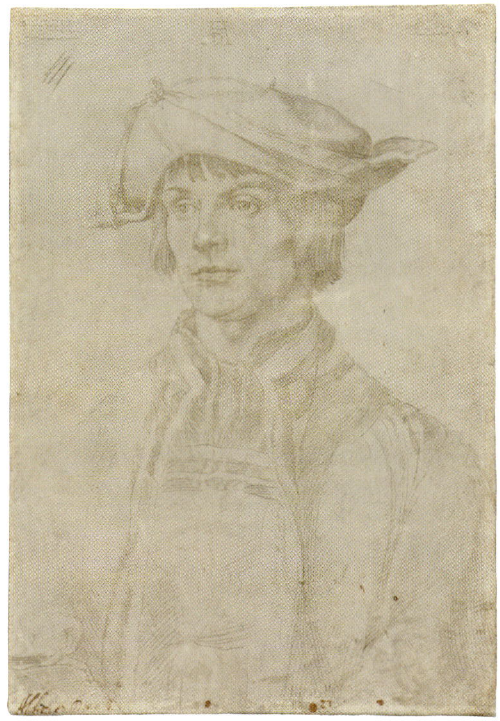

102. Albrecht Dürer 1471–1528
Lucas van Leyden. Silverpoint on grey-white prepared paper, 25.7 x 18 cm
Wicar bequest, 1834. Inv. PL. 918

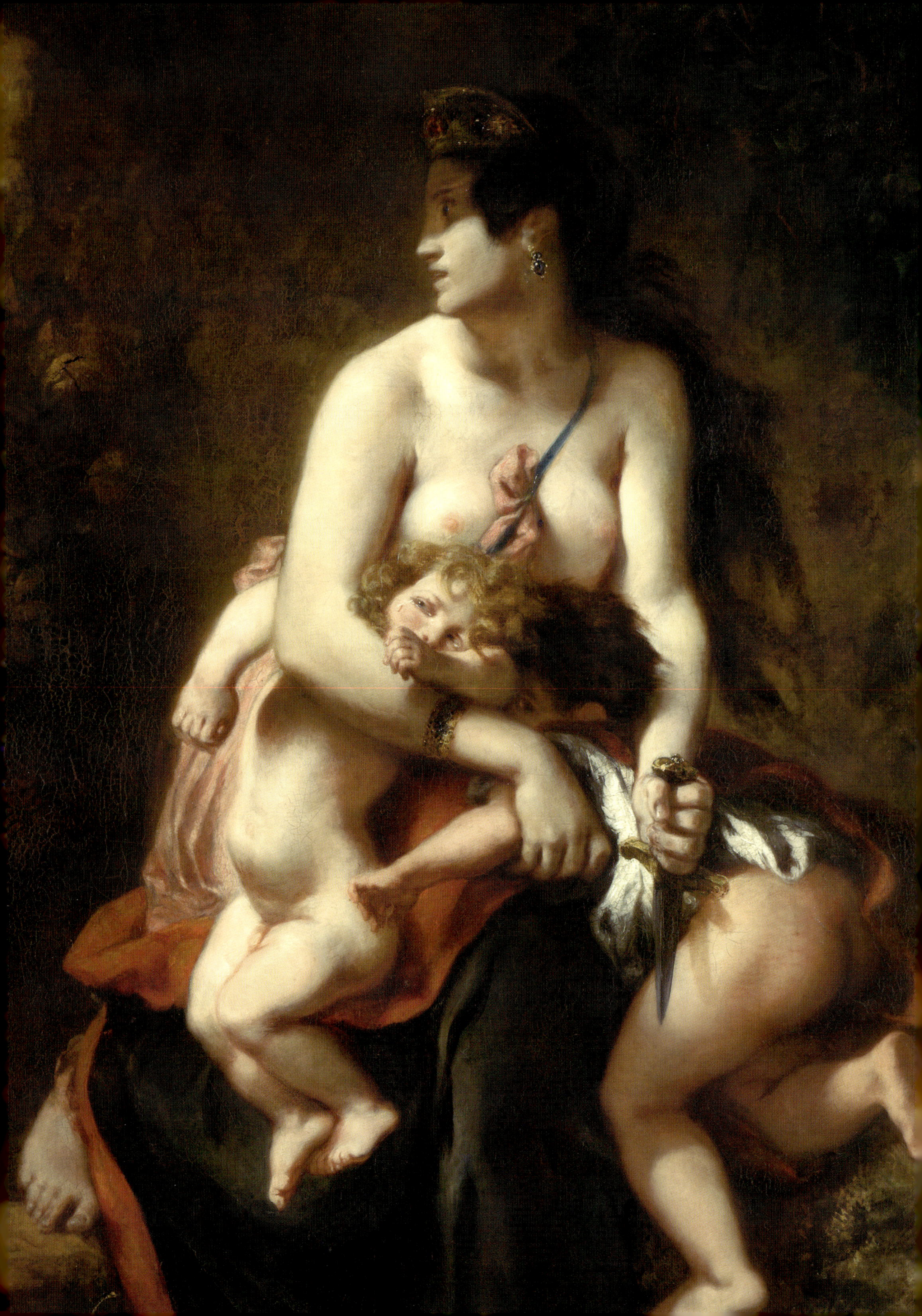

The Nineteenth and Twentieth Centuries

Painting

Research conducted on 19th-century French painting in the past twenty-five years has led to the rediscovery of the Lille collection's exceptional wealth in detail and diversity, placing it at least on a par with Lille's other great collection, the 17th-century Flemish and Dutch School, which is widely known. However, unlike the latter, 19th-century French painting was mainly acquired in pace with the art as it developed over time. The most significant demonstration of this is the entry of essential works as soon as they were acquired by the state at the Salon, for example Delacroix's *Medea* in 1838 and Courbet's *After* 103
Dinner at Ornans in 1849. 102

The Lille museum seemed to become an annexe of the Musée du Luxembourg in Paris, impervious, like it, to Impressionism. This resulted from the sustained, concerted action of an outstanding curator, Edouard Reynart, who introduced artists (Corot, Courbet, Carolus-Duran) to collectors (Camille Benoît) and art critics (Leroi, a.k.a. Gauchez) in Paris. The two large fine arts exhibitions held in Lille in 1866 and 1881 also contributed to the movement. The acquisition policy, which slowed to a standstill in the 20th century, was brilliantly revived by the daring acquisition of *Ruggiero and Angelica* by Joseph Blanc in 1975, the exceptional bequests and donations of André and Denise Masson (in 1949 and 1979) having filled the gap in Impressionism. ADW

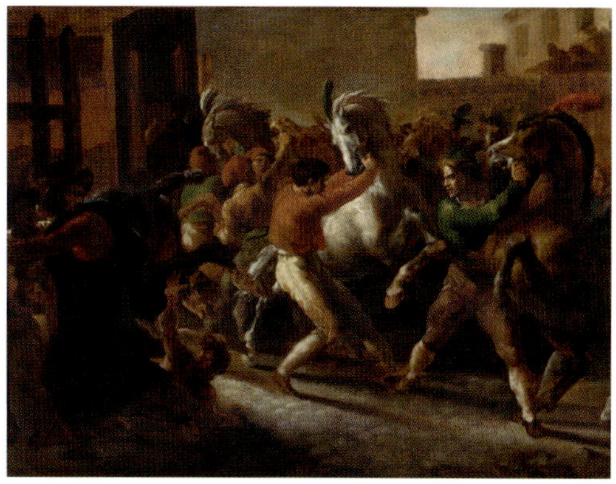

104. Théodore Géricault 1791–1824
Study for 'The Race of the Riderless Horses in Rome', 1817. Oil on paper on canvas, 45 x 61 cm
Mme Maracci bequest, 1901. Inv. P. 475

Romanticism

In the early 19th century, painting was transformed under the influence of several artists who moved away from the Neoclassical principles advocated by David. A forerunner of the movement, Théodore Géricault brought back from his trip to Rome in 1816 several compositions re-creating the Italian city's lively atmosphere. In the study for the *Race of the Riderless Horses in Rome*, the 104
paint has been distributed rapidly, expressing the fiery spirit of the animal that Man struggles to master. Others also exploited the spectacular, but taking a dramatic approach, as in Charles Desains's depiction of a young woman's suicide. The careful brushwork and flawless drawing of his *Suffocated Woman* re- 106
call scenes by Boilly, but the choice of subject links it to concerns of the Romantics.

The development of the genre scene associated with an enthusiasm for the Middle Ages gave rise to what is known as the 'troubadour' style. The artists connected with it drew upon national history and literature for subject-matter, which they painted with a precision worthy of the 17th-century Dutch masters, multiplying details, costumes and accessories likely to evoke the Middle Ages. This is seen in Coupin de la Couperie's *Ill-fated Love of Francesca da Rimini*, illustrating a passage from Dante's *Inferno* (Canto V).

Seeking subjects with the potential to move viewers, many artists of this generation found inspiration in the novels of the British author Walter Scott adapted for the theatre, like Eugène Isabey in *The Arrival of Mary Stuart* or

103. Eugène Delacroix 1798–1863
Medea, Salon of 1838. Oil on canvas, 260 x 165 cm
Acquired by the state for the Lille museum, 1838. Inv. P. 542

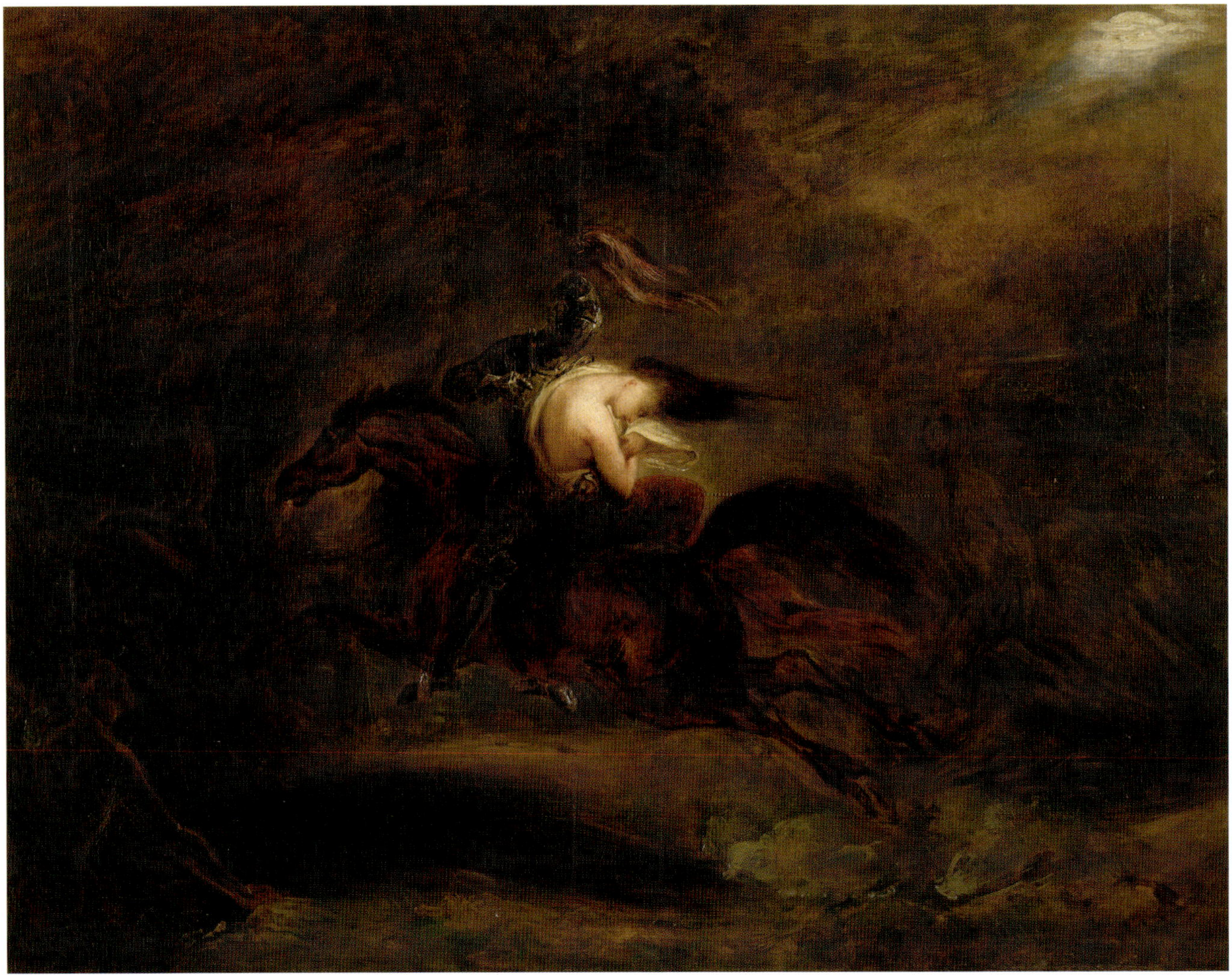

105. Ary Scheffer 1795–1858
The Dead Ride Fast.
Oil on canvas, 59 x 76 cm
Alexandre Leleux bequest, 1873. Inv. P. 468

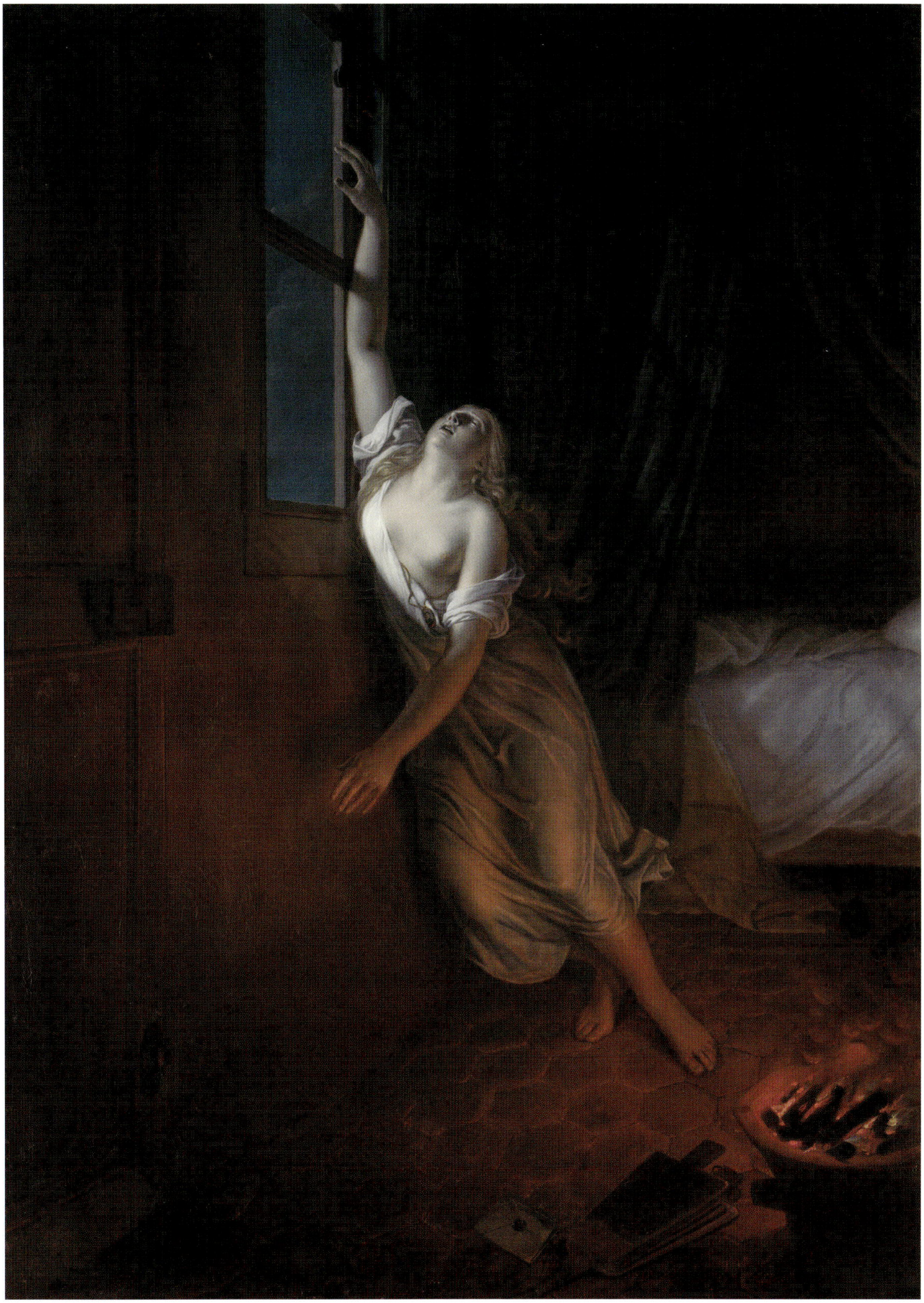

106. Charles Desains 1789–1843
Suffocated Woman, Salon of 1822.
Oil on canvas, 134.5 x 99 cm
Purchased, 1977. Inv. P. 1938

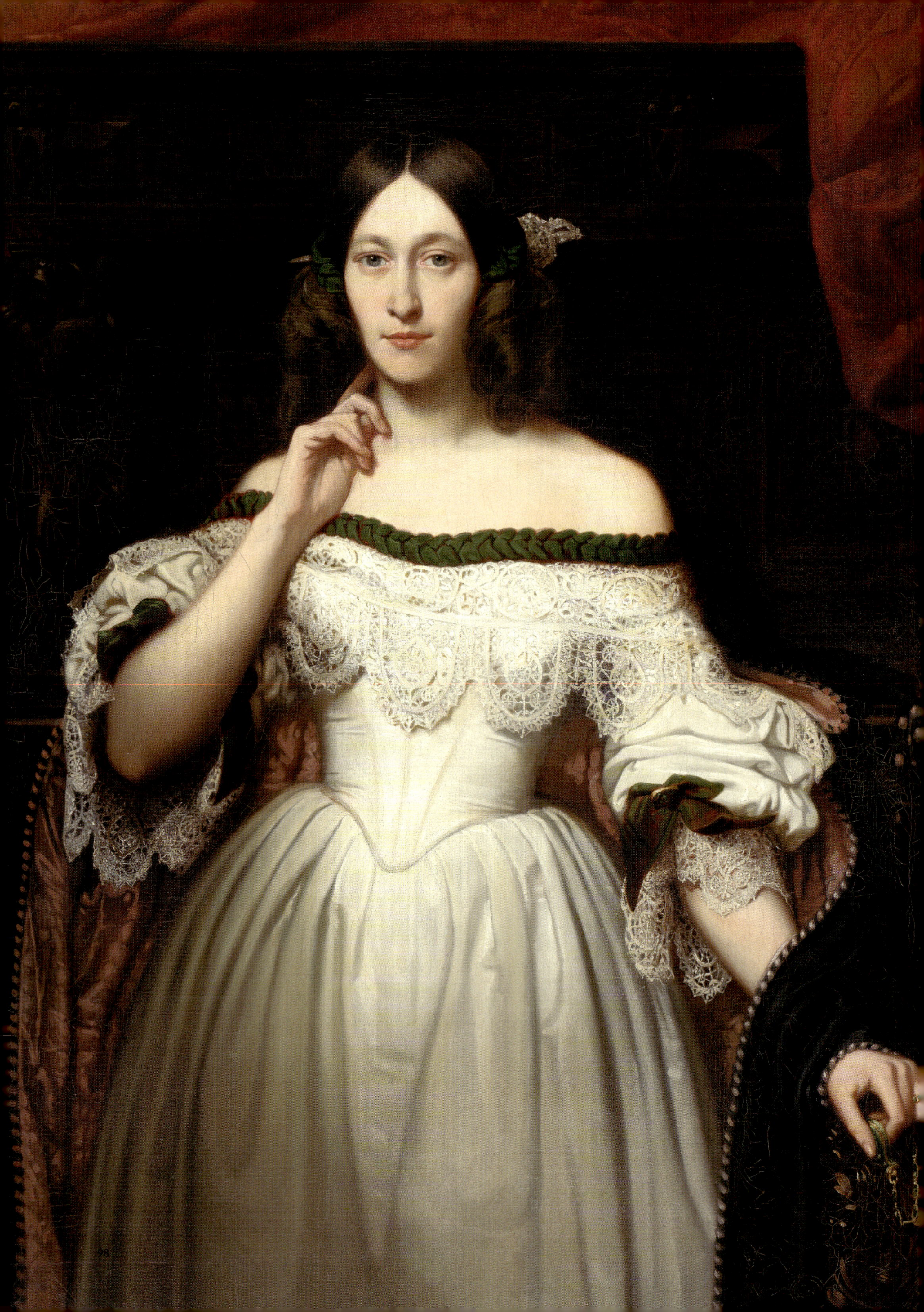

Camille Roqueplan in *The Death of Morris the Spy*. In *The Dead Ride Fast*, the 105
ghostly figures of Ary Scheffer are perfectly suited to the German legend they are taken from. In the 1830s, while the taste for pathos remained, the concern for historical accuracy grew stronger, the formats larger, as can be seen in Charles de Steuben's *Joan the Mad Awaiting the Resurrection of Philip the Handsome, Her Husband*.

If *Medea* refers to Greek mythology, the classical painters' main source of inspiration, the work none the less reflects the aspirations of the Romantic generation. Delacroix chose one of the most emotionally charged instants, when Medea, betrayed by her husband Jason, decides to murder their two children. In 1824, Delacroix undertook a series of experiments – no fewer than thirty-one drawings and a painted sketch now at the Lille museum – which resulted in the painting of 1838 that expresses the fiery impulse of Medea's act. *Susannah and the Elders* also reveals the rapid gesture of the painter, who suffused this sketch with all his expressive power. Delacroix's talent as a colourist, readily comparable to Rubens, finds an outlet in still life, of which the *Rustic Bouquet* is a remarkable example.

The Followers of Ingres

In contrast to Delacroix's style, the precise drawing of Ingres is reflected in the students of the studio he founded in 1824. His admiration for Raphael and the Italians of the Quattrocento induced some disciples like Hippolyte Flandrin to turn toward religious art. *The Scattering of the Tribes*, a finished study for the decoration of the nave of Saint-Germain-des-Prés, which he worked on between 1842 and 1864, also conveys a good knowledge of antique sculpture. Reference to mythology was part of the teaching of Ingres, as indicated by the *Birth of Venus*. Drawing inspiration from Ingres's 1848 painting of the same title, Amaury-Duval revisits the antique ideal of beauty with a concern for stylization.

Recalling the influence of a trip to Italy, an essential stage in artistic training, the more realistic *Rest* by Henri Lehmann depicts two Italian peasants. *The Republic*, a majestic and impassive figure, was entered by Jules Ziegler, one of the group's most ambitious painters, in the competition organized by the state in 1848 to decorate the City Hall. Victor Mottez, in the portrait of his
wife Julie (1805–1845), sought to transcribe the beauty of the model and render 107
details like the hairdo and the embroidery of the dress precisely, conveying a graphic sense inherited from the master. Portraits of Charles Benvignat and Blanquart-Evrart, notable citizens of Lille and friends of the painter, attest to the ties he kept with his native region. Another aspect of Mottez's career, the abundance of religious subject-matter, appears in the *Resurrection of the Dead*, a later work. Even if he was not a student of Ingres, Antoine Lecomte du Noüy particularly admired his refined style, which he tried to imitate in the *Portrait of Mademoiselle E. T.*

Orientalism

The call of adventure and the thirst for new horizons induced artists to travel ever farther. The colonization of Algeria, which began in 1830, increased interest in the East, leading a number of painters – Descamps and Marilhat, as well as Delacroix – to undertake the voyage to Africa. In 1831, Marilhat embarked on a journey that took him from Greece to Syria, through Libya and Egypt. When he returned to France, he executed many compositions similar to *Oriental Landscape*, which contributed to the success of Orientalism in France. Some artists travelled with the army and recounted their exploits. Adrien Dauzats took part in the 1839 expedition through the passage of the Iron Gates. In the Lille painting, exhibited at the Salon of 1853, the rocks

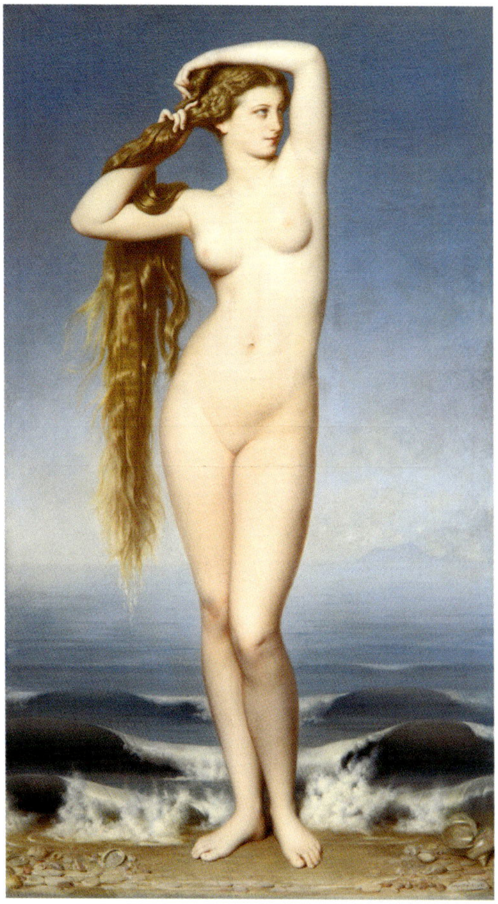

108. Amaury-Duval 1808–1885
The Birth of Venus, 1862, Salon of 1863. Oil on canvas, 197 x 109 cm
Acquired at the Lille fine arts exhibition of 1866. Inv. P. 506

107. Victor Mottez 1809–1897
Julie Mottez, Salon of 1834.
Oil on canvas, 125 x 105.5 cm
Gift of Henri Mottez, 1934. Inv. P. 1698

seem to overrun the canvas, magnifying the monumentality of the reputedly unnegotiable pass.

Sometimes, the celebration of battles took a back seat to the observation of the daily life of local tribes, rural scenes, as in Adolphe Leleux's *Threshing Wheat in Algeria*, or, at all events, the discovery of an unknown culture that was readily likened to some ancient civilization. In Théodore Chassériau's
109 *Arab Merchant Showing a Mare*, the frieze-like composition, city in the background and young woman carrying an amphora evoke the peaceful atmosphere of a Bible scene. Sometimes, curiosity about this civilization transformed the painter into an ethnologist: *The Jewish Bride* by Alfred Dehodencq and *In the Harem* by Benjamin Constant are pretexts for studying unfamiliar customs that, as often, idealize oriental women. MM

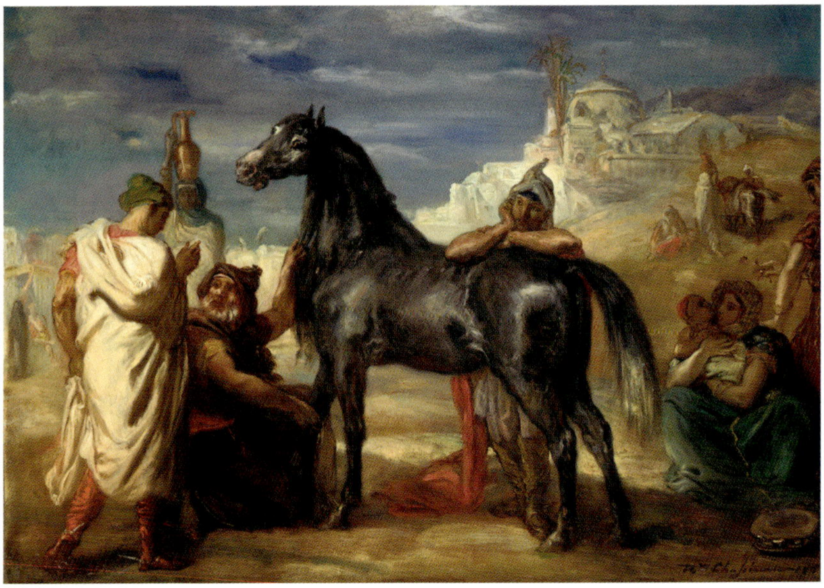

109. Théodore Chassériau 1819–1856
Arab Merchant Showing a Mare, 1853.
Oil on panel, 40.5 x 54.5 cm
Deposit of the Musée du Louvre, 1937. Inv. P. 1710

Realism and Naturalism

Gustave Courbet, the genius of the century who succeeded in toppling the supremacy of Delacroix and Ingres, is represented at the museum by a group of a quality that is unusual outside Paris. Courbet created a Realism distinct from that of Millet. Faithful to his native soil, Ornans, which he would paint
112 without respite, Courbet caused a sensation at the 1849 Salon with *After Dinner at Ornans*, a commonplace scene treated in beige and grey monochrome, which he elevated to the rank of a history painting by its format: the autumn afternoon, stained tablecloth, nodding guests and huge dog squeezed under a chair are all components of this manifesto of Realism that led to *A Burial at Ornans* a year later.

Of equal stature, Jean-François Millet favoured naturalism – the inclination to restore a direct vision of nature and peasant life, a consequence of the
110 Revolution of 1848. After *The Angelus*, Millet conceived *La Becquée* ('The Morsel in the Beak'), comparing a mother and her children to a bird nourishing its young, while the father tills the garden behind the house. Representative of the universal scope of Millet's art, it is one of the museum's most highly regarded paintings. It attempts to reconstruct the majesty of toiling in the fields – in this case around Barbizon, where the painter lived from 1849 – bathed in the serenity of harmonious colouring.

Two large naturalist paintings met with success at the Salon of 1859, one by Jules Breton, the other by Amand Gautier. Breton too painted scenes of the life of his native region of Courrières, in Artois, but in a more narrative and

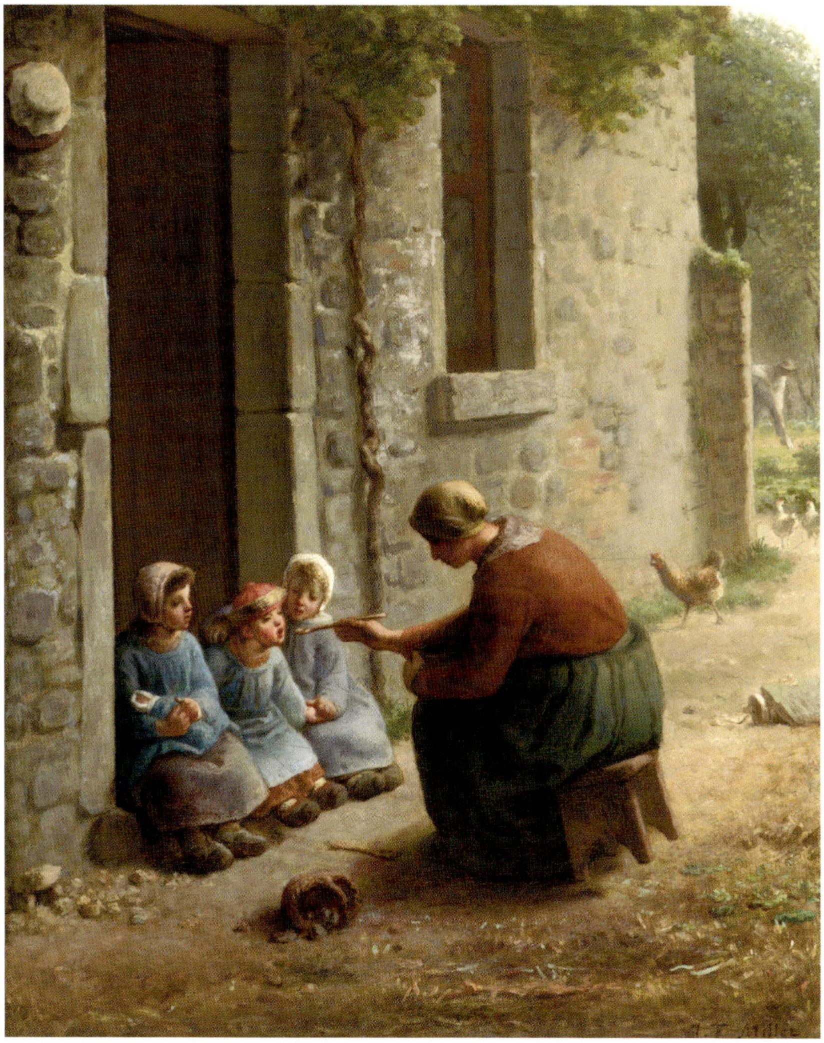

110. Jean-François Millet 1814–1875
La Becquée ('*The Morsel in the Beak*'),
c. 1860. Oil on canvas, 74 x 60 cm
Gift of Mme Maracci, 1871. Inv. P. 543

objective manner than Millet. Having witnessed the raising of an outdoor Crucifixion group in his youth, the painter re-creates this rustic scene with *111*
fervour and precision, incorporating portraits of his family. Gautier, a very loyal friend of Courbet and sensitive to the prisonlike atmosphere in hospitals and convents, produced *The Nuns' Promenade*, which earned Baudelaire's praise. Using a restricted chromatic range, he makes palpable both the monotony of the nuns' life and the sensation of suspended time. Two portraits executed in testimony to friendship stem from the Realist spirit, which leaves no room for seductive or anecdotal concessions: Courbet's *Amand Gautier* (1867) and Gautier's *Docteur Gachet* (1860). Influenced by Ribera, *St Vincent* (1867) and the mysterious *Self-portrait* (*c.* 1880) of Théodule Ribot show a surprising naturalism, above all in their vigorous and contrasting treatment.

The following generation adhered to Courbet's inspiration in regard to the tradition of popular subjects but organized them in light of Impressionism, with bright colours: *Louise Cattel, Wet Nurse* by Alfred-Philippe Roll (1894), *113*
The Quai de La Villette by Henri Gervex (1882) or in the Flemish manner of the 17th century, like *The Fish Market* by Victor Gilbert (Salon of 1880).

ADW

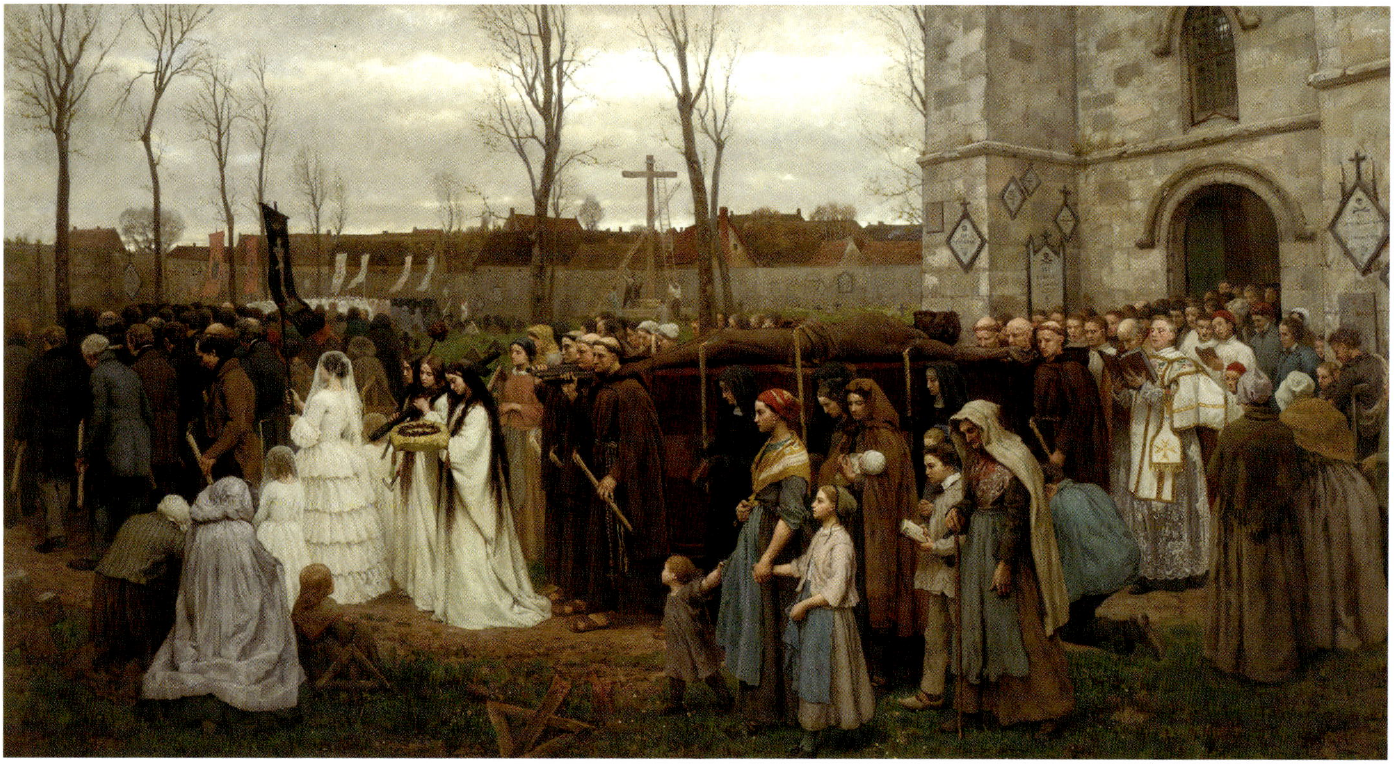

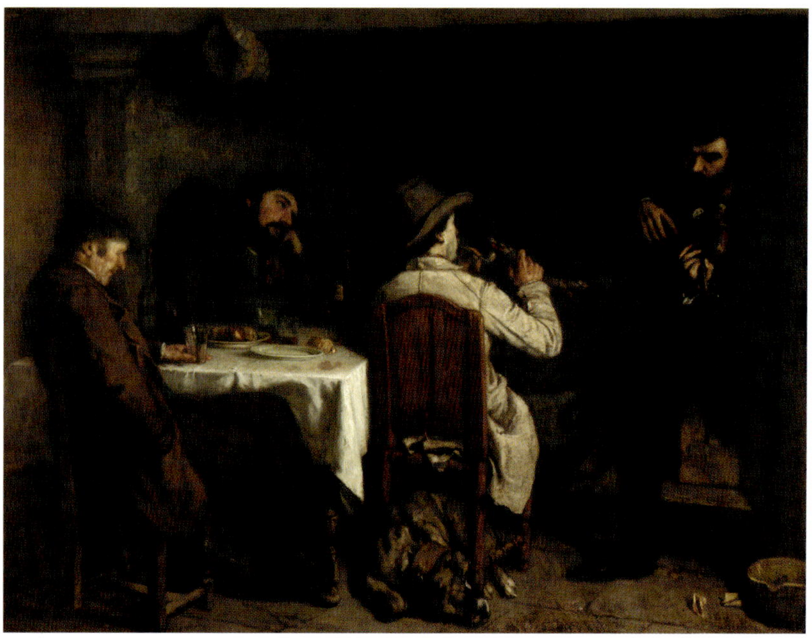

111. Jules Breton 1827–1906
Raising an Outdoor Crucifixion Group, 1858, Salon of 1859. Oil on canvas, 135 x 250 cm
Acquired from Mr Pereire at the Lille fine arts exhibition of 1866. Inv. P. 524

112. Gustave Courbet 1819–1877
After Dinner at Ornans, Salon of 1849. Oil on canvas, 195 x 257 cm
State consignment, 1849. Inv. P. 522

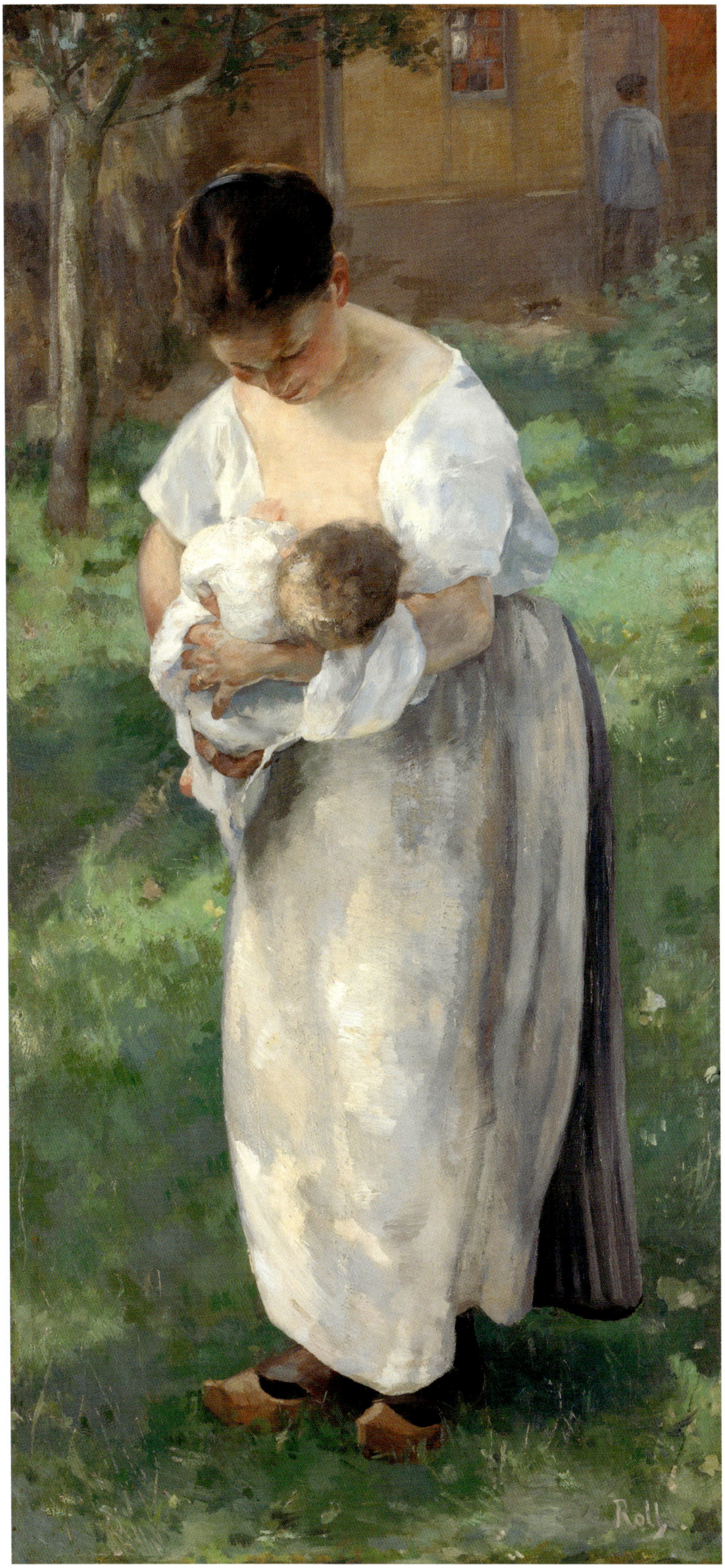

113. Alfred-Philippe Roll 1846–1919
Louise Cattel, Wet Nurse, Salon de la Société Nationale des Beaux-Arts, 1894. Oil on canvas, 157 x 74 cm
Léonard Danel donation, 1904. Inv. P. 550

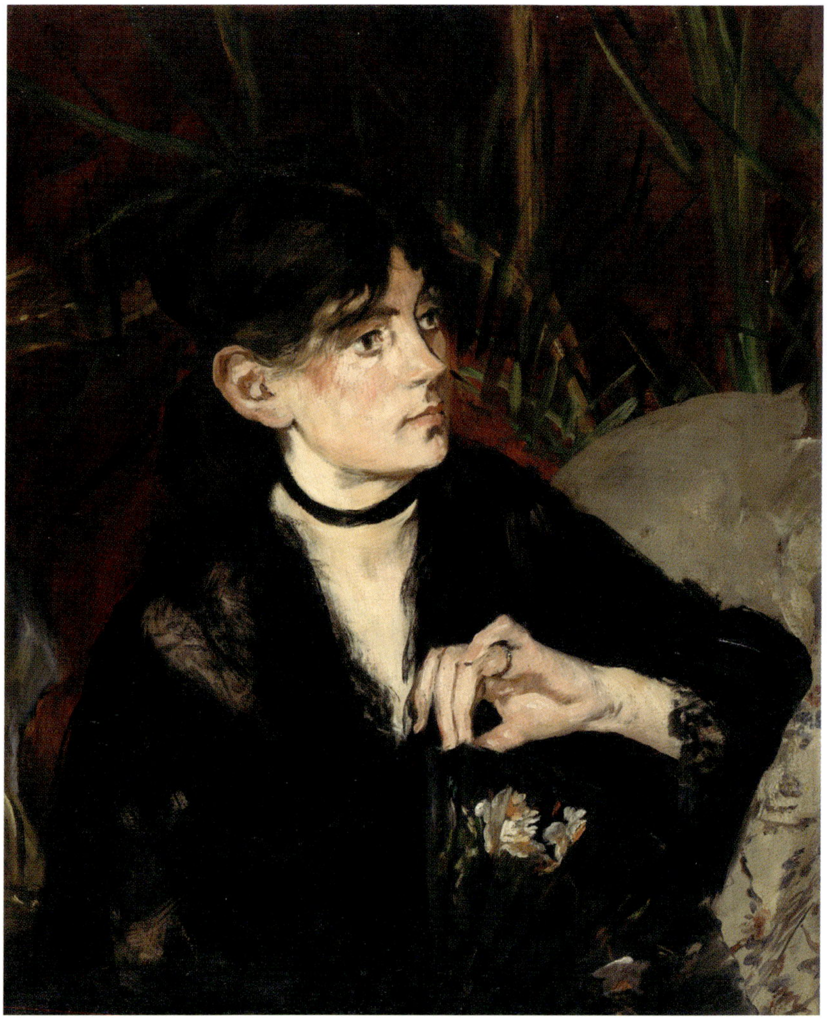

114. Edouard Manet 1832–1883
Berthe Morisot with a Fan, 1874.
Oil on canvas, 61 x 50 cm
Deposit from the Musée d'Orsay, 2000. Inv. D. 2000.1.1

Academicism and Modernity

Three paintings glorify the official art of the Second Empire, based on the pre-eminence of the Old Masters and the nude, before academicism became ossified: *Torment of a Vestal* by Paul Baudry (1875), done the year after the painter's return from Rome; *Adam and Eve* by Léon Bonnat, sent from his residency at the Académie de France in Rome; and, above all, Alexandre Cabanel's *Nymph Abducted by a Faun*, a work acquired by Napoleon III (the Bonnat and the Cabanel were exhibited at the 1861 Salon). On the other hand, Charles
118 Chaplin ventured an intimate portrait of the collector Ernest Feydeau, where sobriety and silvery-golden tones recall the timeless art of Chardin.

In the 1860s, Edouard Manet, the inspiration behind Impressionism, waged a new aesthetic battle under the double influence of Velázquez and Courbet that lastingly altered the course of painting. The modernity and authenticity of his subject-matter and his bold style of painting earned him an unequalled
114 status, shown off in the 1874 portrait of Berthe Morisot, his sister-in-law and, on a number of occasions, his model, absorbed in thought. Carolus-Duran, a citizen of Lille who was close to Manet, adhered to this modern language, but in a more literary vein: a vigorous autobiographical painting composed on the
115 occasion of his marriage, *The Kiss* (1868) represents him passionately embrac-
116 ing his young wife. In the same way, *Henri Regnault Dead on the Battlefield*, a sketch painted two years later portraying a painter who showed bright promise but was killed at Champigny-sur-Marne in 1871, forcefully proclaims his stylistic kinship with Manet in the lively and synthetic use of line.

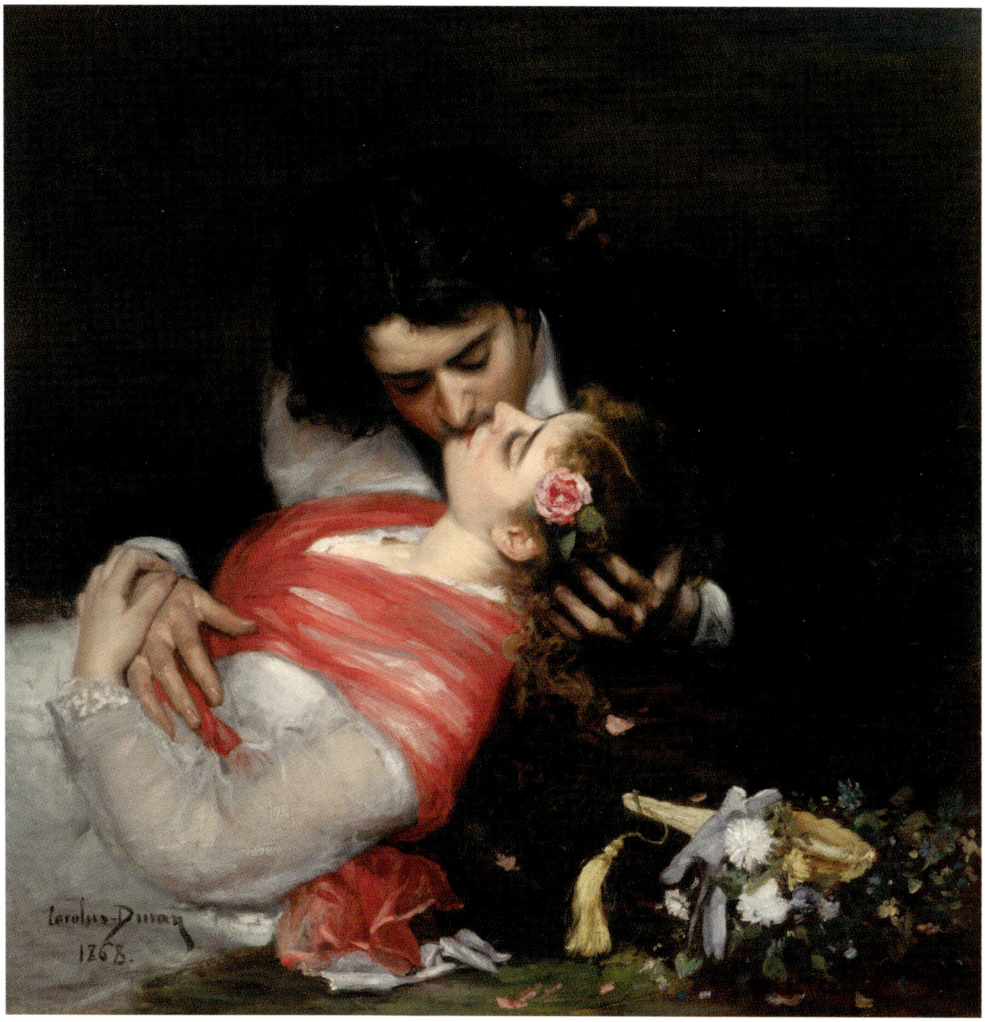

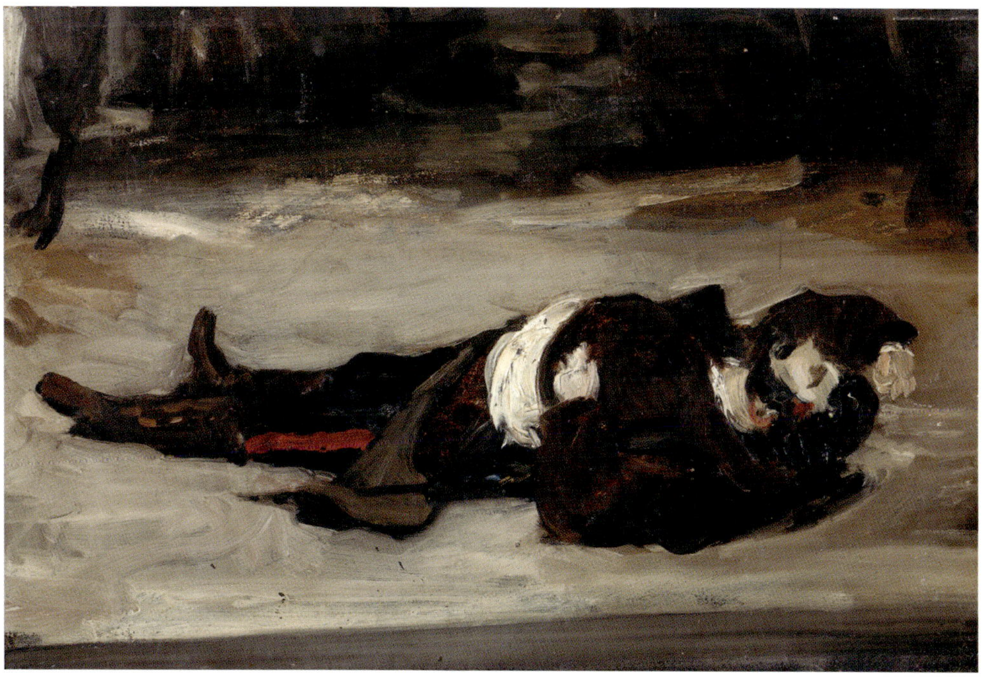

115. Carolus-Duran 1837–1917
The Kiss, 1868.
Oil on canvas, 92 x 91.5 cm
Gift of Mme Buyse, 1986. Inv. P. 1984

116. Carolus-Duran 1837–1917
Henri Regnault Dead on the Battlefield. Oil on mahogany panel, 35 x 53 cm
Acquired 2004 with the support of Crédit Immobilier de France and White Public Relations Tokyo. Inv. P. 2056

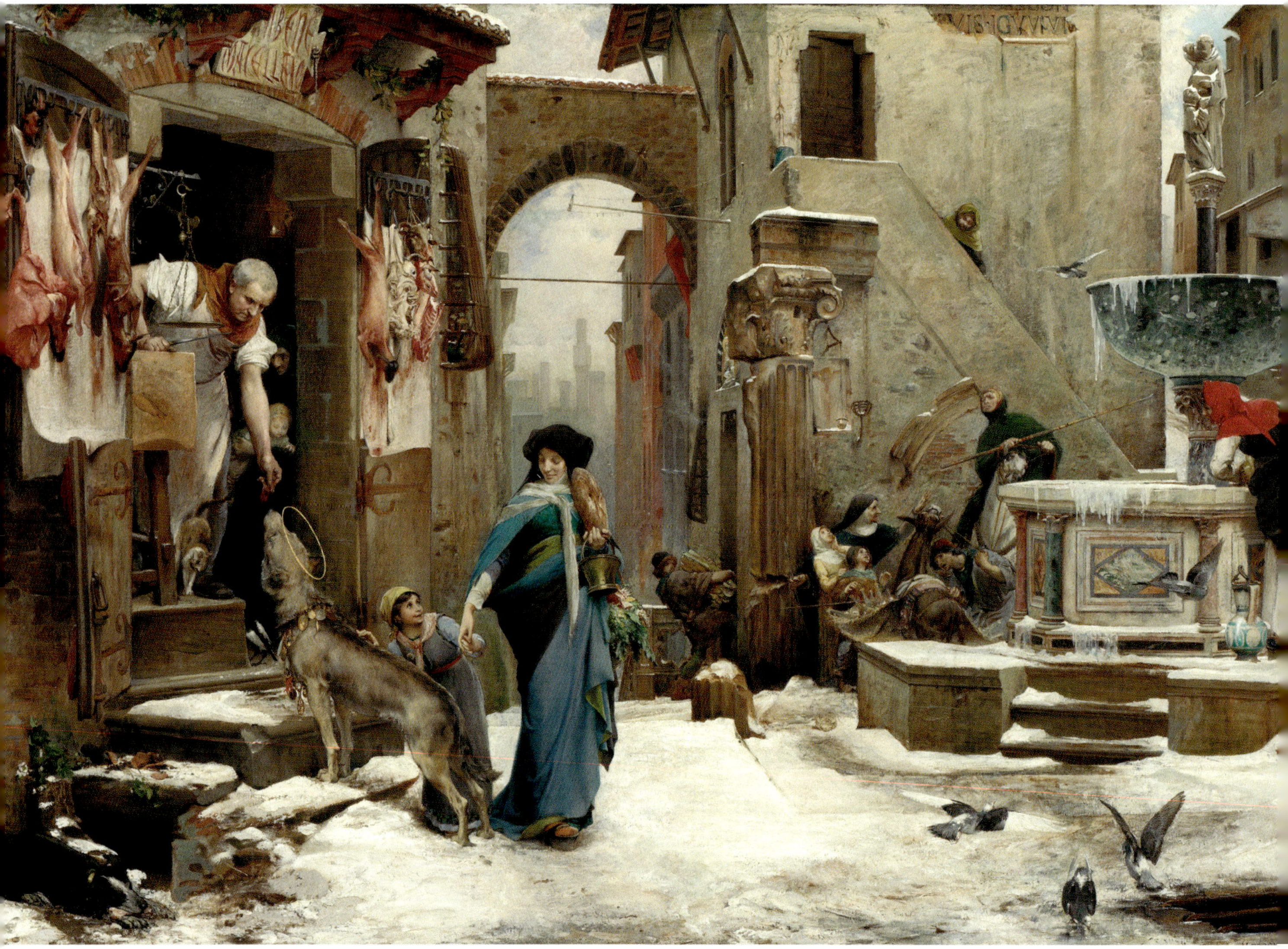

117. Luc-Olivier Merson 1846–1920
The Wolf of Gubbio, 1877, Salon of
1878. Oil on canvas, 88 x 133 cm

Acquired at the Lille fine arts exhibition of 1881.
Inv. P. 500

Luc-Olivier Merson, too, abandoned mythological themes, preferring to
paint anecdotes of religious history, such as *The Wolf of Gubbio* (1877), about 117
a wolf that terrorized the surroundings of the town until St Francis of Assisi
tamed him: mysticism and Realism join forces to offer one of the most touchingly refined scenes in the museum's collection. In a personal, lyrical mode supported by an elliptical, virtuoso craftsmanship, Alfred Agache, also of Lille, painted allegories propelled by contemporary references, like his muse, the proud, modern young woman personifying *Vanity* (1890; see cover). ADW

Landscape

The development of landscape was one of the 19th century's main characteristics. Exhorted to leave their studios, artists increasingly made quick sketches from nature, following the recommendation of Pierre-Henri de Valenciennes. Valenciennes nevertheless extolled the importance of ancient architecture, which he introduced into his *Historic Landscape*.

The journey to Italy that Valenciennes advised future landscape painters to make was a fundamental stage in the training of Camille Corot. In
Rome in 1825, he made many architectural views, particularly of the Castello 119
Sant'Angelo. The studies of the site he tirelessly produced resulted in a unique rendering without artifice, emphasizing contrasts of light and shadow.

Among the Romantic painters' aspirations, the contemplation of nature was a favourite activity for stimulating the imagination. Georges Michel in *Environs of Paris* and *Seacoast*, and Paul Huet in *Effect of Evening*, express the mystery and melancholy of a rural setting. Like Huet, Constant Troyon was drawn to the Forest of Fontainebleau and Barbizon. His attention to transcribing effects of light in a mosaic of coloured strokes applied in a thick layer is already near to Théodore Rousseau and Charles Daubigny. Constant Dutilleux, a close friend of Corot, did likewise with the freshness of vision in *Beech
Grove in the Forest of Fontainebleau*. The broad panorama of *The Seine at Ville-* 120
neuve-Saint-Georges by Théodore Rousseau attests to the universal dialogue of trees and water, and the organic cult of nature that already haunted the painter before settling in Barbizon (1848). Also familiar with this area, Charles Daubigny liked to visit the banks of the Oise, trying to reconstruct the fleeting instant, as in *Sunrise: Banks of the Oise* (1865).

Three paintings illustrate Courbet's attraction to landscape. The first,
Seascape: View of Honfleur (1841–45), from his youth, reflects a fascination with 121
the sea that remained with him for his entire career. The second, *Garden of the Abbey of Loos* (1851) – recording a visit to Lille – examines nature's sombre and mysterious depths. The third, *The Meuse at Freyr* (1856), arose from one of the artist's sojourns in Belgium, near Dinant, where he sought to render the materiality of the cliffs, which recall Ornans, rather than re-create the limpidity of the water and air.

Eugène Boudin, who was related to Troyon, Corot and Daubigny, none the less avowed his predilection for the seacoasts of Normandy and Brittany, as in his masterpiece *Camaret Harbour, Stormy Sky* (1873), whose brisk, supple brushwork and fine contrasts of light make the clouds sweep across the sky. Ludovic Lepic turned his attention to the observation of variations of light at Berck, on the coast of the English Channel, making many views at every time of day and
year, such as *Fishing Boats Returning to Berck* in heavy weather (1877). 123

Awakened to a feeling for nature by Boudin, Claude Monet demonstrates his exceptional technical mastery and attention to the ceaseless,
diffuse movement of light effects, particularly in the frozen winter, in *Ice* 122
Floes (1880), where the Seine is congested with ice. Alfred Sisley proposes a version tinged with melancholy in the blended tones of *Port-Marly, White
Frost* (1872). Monet's *Houses of Parliament, London* (1904) belongs to a series of 124

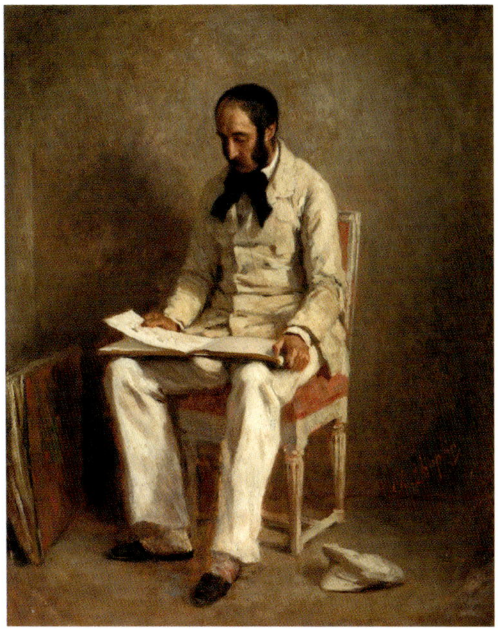

118. Charles Chaplin 1825-1891
Ernest Feydeau. Oil on canvas,
27 x 22 cm
Gift of Alain Feydeau, 2002. Inv. P. 2050

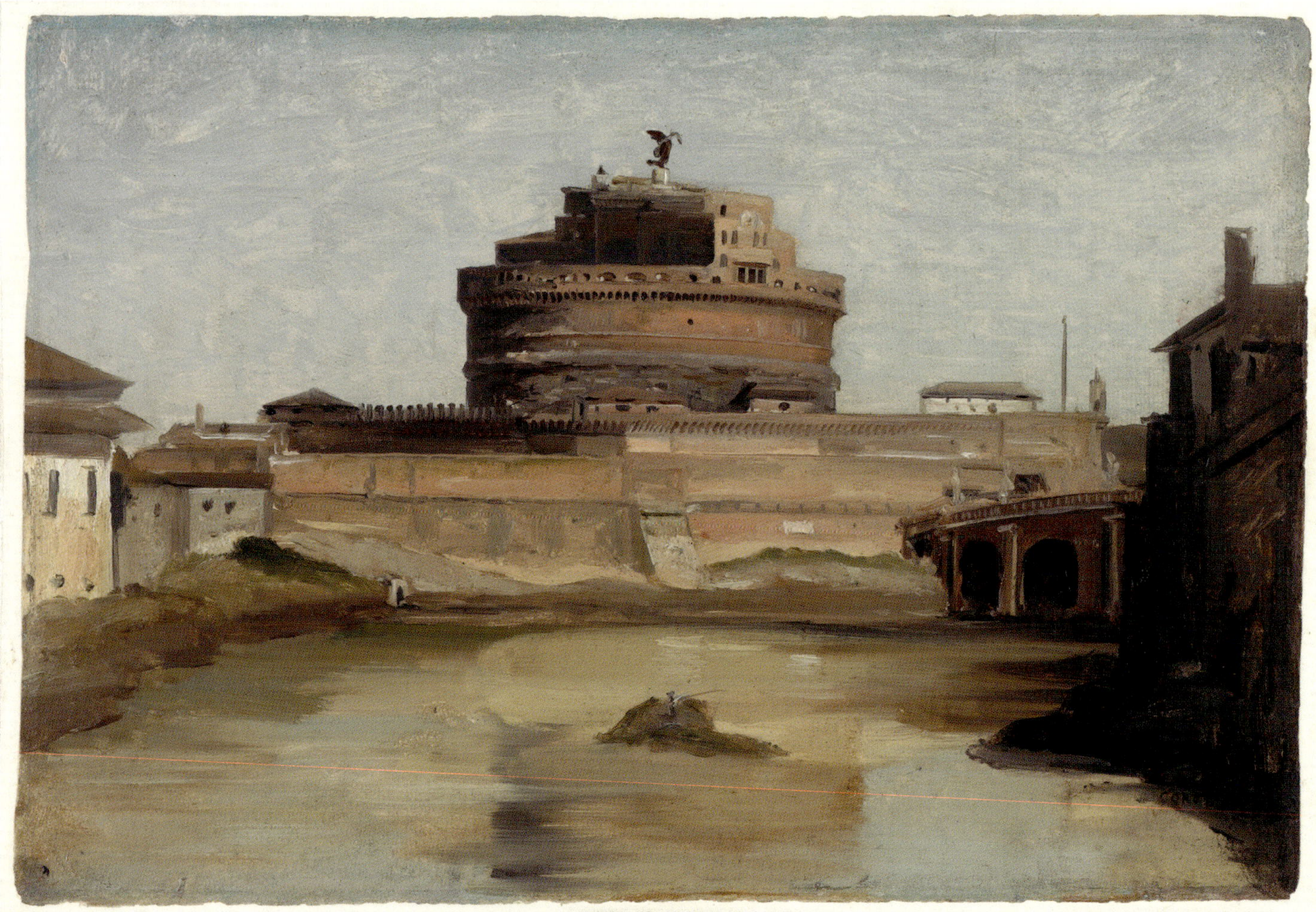

119. Jean-Baptiste-Camille Corot 1796–1875
Castello Sant'Angelo. Oil on paper
on canvas, 27 x 40 cm

Camille Benoît bequest, 1882. Inv. P. 544

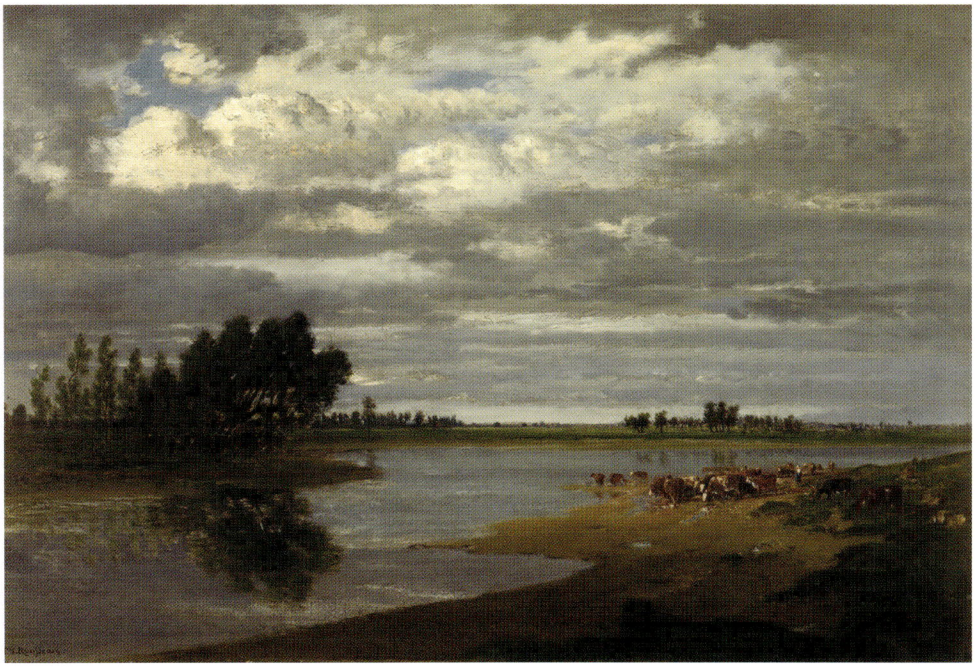

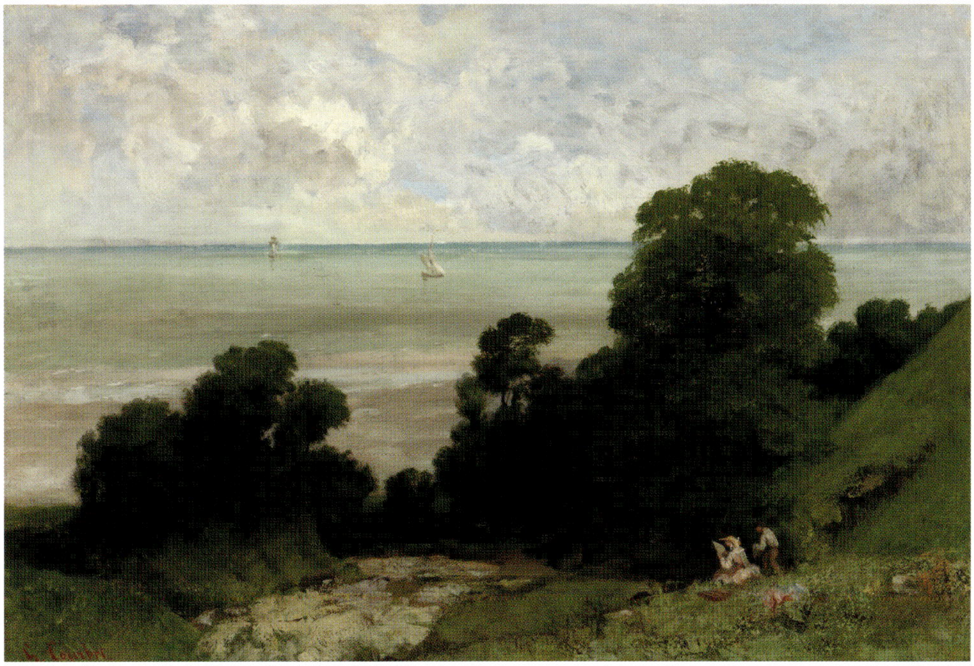

120. Théodore Rousseau 1812–1867
The Seine at Villeneuve-Saint-Georges.
Oil on panel, 32 x 49 cm

Mme Maracci bequest, 1901. Inv. P. 546

121. Gustave Courbet 1819–1877
Seascape: View of Honfleur, c. 1841–45.
Oil on canvas, 43.5 x 65 cm

Acquired from the artist by Auguste Richebé, mayor of Lille, who donated it in 1861. Inv. P. 545

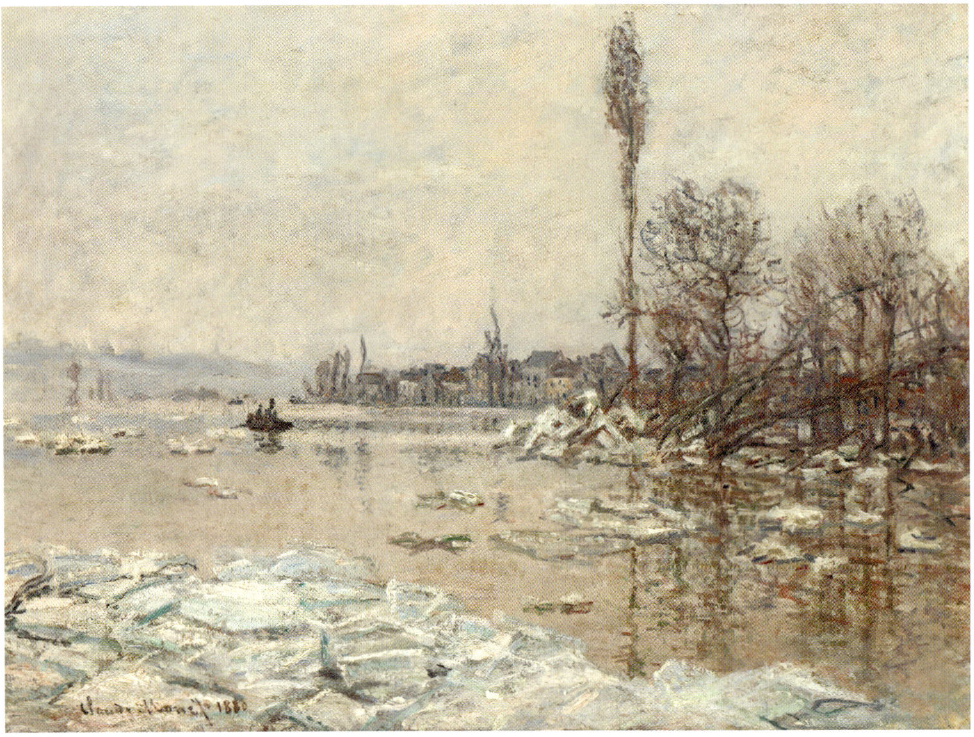

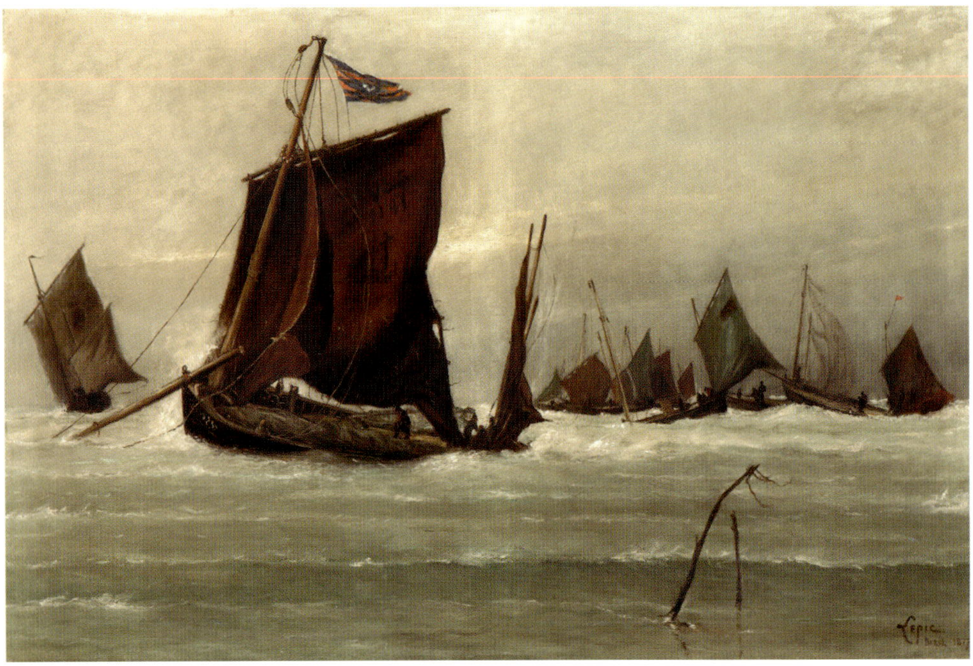

122. Claude Monet 1840–1926
Ice Floes, 1880. Oil on canvas, 72.3 x 99.3 cm

Collection of Maurice Masson, acquired by *dation* to the state on condition of permanent deposit at the Lille museum, 1974. Inv. P. 1891

123. Ludovic-Napoléon Lepic 1839–1890
Fishing Boats Returning to Berck, 1877. Oil on canvas, 127 x 246 cm

Gift of the artist (under the name of Van der Hoost), 1877. Inv. P. 730

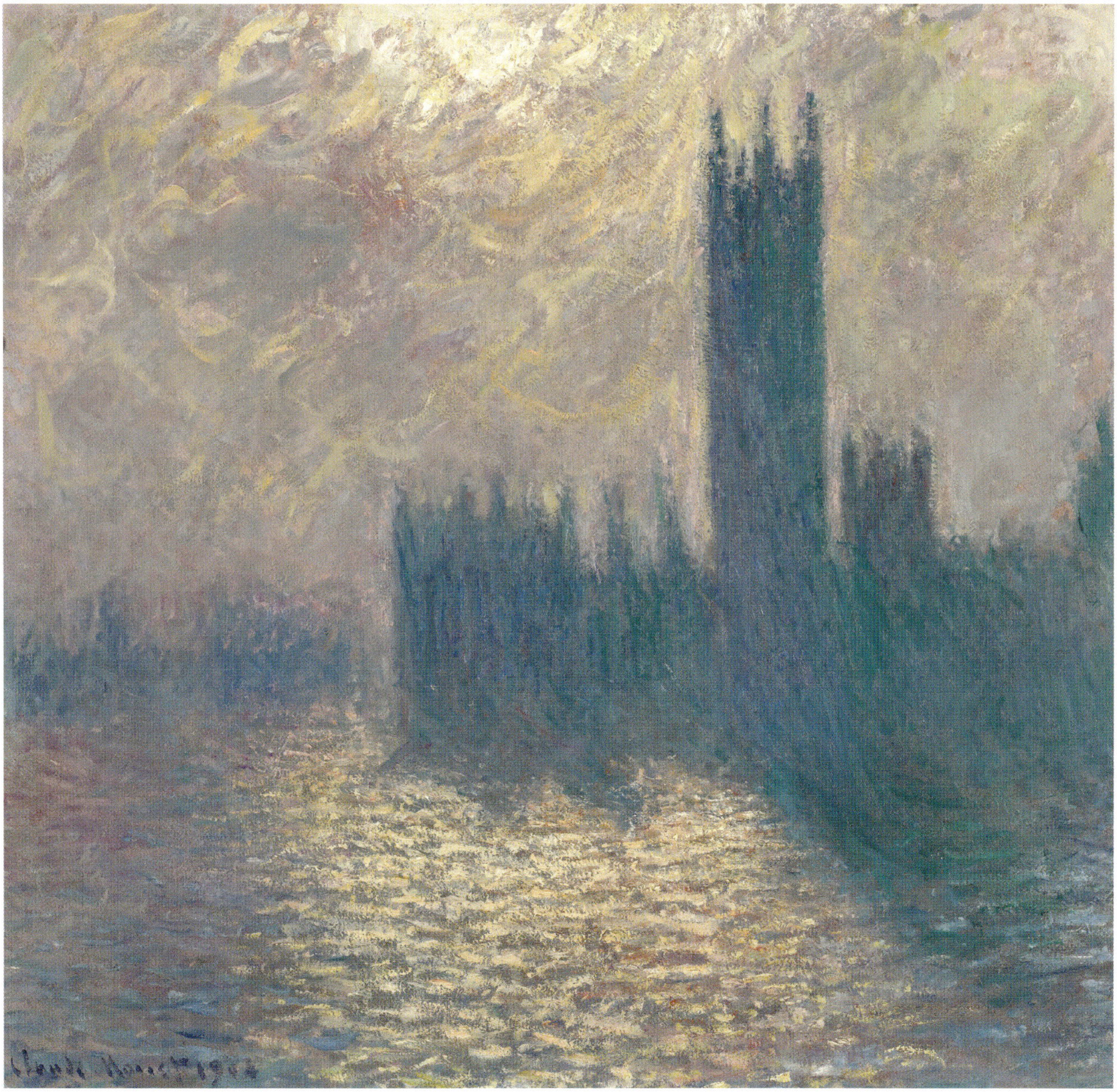

eleven paintings undertaken after sojourns in the British capital (1899–1901). The architectural monument dissolves into the vibrating, mist-filtered light. *Vétheuil, Morning* (1901) also belongs to a series of this type, which Monet created toward the end of his career. ADW & MM

124. Claude Monet 1840–1926
Houses of Parliament, London, 1904.
Oil on canvas, 81.5 x 92 cm
Maurice Masson bequest, 1949. Inv. P. 1734

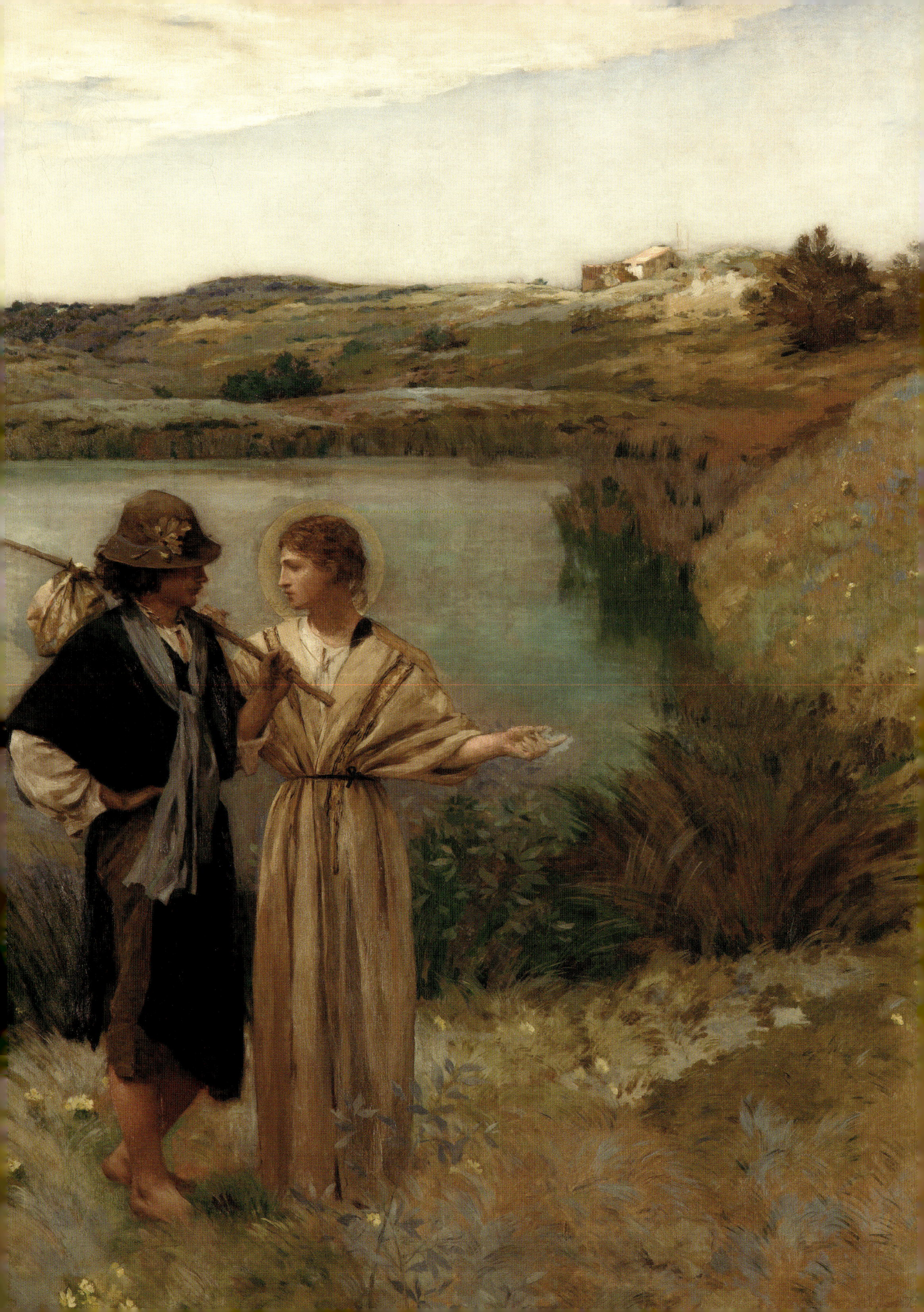

Symbolism

Late 19th-century Symbolism is well represented at the museum. This widespread movement wears many faces, according to whether its inspiration is literary, oneiric or allegorical. The first of the Symbolists is incontestably Puvis de Chavannes, whose vast canvas *Sleep* is one of his first works to attract notice 126 (Salon of 1867). Derived from Millet's naturalism, the formula it invents evokes contented repose after a day of labour in the distant past, a scene drawn from Virgil's *Aeneid*. Treated in the tones of beige, blue and pink dear to the painter, the vision conveys a sense of torpor. Jean-Charles Cazin's *Tobias and the Angel*, 125 the object of great fascination at the 1880 Salon, exploits a monumental naturalism that accommodates the dunes of his native Boulonnais region, imbued with a mystic serenity. In the elegant female figure *Erigone, or Autumn* (*c.* 1875), 127 Gustave Moreau uses the linear drawing and refined palette inherited from Chassériau, whom he admired, to unveil his fantastic world, corresponding to a literary Symbolism.

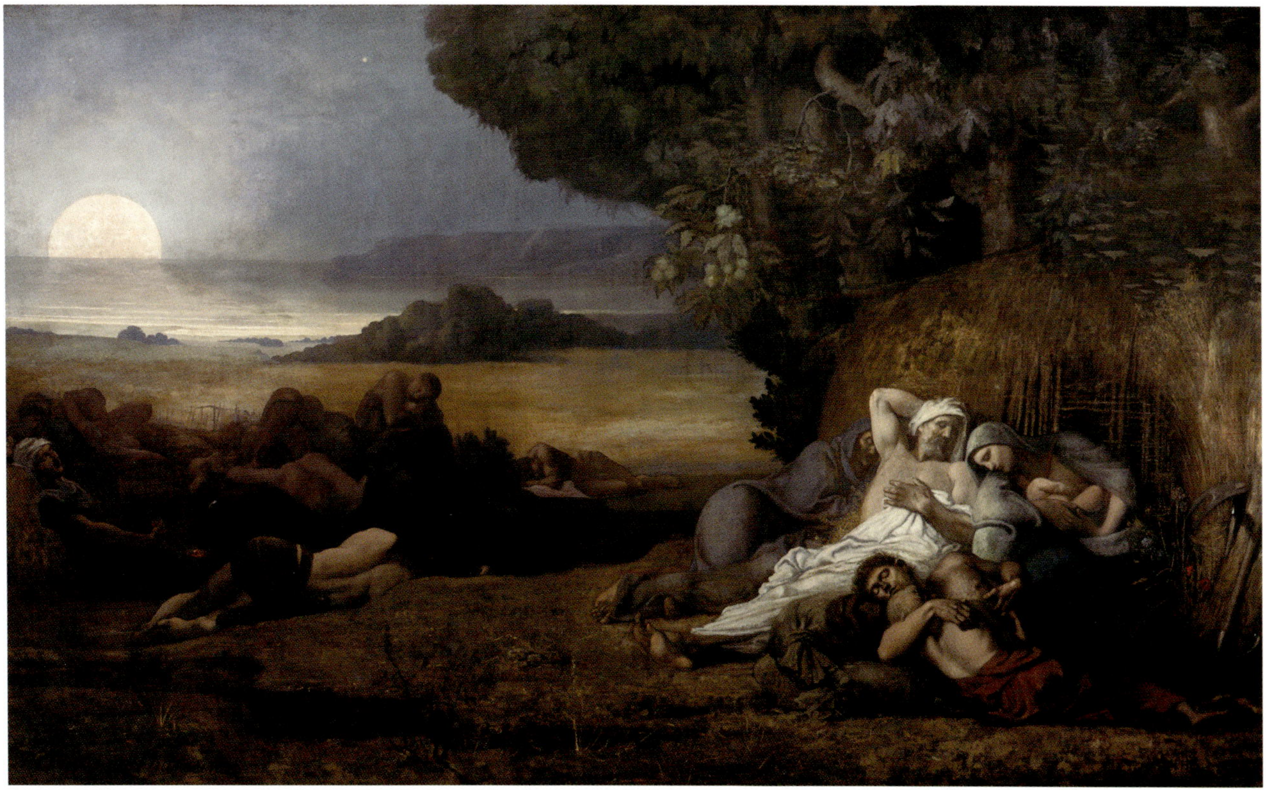

126. Pierre Puvis de Chavannes 1824–1898
Sleep, Salon of 1867. Oil on canvas, 381 x 600 cm
Acquired with matching funds from the state, 1888. Inv. P. 625

125. Jean-Charles Cazin 1841–1901
Tobias and the Angel, Salon of 1880. Oil on canvas, 186 x 142 cm
Acquired 1880. Inv. P. 568

Odilon Redon's singular breadth is evident in the works on deposit from the Musée d'Orsay, *Silence* and *The Gaze*, unfurling the complex, precious richness of the author's dream world. Eugène Carrière, a friend of Puvis de Chavannes, devised an intimist Symbolism, favouring tender portraits of those close to him, such as *Madame Carrier* and *Lise at the Piano*, bathed in bistre mist. The vaporous *Self-portrait* of Henri Fantin-Latour at the age of seventeen also partakes of this intimist vein and reveals the young painter's coming attraction to the world of enchantment. ADW

Post-impressionism

At the last Impressionist exhibition in 1886, a new generation of artists appeared: the Neo-Impressionists, who restored the form that had been drained empty by the Impressionists. Georges Seurat became their leader, perfecting the technique of pointillism, which involves the systematic juxtaposition of

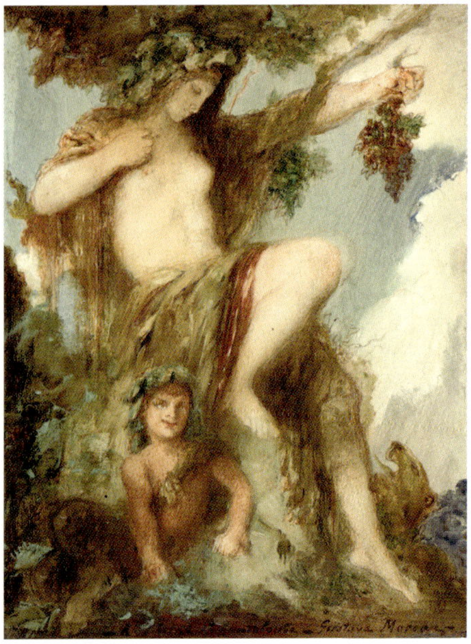

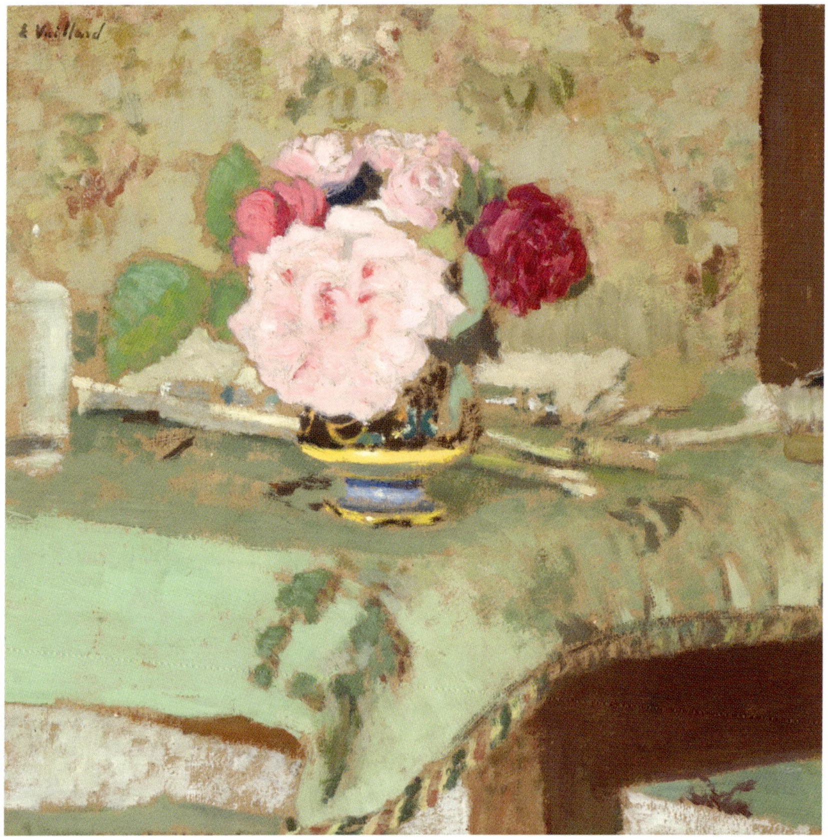

127. Gustave Moreau 1826–1896
Erigone, or Autumn, c. 1875.
Oil on panel, 23 x 18 cm
Purchased from the Mr A. Cantaloube sale, 1883.
Inv. P. 609

128. Edouard Vuillard 1868–1940
Bouquet of Roses. Oil on cardboard, 32.7 x 33 cm
Acquired from Mlle Denise Masson, 1973. Inv. P. 1878

tiny brushstrokes in pure colour. *Landscape at Grandcamp*, from 1885, illustrates his theory in a harmoniously balanced composition while expressing modernity. Under this aesthetic influence, academic painters like Henri Martin then experimented with the divided brushstroke in their own fashion. *Young Breton Woman by the Sea* combines a brown-and-ochre pointillism with a subject for meditation evoking the School of Pont-Aven. Ernest Laurent's canvas *In the Garden* (1904) is an intimate family scene in which the distribution of the coloured masses is barely separated.

Still in reaction against Impressionism, the painter Emile Bernard, from Lille, simplified forms as enclosed areas of flat colour, consequently formulating the principles of Synthetism. The glass painting depicting *Women Picking Pears* (1888) is a successful application of this technique: the ornamental stylization fosters the expression of the imagination. Bernard returned to a more
129 classical conception of painting with *Nymphs after Bathing* (1908), where buxom young women animate a mythological composition recalling the pastoral scenes of Titian. During the same years, however, Edouard Vuillard pursued
128 the lessons of Bernard's Synthetism, seeking a decorative effect. His *Bouquet of Roses*, composed of monochrome bands and the patterns of the wallpaper and tablecloth, confirms his talent as a colourist. This return to reality is found in the painting of Pierre Bonnard, which resembles the Impressionism then being denounced by the avant-garde. *Landscape, Le Canet* (1924), a composition of oblique and contrary planes, is flooded with light. With Bonnard, the vision of nature takes on an almost methodically ordered sensuality. MFB

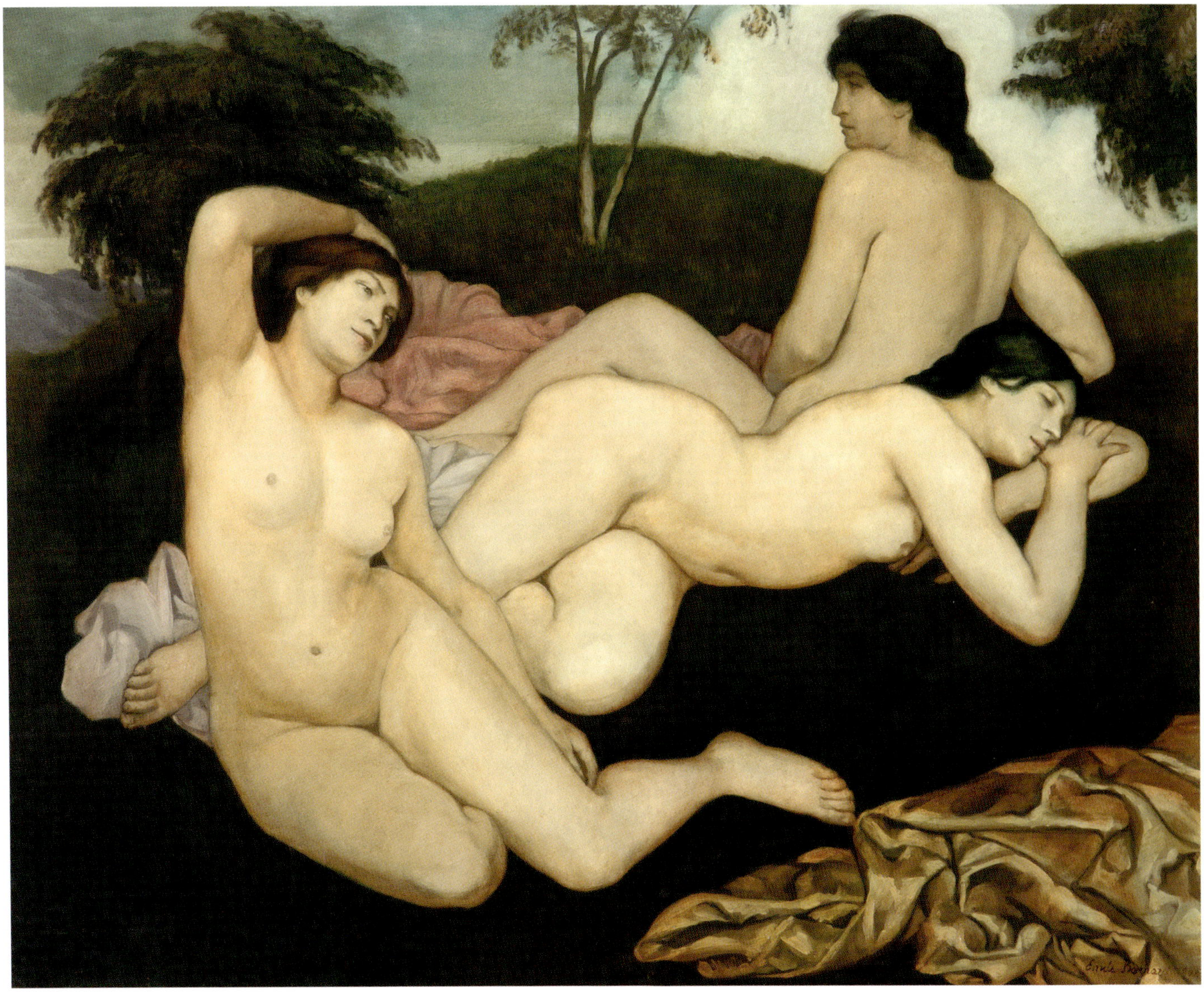

129. Emile Bernard 1868–1941
Nymphs after Bathing, 1908.
Oil on canvas, 121 x 151 cm
Deposit from the Musée d'Orsay, 1997. Inv. D. 97.4.7

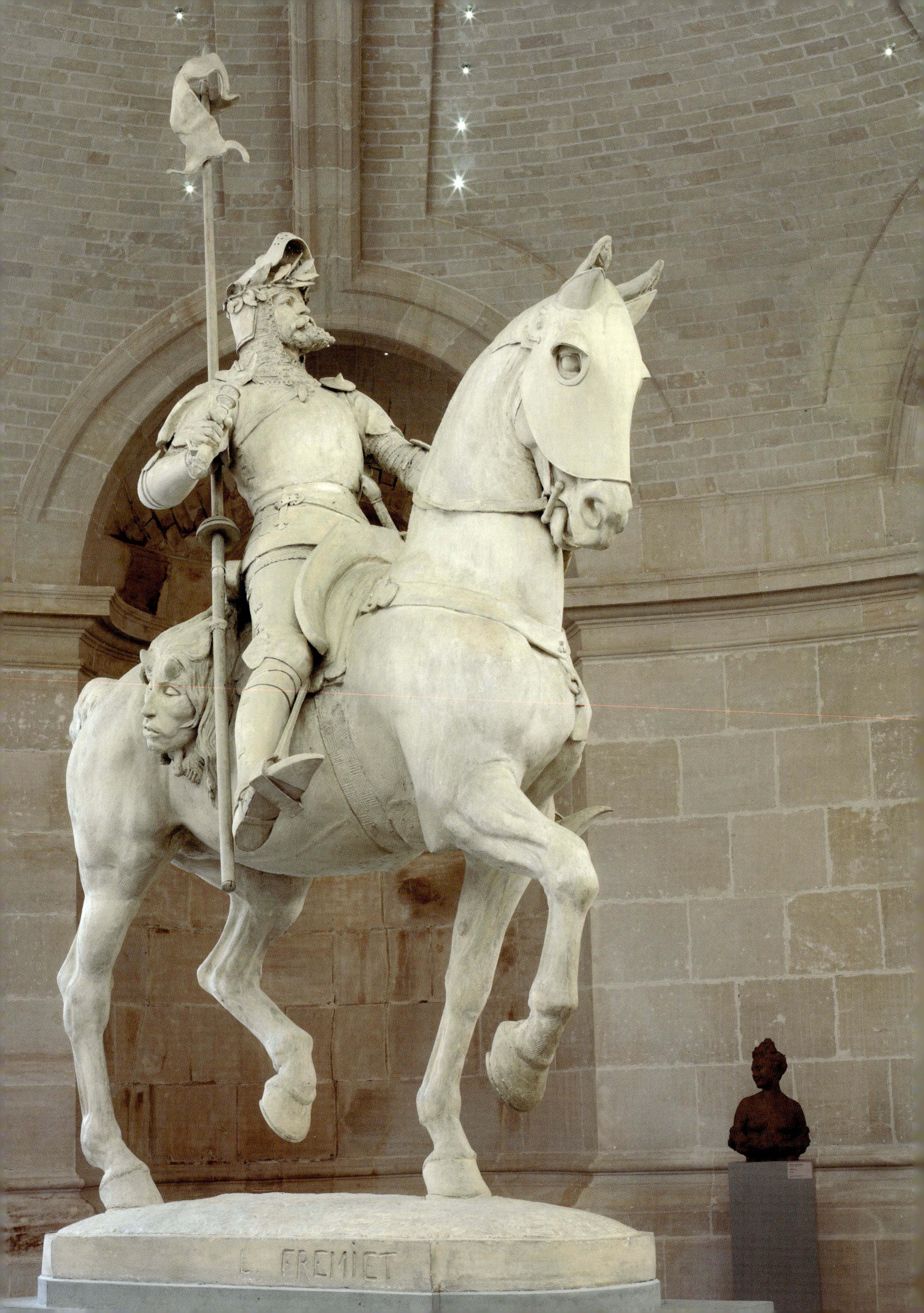
L. FREMIET

Sculpture: Houdon to Bourdelle

The 'sculpture museum' was the last 'museum' to take shape, in 1892, in the new Palais des Beaux-Arts. Installed in the entrance on the Place de la République side, it included two monumental – and rare – plaster models, Frémiet's *Knight Errant* (1878) and Barrias's *Defence of Saint-Quentin* (1881). If 130 state consignments consisting of works purchased from the spawning ground of the Salons contributed to building the collection, donors – from sculptors including Carpeaux himself, and their families, like those of David d'Angers, Dantan, Bartholdi, Cavelier and Lacombe – followed close behind, attracted by the energy of the sculpture museum.

A century later, exhibited in the west of the building, the collection exerts the same presence in the renovated museum. The sculpture collection, one of the most representative and richest panoramas of 19th-century French sculpture outside Paris, is reinforced by the interplay of correspondences with the paintings presented in the galleries above.

By way of tribute, let us mention the marvellous *Wax Head*. The first 1 masterpiece to enter the museum (1834), it quickly became an emblematic figure. Given in the 'time of Raphael', it has resisted many attempts at attribution but has since lost some of its aura, unjustly so. Another masterpiece, and a source of public favour, has never been refuted: *Napoleon I, Protector of Industry* by Henri Lemaire (1854), transferred from the Old Stock Exchange, shows the emperor with the attributes of flax and sugar beet cultivation, developed in the North on his initiative.

The humanism and smiling grace of the Enlightenment are embodied in busts by the best sculptors of the 18th century: *Le Fèvre de Caumartin* (1779), intendant of Flanders and Artois, by Houdon and *The Architect Charles de* 131 *Wailly* (1789) by Pajou, who created a portrait of his close friend in casual attire, the face twinkling with mischief. In their wake, let us also recall the region's native sculptors: Roland (*Mme Roland*) and Corbet (*Bonaparte*). The heroism dear to the Neoclassicism that ruled the arts from the 1780s ensured Roland's success with *Cato of Utica* (plaster, 1782) and confirmed Chaudet's supremacy with the valiant group *The Rest of Belisarius* (1789), a noble echo of 133 the *Belisarius* by the painter David. Antiquity's hallmark moral virtues suffuse two powerful, smoothly treated male statues: *Cincinnatus* (plaster, 1834) and *Spartacus Breaking His Chains* (plaster 1824; bronze, 1847), to lead the slave re- 132 volt. These are the first successes of Foyatier, from whom the king commissioned the marbles for the Tuileries Gardens.

Starting from the 1830s, sensuality and movement mitigated the antique ideal of the older generation. Thus, *Satyr and Bacchante* by Pradier, according 138 to Flaubert the 'last of the Greeks' (1834, marble version at the Louvre), provoked a scandal through the voluptuous character of the group, along with portraits of the sculptor and his mistress. In parallel, David d'Angers developed a Romantic lyricism, discernible in the low relief *France* (*c.* 1822) and amplified in the series of four terracotta models *The Benefits of Printing* on the main continents, reliefs for the Gutenberg Monument in Strasbourg (*c.* 1840). The organizing principle of each is similar: exemplary personalities – Voltaire, Descartes and Luther in the relief *In Europe* – crowd around a printing press to celebrate this modern invention, a source of progress. Préault, the impetuous Romantic, glorified 'expression through contraction' and attained a great freedom of line in portraits of his contemporaries, friends and acquaintances: the painter Descamps, the writer Mallefille, the teacher Périgot, subjects of a superb series of forty bronze medallions (1829–62).

Carpeaux renewed the 18th-century portrait tradition, the feeling for nature and plastic richness in the medallion *Edouard Reynart* and the bust *Princess*

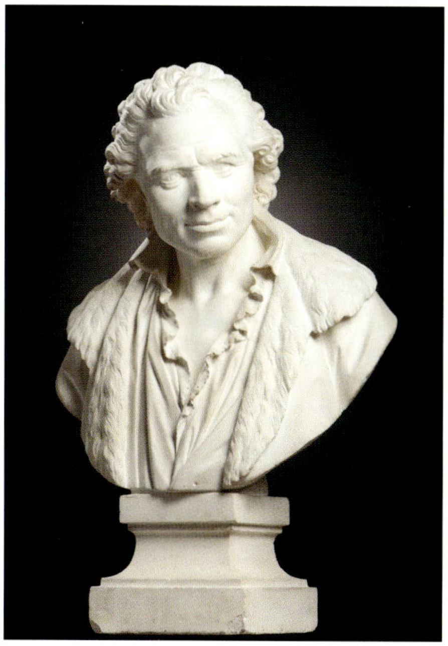

131. Augustin Pajou 1730–1809
The Architect Charles de Wailly, 1789.
Plaster, 55 x 52 x 25 cm
Acquired 2000. Inv. 2001.2.1

130. Emmanuel Frémiet 1824–1910
Knight Errant, Salon of 1878.
Plaster, 323 x 140 x 265 cm
State consignment, 1886. Inv. Sc. 13

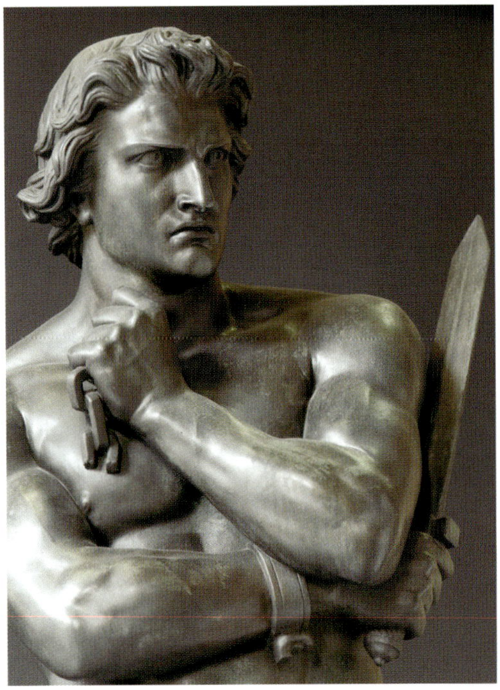

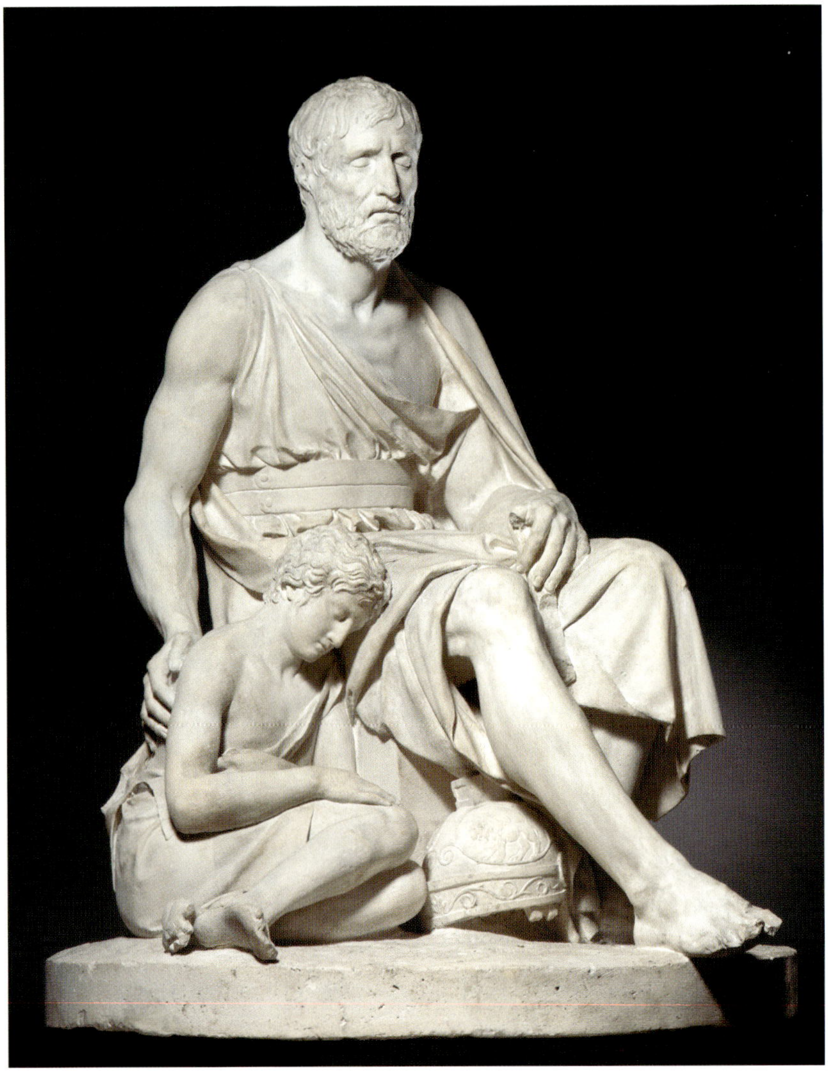

132. Denis Foyatier 1793–1863
Spartacus Breaking His Chains.
Bronze (plaster 1824; cast 1847),
215 x 63 x 94 cm
Acquired 1888. Inv. Sc. 5

133. Antoine-Denis Chaudet 1763–1810
The Rest of Belisarius. Plaster,
83 x 62 x 68 cm, 1789.
Deposit from the Musée du Louvre, 1997. Inv. D. 2006.0.2

Mathilde. However, eclecticism won out in the second half of the century with the enthusiasm for rocaille art that led to *Spring* and *Autumn* by Carrier-Belleuse. The Florentine Renaissance and its masters Verrocchio and Donatello became a fertile source in the 1860s, particularly for works by the residents of the French Academy in Rome – Hiolle's *Narcissus* (1868), Idrac's *Cupid Stung by a Bee* (1876) – but also for the residents from Lille of the Wicar Foundation in
135 Rome, such as Hector Lemaire with *Clélia* (1869), an elegant effigy with simple,
137 fluid lines that can be compared to the bust *The Pisan* (1874) by the painter Carolus-Duran, whose attraction to sculpture recalls the mingling of the arts at the century's close.

Defeat in the Franco-Prussian War in 1871 caused a patriotic stir that was expressed in the erection of public monuments: *The Lion of Belfort* by Bartholdi (model, plaster, 1875) celebrates the heroic defence of the city, as well as *The Defence of Saint-Quentin* by Barrias.

Meant to teach history to citizens of the city, monuments glorify the great men of the Third Republic. The cause of particular fervour in Lille for having created the chair in chemistry there, Pasteur is commemorated by the Lille sculptor Alphonse Cordonnier. His work symbolizes the scientist's discoveries
140 in nimbly sculpted studies such as *The Inoculation* and *Fermentation* (*c.* 1896). The plaster model for the Monument to General Faidherbe (*c.* 1891), which stands near the museum, allows viewers to grasp the development of a work subject to the taste of its commissioners. In this respect, the collection is en-

134. Camille Claudel 1864–1943
Giganti, 1885. Bronze, 32 x 26 x 27 cm
Gift of Baron de Rothschild, 1892. Inv. Sc. 15

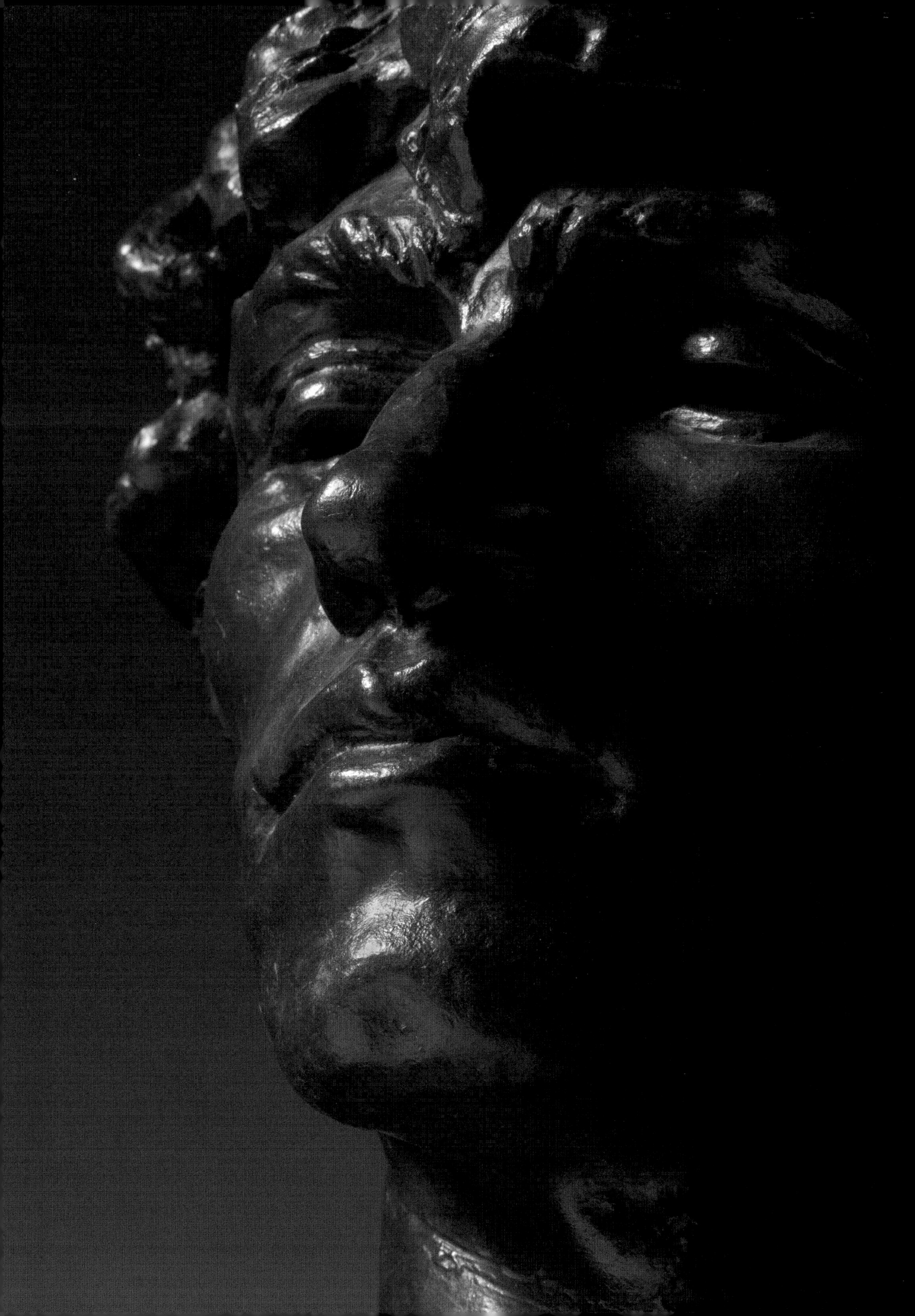

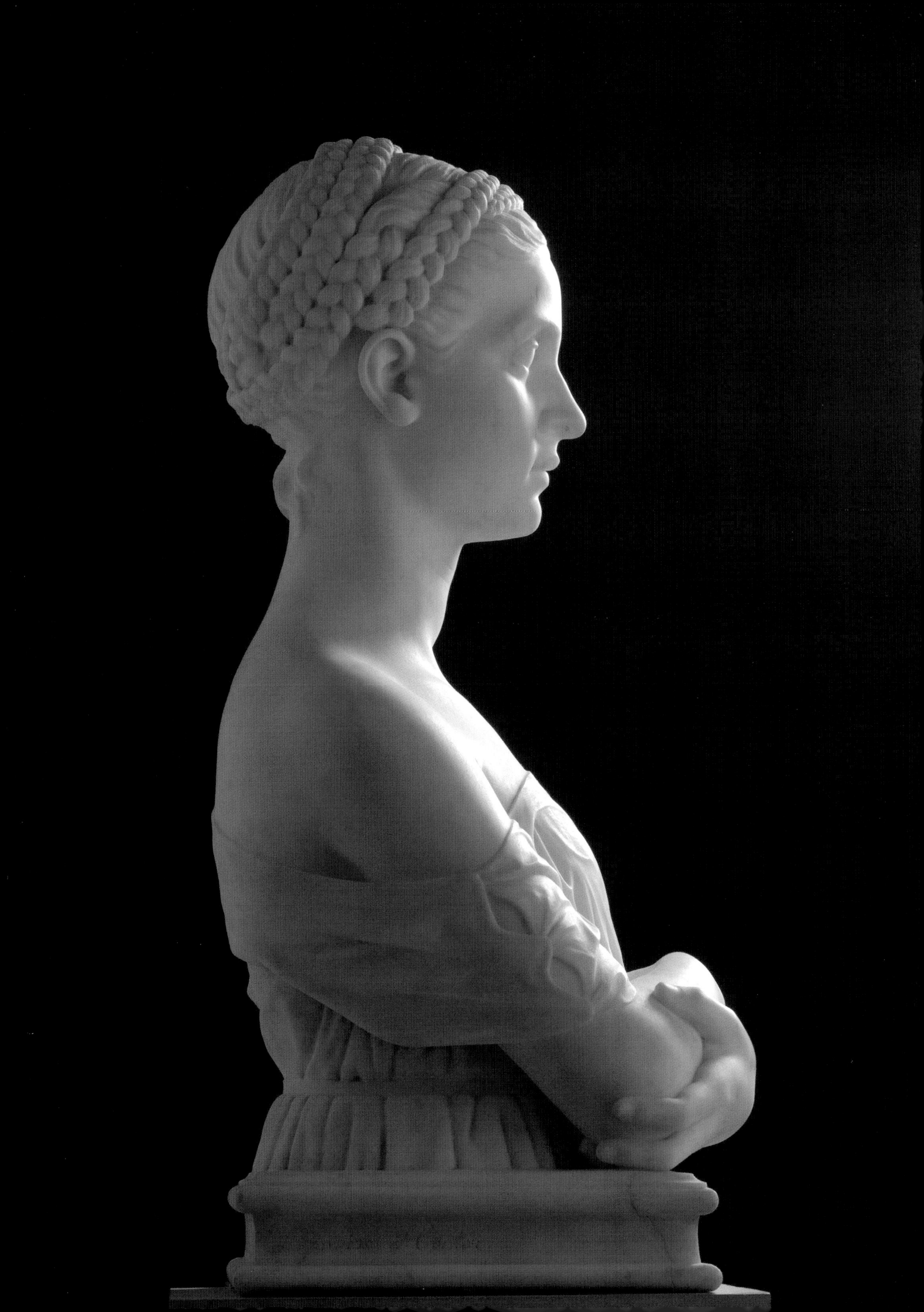

riched through ties with the public statuary of Lille and its creators (Boutry, Desruelles).

The sculptures of Rodin are a strong point of the collection. From the famous Masson collection, like the majority of our Impressionist paintings, the marble *Fallen Angel* recalls the sensual subject-matter of the couple en- 136
twined in *The Kiss*, while the *Standing Female Faun* and *The Toilet of Venus* are connected with Rodin's major project *The Gates of Hell*, inspired by Dante. Likewise, *The Shade* (1880) – an impressive bronze where Rodin gives free rein 139
to an unbridled Romanticism – subjects formal daring to the disarray of a figure overwhelmed by the weight of destiny. The reductions of five figures of

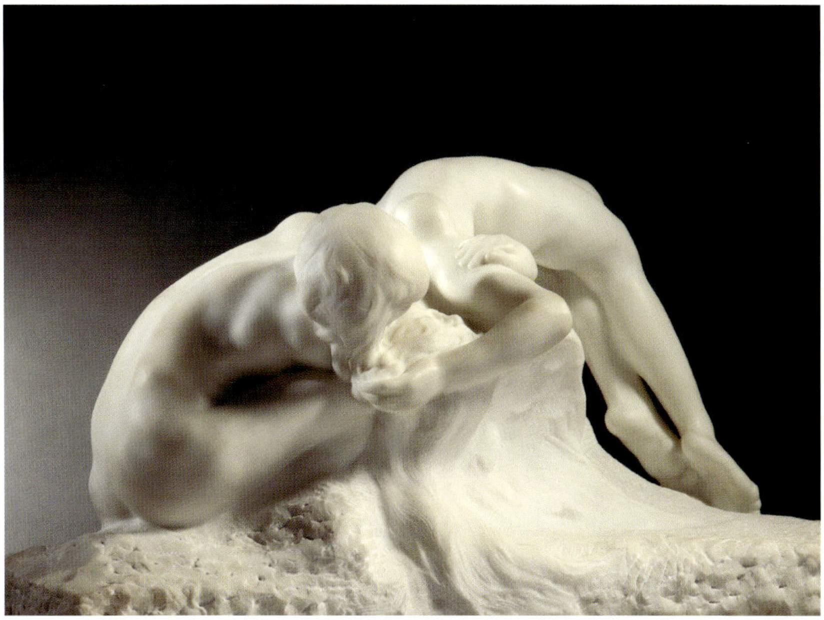

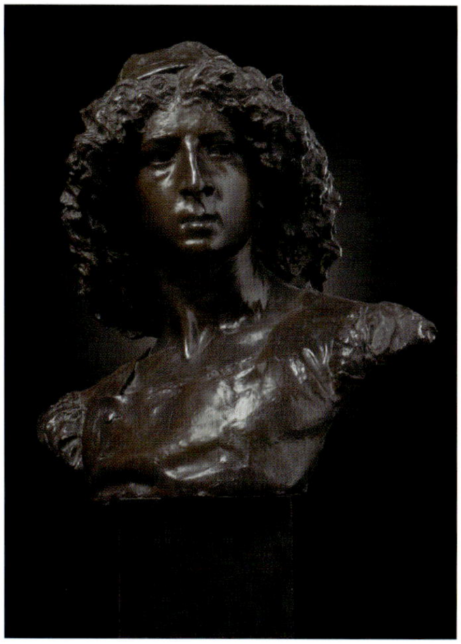

137. Carolus-Duran 1837–1917
The Pisan, 1874. Bronze,
49 x 49 x 30 cm
Acquired 2006 with the support of Crédit du Nord. Inv. 2006.1.1

136. Auguste Rodin 1840–1917
The Fallen Angel. Marble,
41 x 79 x 41 cm
Deposit from the Musée du Louvre, 1975. Inv. D.975.1.1

the *Burghers of Calais*, the *Head of St John the Baptist* and *Brother and Sister* evoke the burgeoning market for multiples. Related to these works in a way are two portraits by Camille Claudel, from her early days in Rodin's workshop: *Louise Claudel*, her younger sister, and *Giganti*, a model from the workshop of Rodin, 134
demonstrate the profound sensitivity and expressiveness of an artist whose art was in osmosis with the master's.

At the turn of the century marked by Symbolism, the powerful *Kneeling* 141
Mary Magdalene, one of two religious sculptures by the Nabi painter Georges Lacombe, illustrates the basic need for a return to sources, here preferably Egyptian, mingled with mysticism. Bourdelle, a marble cutter and friend of Rodin, developed a style of his own, in particular with *Penelope* (1909), which renews ties with Greek archaism. Portraying the features of his first wife, he constructs a strong, eloquent image of marital fidelity.

Then the 'sculpture museum' opens the doors to the 20th century, particularly the sculpture of the region, headed by Jean Roulland and Georges Jeanclos, as well as Eugène Dodeigne, present on the square in front of the museum. ADW

135. Hector-Joseph Lemaire 1846–1933
Clélia, 1869. Marble, 70 x 38 x 33 cm
Acquired 1869. Inv. Sc. 20

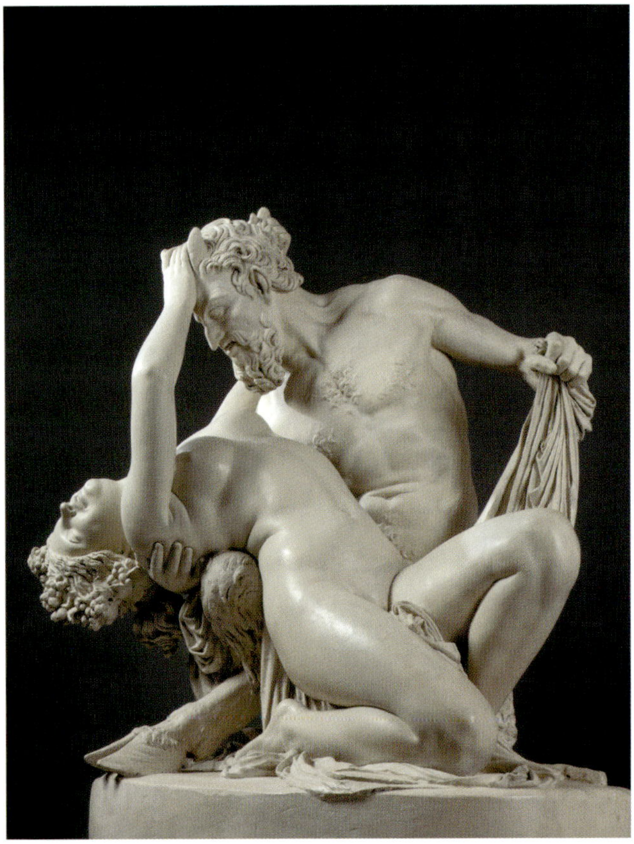

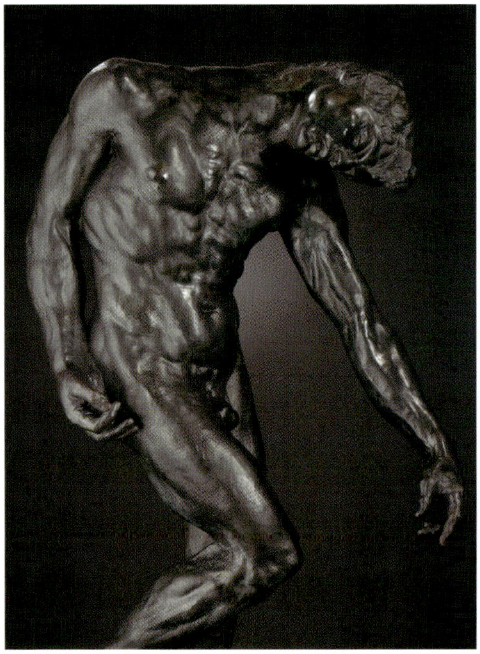

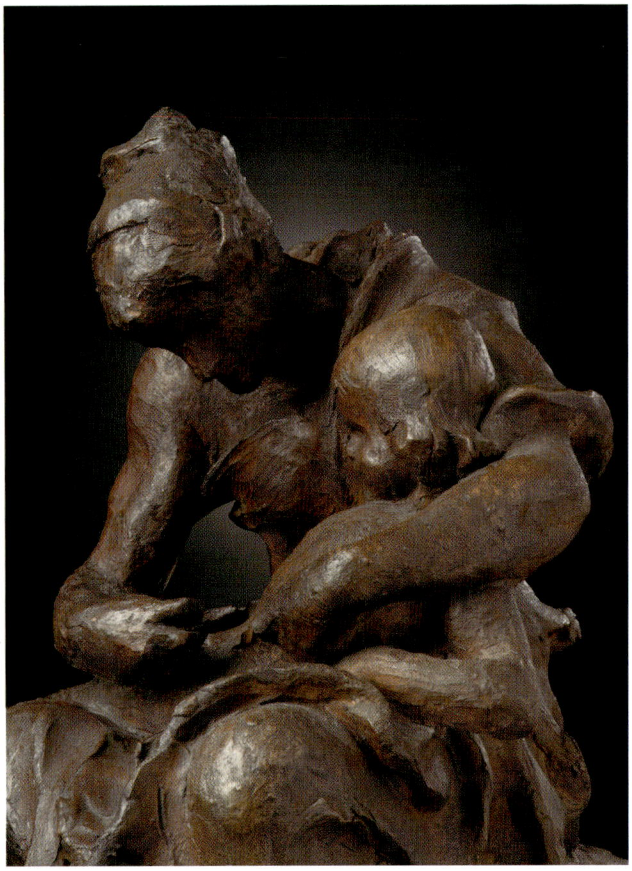

138. James Pradier 1790–1852
Satyr and Bacchante, 1834.
Plaster, 120 x 110 x 82 cm
State consignment, 1889. Inv. Sc. 51

139. Auguste Rodin 1840–1917
The Shade, 1880. Bronze,
192 x 90 x 60 cm
Deposit of the Musée Rodin, 1996. Inv. D. 996.1.1

140. Alphonse Amédée Cordonnier 1848–1930
The Inoculation, 1896. Terracotta,
35 x 23 x 22 cm
Gift of Yvonne Cordonnier, 1932. Inv. SPBS. 34

141. Georges Lacombe 1868–1916
Kneeling Mary Magdalene, 1897
Salon of the Société Nationale des Beaux-Arts, 1899.
Mahogany, 105 x 42 x 53 cm
Gift of Mme Wenger, 1899. Inv. Sc. 132

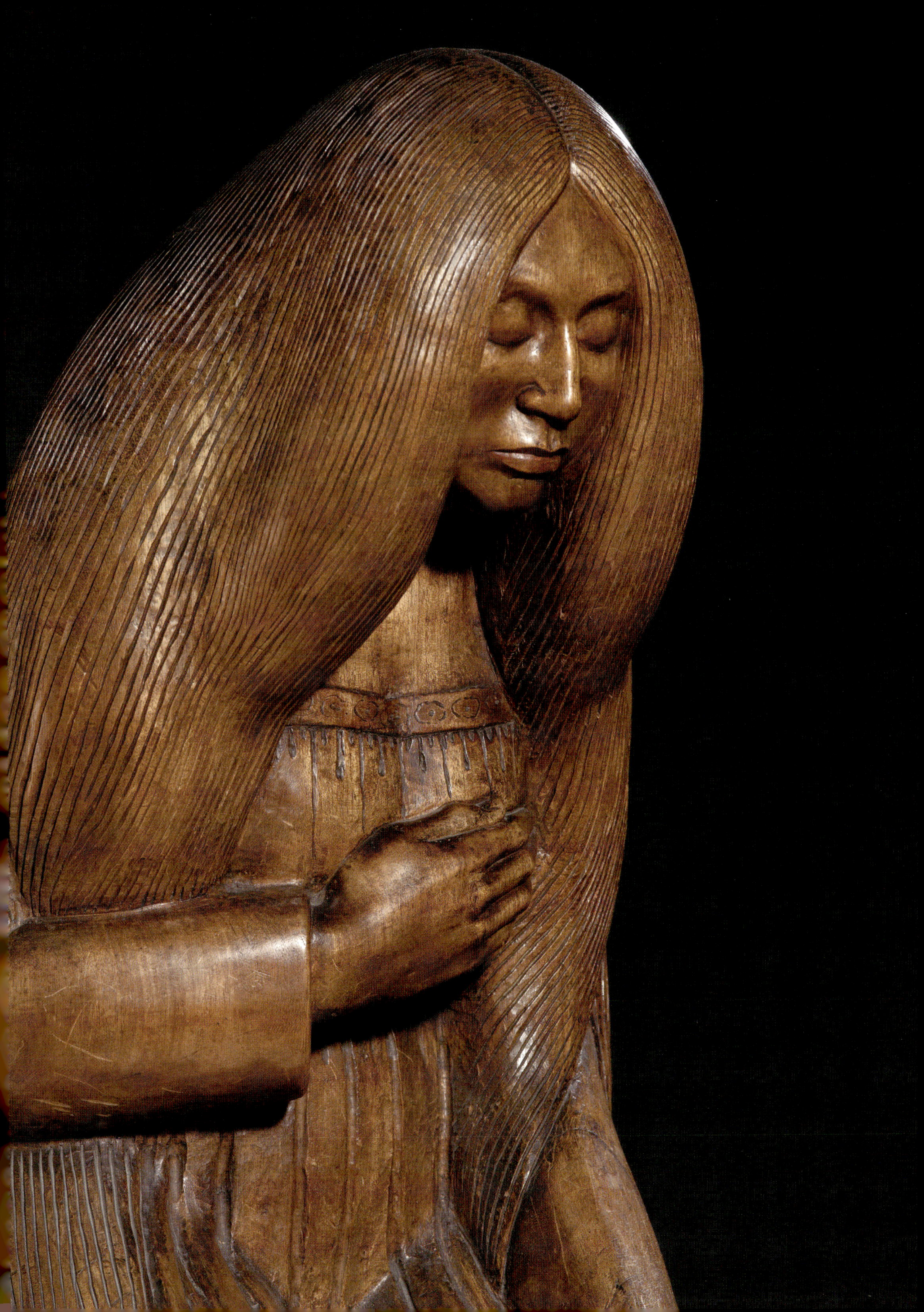

Modern Art

Although the modern art collection of the Palais des Beaux-Arts is relatively small numerically, it reflects the way the curators have understood the art of their time since the beginning of the 20th century.

The presence of avant-garde movements and works of rupture in a fine arts museum attests to daring or excess caution in choosing acquisitions. A museum of fine arts often offers visitors the reassuring face of a guardian of established values. Since the 1960s, the mission of representing contemporary creation has ordinarily been left to contemporary art museums. The panorama of the collection, though not exhaustive, promotes the theoretical coexistence of different modern trends. Two great axes structure the collection: on one hand, a classical figurative art, with the major European artists of the 20th century (a group created by many deposits dating from 1997); on the other, abstract art, focusing on post-1945 'Ecole de Paris' artists.

In the figurative realm, art history accelerated at the beginning of the 20th century. From then on, the only tradition was novelty. Representative

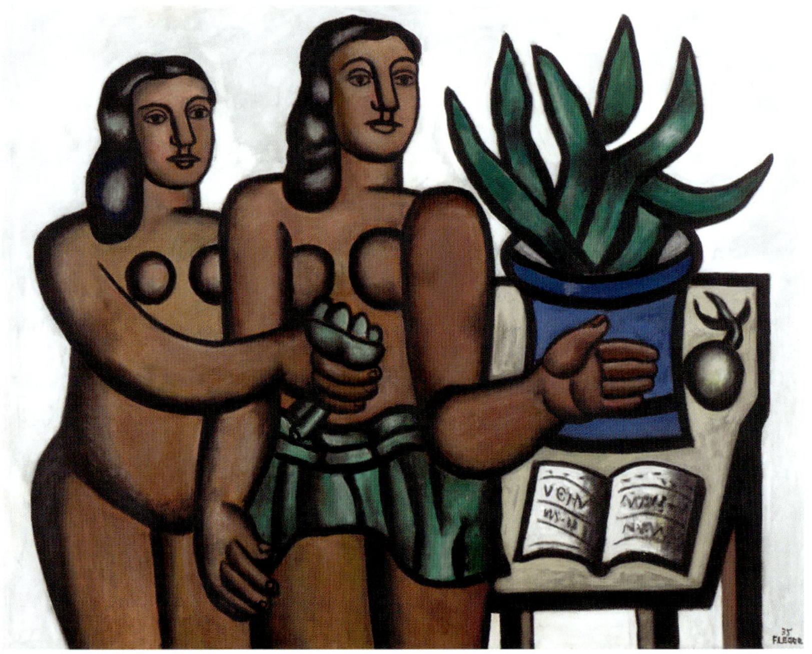

142. Fernand Léger 1881–1955
The Two Women with a Blue Vase, 1935.
Oil on canvas, 114 x 146 cm
Acquired with support from Jacques Segard and Jean Masurel, 1955. Inv. P. 1793

of this tendency – and a masterwork of the collection – is Picasso's *Olga with*
143 *a Fur Collar*, executed in 1923, when the artist returned to realism and the
human figure in a portrait with a conventional pose, but an unconventional
142 absence of colour, laying bare the pictorial material. In *The Two Women with*
a Blue Vase (1935) and *The Butterfly on the Wheel* (1948), Fernand Léger, having come to painting just when concepts were in the throes of upheaval, proved that painting was capable of uniting curves and right angles, flat colour and shading: on coarse, unprepared canvas the colour of raw silk, he created elaborate compositions structured by colour, the figures and objects outlined in black and grey.

Heir to a sense of light and material worthy of the Flemish painters, Con-
144 stant Permeke created *The Stable* in 1933. His dark, sensual palette is the opposite of Léger's. The forms of man and animal merge in a range of blacks and browns warmed with yellow. In this work, Permeke provides a fine example of lyrical and *matiériste* painting, where the subject is central to the composition. Marcel Gromaire and Edouard Pignon, who were born and lived in the

143. Pablo Picasso 1881–1973
Olga with a Fur Collar, 1923.
Oil on canvas, 116 x 80.5 cm
Deposit from the Musée Picasso, 1990. Inv. P. 2004

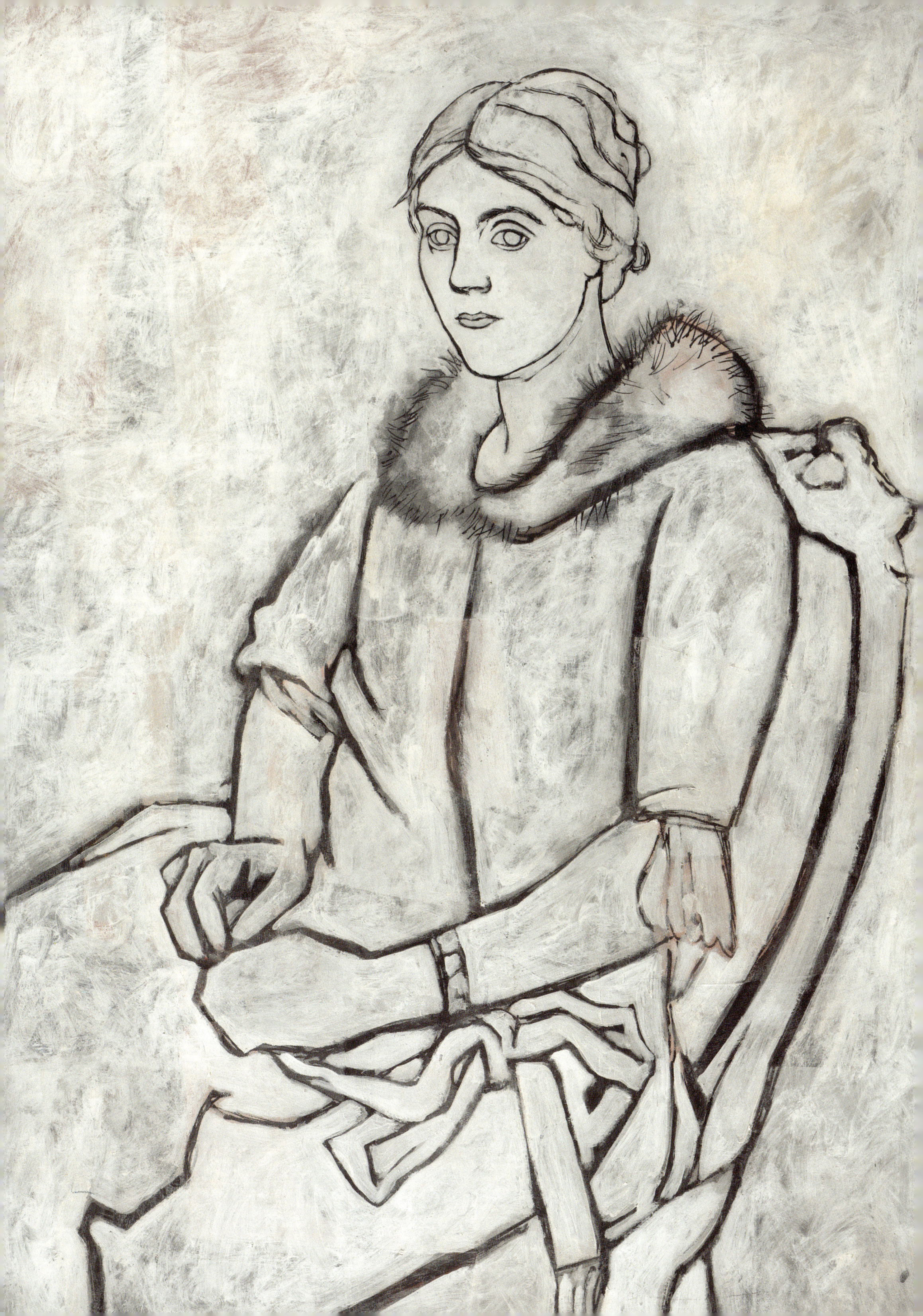

North, deal with subjects from the daily life of the people of their region. Pignon is foremost a socially committed painter (*The Meeting* and *The Dead Workman*), one of the last witnesses of a social history in need of being immortalized. In the 'rustic' fashion of Permeke, he created wide-shouldered, wide-hipped characters with massive silhouettes like the objects surrounding them (*The Flemish Stove*).

Standing apart from movements and schools, Eugène Leroy sought the middle ground between motif and the expressivity of pictorial matter throughout his career. The one never takes precedence over the other, as in *Composition* and *Si peau d'âne m'était conté*, where he pursues his concept with constancy.

The realm of abstraction, modern art's second major mutation, was established by 1910. A phenomenon of rupture and a new path, it was a non-descriptive expression, forgoing the illusion of the external world. The artist does not name or describe, but expresses.

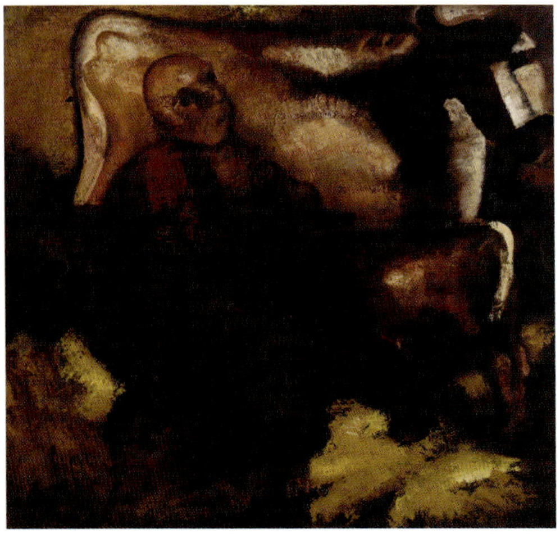

144. Constant Permeke 1886–1952
The Stable, 1933. Oil on canvas,
165 x 181 cm
Deposit from the Centre Georges Pompidou, 1997.
Inv. D. 97.8.5

Sonia Delaunay, a pioneer of abstraction, was among the first Cubists. In
146 *Rhythm-Colour 1076*, the space is organized in planes of shaded colours with contrasts of forms, tones and value, ending up in a joyful, infinitely flexible composition.

Very close to Sonia and Robert Delaunay, Serge Poliakoff moves beyond
145 the coldness of geometric abstraction in *Composition*. The forms are not hardened by surrounding lines, and thus the power of colour is heightened. This painting is one of numerous gifts to the museum in the 1950s by the Amis de l'Art Contemporain. Their manifest will was to create a representative group of works by the artists of the second School of Paris and the various abstract currents. *Art informel* painters like Mathieu, Bryen and Atlan put the gestural element of painting to the fore. Lyrical Abstraction is also represented by artists like Bissière, Manessier and Estève, who provided an alternative to geometric abstraction after 1947.

Among these painters who worked in Paris, Maria Helena Vieira da Silva stands apart. In *The Lock* and *The Barrier*, the space is limitless, and shapes near to reality become abstract, intermingling and embedding themselves in a distension of forms.

At the time when abstraction lost its leading role in modernism, Martin Barré devised a personal language wherein art and technique join forces (*Composition*, 1956). His works aim for the essence, the simplification of the visible, as in *Ochre Pink and Grey Blue* (1976).

The desire of the current chief curator, Alain Tapié, is to strengthen the value of the collection by veering towards a kind of painting that is more sensitive to the dynamic of sensations and the expressiveness of the materials, with artists like Eugène Leroy and Paul Rebeyrolle. DR

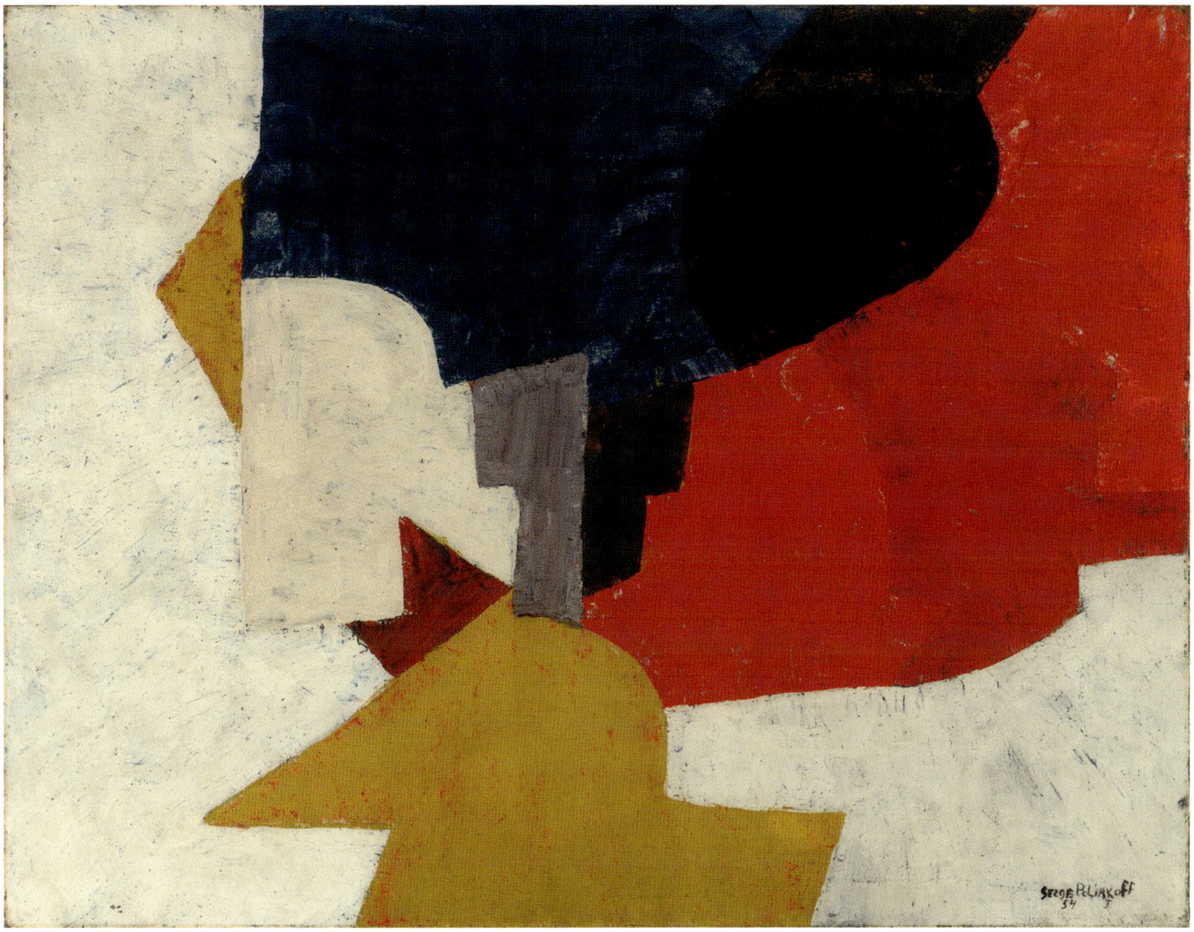

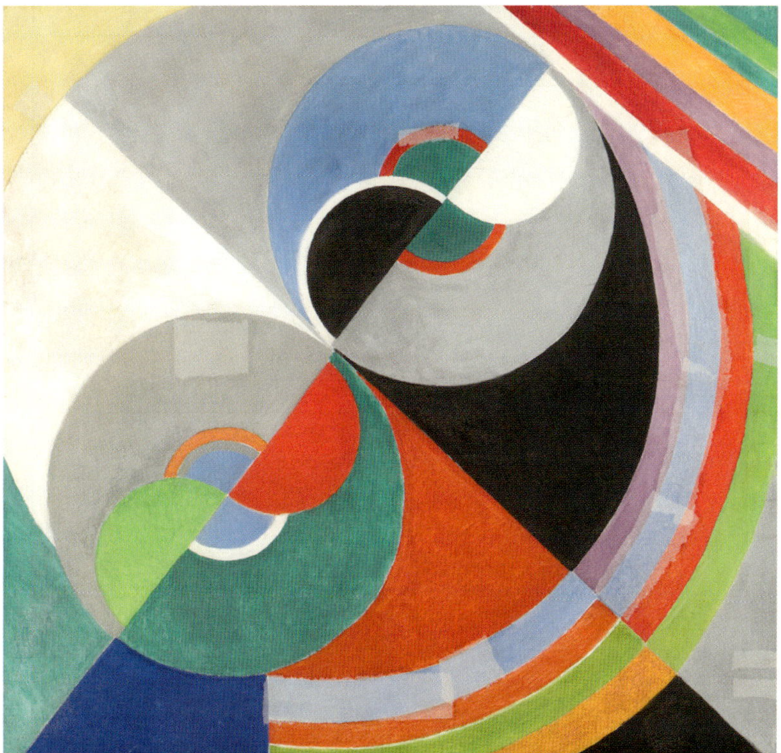

145. Serge Poliakoff 1906–1969
Composition, 1954. Oil on canvas,
89 x 116 cm
Donation of the Amis des musées, 1955. Inv. P. 1789

146. Sonia Delaunay 1885–1979
Rhythm-Colour 1076, 1939.
Oil on canvas, 154 x 158 cm
State consignment, 1966. Inv. D. 66.5

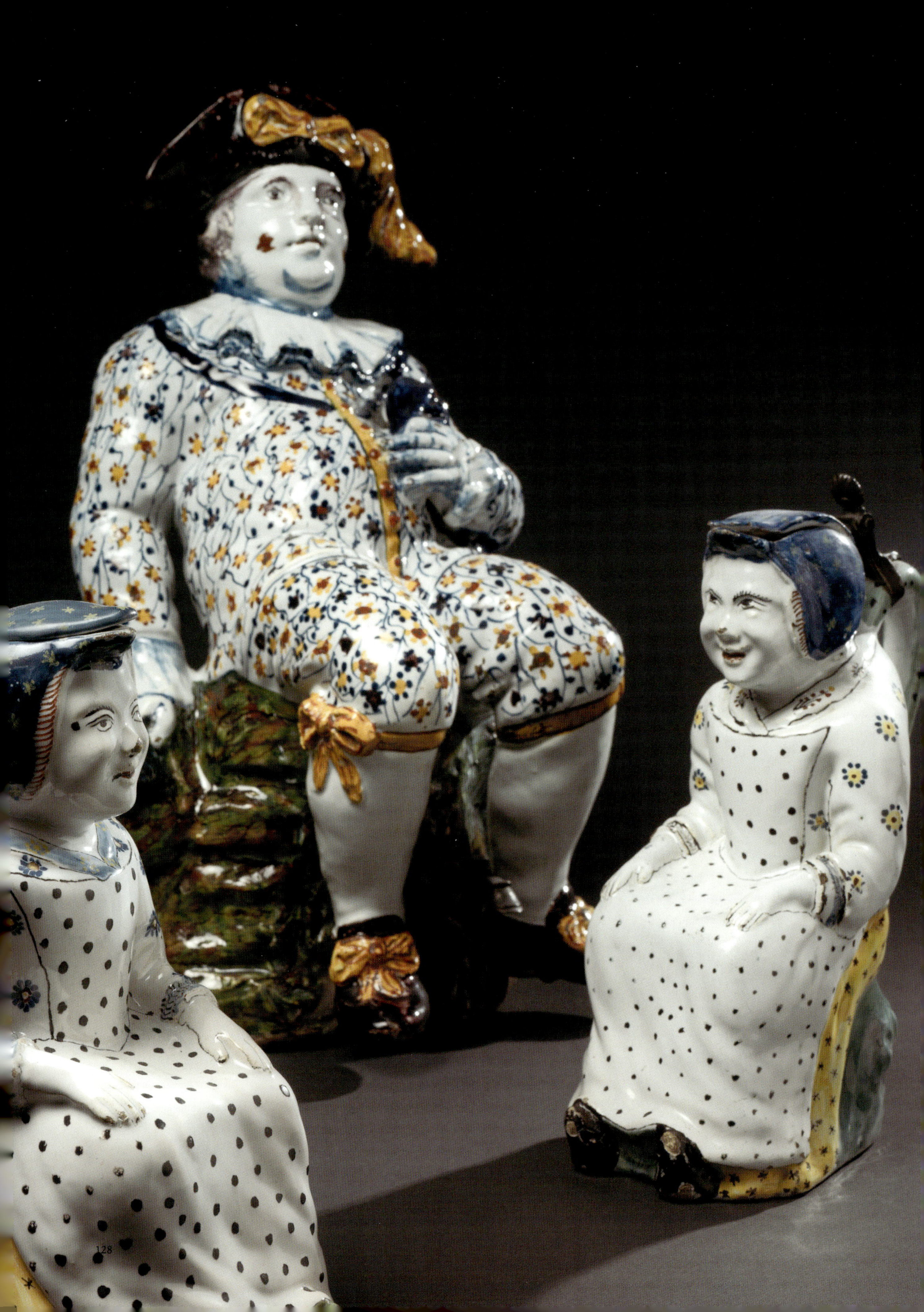

The Ceramics and Numismatic Collections

The Ceramics Collection

Cultural curiosity in the second half of the 19th century was drawn to the decorative arts. With the change from handcrafting objects in series to industrial mass production, amateurs and collectors developed an inordinate taste for the rare object as testimony of the skills and art of living that were looked upon with nostalgia at the dawn of the 20th century. The Nord region of France, with its longstanding ceramics tradition in centres as varied as Lille, Saint-Amand, Saint-Omer and Aire-sur-la-Lys, was home to great collectors whose donations and bequests added significantly to Lille's holdings: among others, the Verly-Lecoutre de Beauvais bequest in 1914, the Baron de Vicq bequest in 1881 and 1891, the bequest of Dr Trachet in 1949 and that of André Cateaux in 1975. The taste of these art lovers and patrons shaped the museum's collections. They were often friends of the curators, with whom they exchanged letters and study topics, seeking to pinpoint a place of manufacture. For this reason, a great deal of documentary evidence remains, notably the correspondence between Désiré Riocreux, curator of the Sèvres museum, and Jules Houdoy of Lille, a specialist in earthenware, who wrote *Histoire de la Céramique lilloise* in 1869, which was the authoritative study in its day. The same year, the city of Lille founded a ceramics museum, composed essentially of tin-glazed earthenware from the North of France, Holland and Rouen.

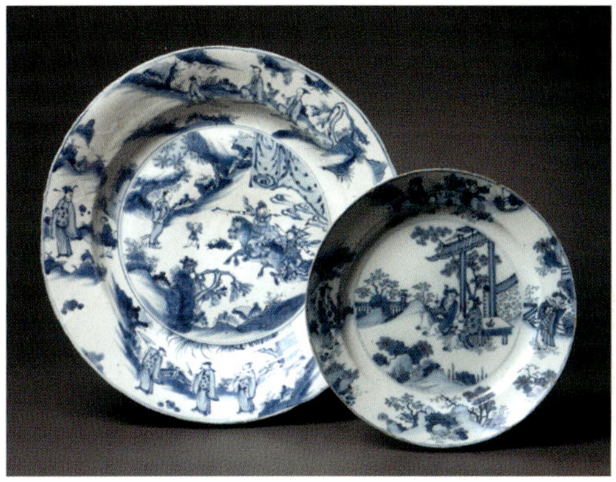

148. Left: Plate, hard-paste porcelain with monochrome blue decoration (China, Transition Period, 1620–83). Right: Plate, tin-glazed earthenware with grand feu monochrome blue decoration (Delft, 1660–1690).

The collections on display today were formed from this original nucleus,
inventoried at more than 2500 pieces. In 1696, Jacques Febvrier, a native of
Tournai, and Jean Bossut, a native of Ghent, submitted a request to the city
council asking for permission to found an earthenware manufactory in Lille.
This request was motivated by their discovery of 'earth well suited to making
earthenware in the Dutch manner', which gives an indication of just how
much Lille's production was influenced by the manufactories in the Nether- *147*
lands. The highly prestigious Dutch producers had made great advances after
1647, when political problems in China abruptly put an end to imports by the
Dutch East India Company, established in 1602. Through the technical and
artistic quality of their glazed earthenware, they managed to take over the
market held by Chinese porcelain. Europeans did not yet possess the secret *148*
of manufacturing hard-paste porcelain (1708) but were successful in imitating
it convincingly thanks to an improved glazing technique. In Delft, the fine,
glossy lead-based glaze *kwaart* and, in Lille, the rich glaze made plentiful by
imports of English tin at reduced duty enabled these manufacturers to achieve
a remarkable expansion that contributed to the regions' economic wealth in
the 18th century. Rouen earthenware, which developed in the Italian tradition,
had been celebrated since the 16th century and was the joy of collectors. In
Lille, Rouen-style embroidery decoration in blue monochrome and, later,
polychrome met with considerable success. The manufactories of Febvrier,
then of Boussemart and Dorez, made such frequent use of it that the attribu- *149*
tion of pieces to a specific manufactory is still often confused.

147. Pulchinella water jug with handle, tin-glazed earthenware (delftware, late 18th century); two 'Jacqueline' jars in the form of seated women, polychrome glazed earthenware (Lille, 18th century)

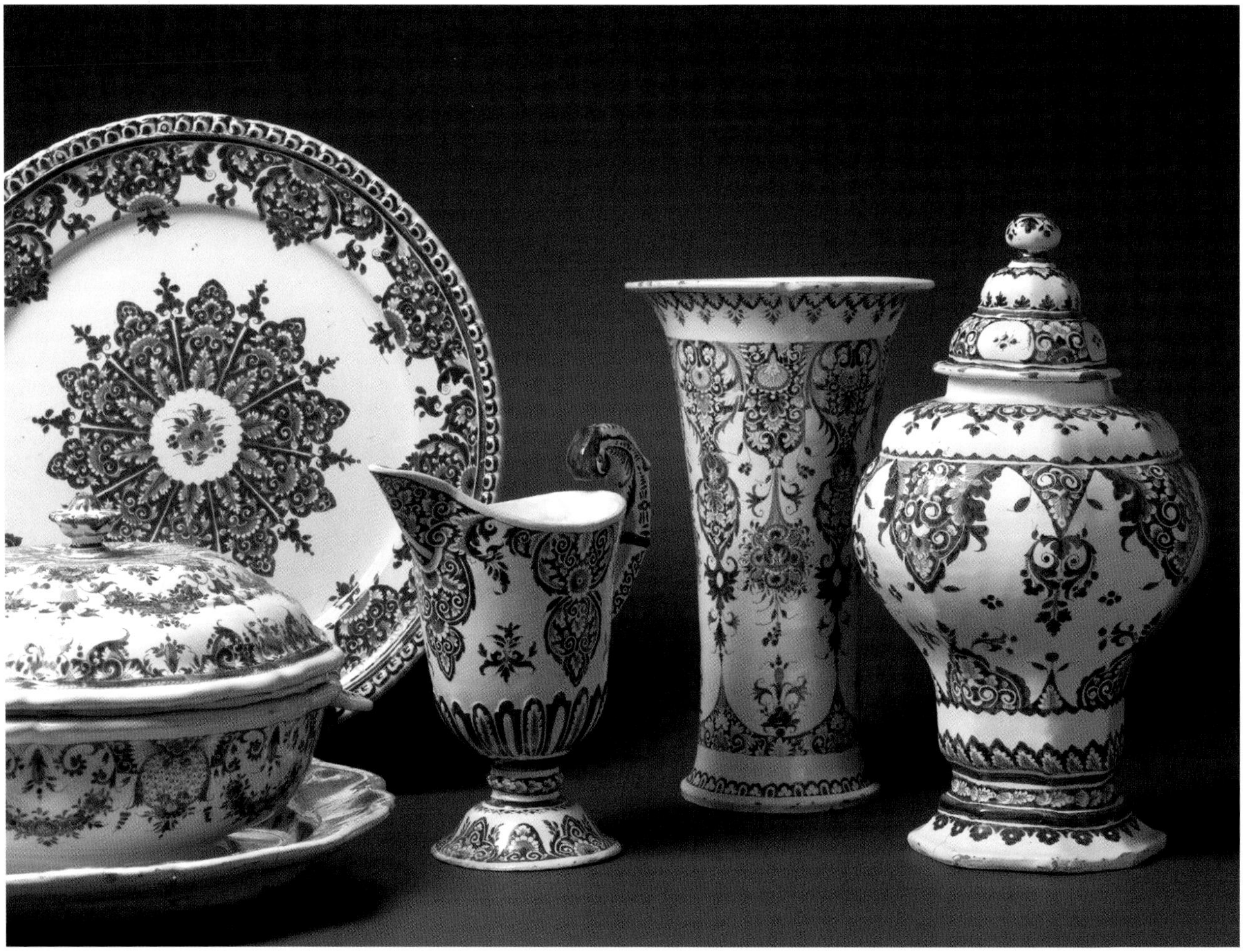

149. Left to right: tureen and underplate, tin-glazed earthenware with grand feu monochrome blue decoration (Rouen, *c.* 1740); plate (Lille or Rouen, first half 18th century); helmet-shaped ewer, tin-glazed earthenware (Lille, 18th century); conical vase, tin-glazed earthenware (Rouen, 18th century); covered vessel in the form of a faceted baluster, tin-glazed earthenware (Lille, 18th century).

The arrangement of Lille's ceramic collection clearly demonstrates the close connections between the production of Lille, the Netherlands and Rouen. During the museum's renovation in 1997, the Musée national de Sèvres deposited a large number of outstanding 18th-century pieces from Rouen and Lille that make these connections all the more evident.

A large display case of Chinese and Japanese porcelain further enriches the comparison ceramics lovers like to make between pieces from different areas. The other fundamental approach in the ceramics gallery highlights the collection's European composition. In addition to the Netherlands and Belgium, Germany, Italy, Spain, Sweden, Central Europe and England are represented by strong original pieces that would not be out of place in their own national museums. The composition of the ceramic collection at Lille's fine arts museum coincides with the city's desire to stand at the heart of Europe as a crossroads of diverse cultural currents.

The collection of 18th-century porcelain from Lille and elsewhere adds to the attraction of a gallery that, in its didactic intent, provides inquisitive visitors with a good introduction to ceramics. AC

The Numismatic Collection

The museum has a large numismatic collection. A selection of coins, medals and seal matrices is presented in a display case designed for these objects, whose dimensions require thorough attention in order to discover their secrets and their beauty.

Coins

The most remarkable of the medieval coins are from the collection of the banker Achille Vernier (1834–1917). The collection, which was studied by the Belgian numismatist Serrure in 1880, was acquired by the museum in 1900, enlarging the existing holdings of several thousand pieces. A series of superb examples, some exceedingly rare, beckon us to an overview of the history of Flanders.

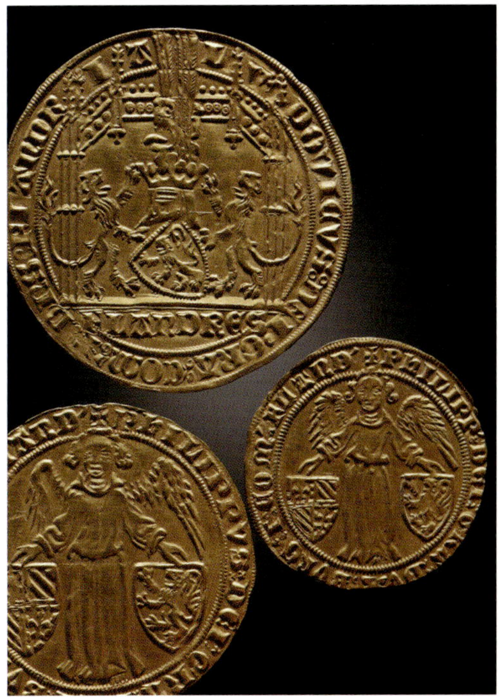

First come the silver *denarii* of the first counts and the 10th-century coin of Baldwin V. Inspired by the Carolingian *denarius*, it bears a stylized image of a temple portico. The 'small silver *denarii*' on display provide a hint of the wide variety of small-format issues with a high silver content minted for the counts, towns and great abbeys of Flanders, Hainaut and Artois in the 11th and 12th centuries.

The commercial development of the Northern Provinces in the 13th century is reflected in the *groot* of Marguerite of Flanders, worth two-thirds the value of the silver *gros* of St Louis, and the *esterlins* of Count Guy of Dampierre, which imitate the English penny.

In the mid-14th century, a hundred years after France, Flanders saw the return of gold coinage with the florin, imitating the Florentine type with the large fleur-de-lis, then the *écu*, the gold *chaise* and the royal, patterned after the French royal coinages. The Flemish sculptors chiselled veritable gems, examples of Gothic art at its pinnacle. The *lion d'or* of Louis of Mâle (1346–1389) *150*
represents the heraldic animal of Flanders in a rib-vaulted building. The creative originality of the craftsmen lasted through the 'Autumn of the Middle Ages'. With its gold and silver coins, *groten* and double *groten*, Flemish coinage is independent of French influence.

150. Gold 'Flandres' of Louis of Mâle
Ange and *demi-ange* of Philip the Bold, Duke of Burgundy

The dukes of Burgundy of the house of Valois, heirs of the counts of Flanders, continued this splendid series of original and varied types, in particular gold coins: the *ange* and its sub-denominations, the much rarer *demi-ange* *150*
and the *écu* with two escutcheons and helmets penchant of Philip the Bold (1389–1404). The different series issued show the development of the value of coins and economic fluctuations. Periods of monetary stability alternated with periods when new mintings were introduced.

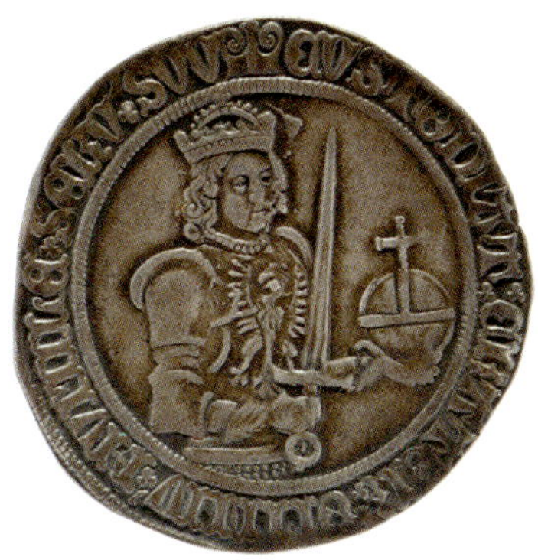

The *cromsteert* (Middle Dutch for 'curled tail'), inaugurated under John the Fearless, shows the heraldic lion of Flanders represented with this trait. This issue was extended during the first part of the reign of Philip the Good (1419–1467). After a realignment of weight and alloy, it was replaced in 1433 by the *vierlander* ('four nations'). This new coin was minted in Flanders, Hainaut, Brabant and Holland. A splendid half *ridre* ('rider'), a gold coin of the *vierlander* system, is presented here. Fifteenth-century coinage is continued by the series of gold florins portraying St Andrew, patron of Burgundy, made under Philip the Good and his successors. It ends with the magnificent large silver *real* of *151*
1487. Two examples of this very rare coin show the head of Maximilian of Habsburg, Holy Roman King, crowned and holding a sword and an orb surmounted by a cross on the obverse, and on the reverse, a curious monogram combining the initials of Maximilian and his son, Archduke Philip the Handsome. His *toisons d'or* and *toisons d'argent* are in exceptional condition, just like the gold *real*, the silver florin of Charles V and the principal denominations of

151. Large silver *real* depicting Maximilian I of Habsburg, 1487

the system current at the time of Philip II of Spain, sovereign of the Netherlands and Count of Flanders.

152 Two specimens of the rare half *daaldre*, a silver coin issued in 1582 by François d'Alençon (d. 1584), brother of King Henry III of France who intervened in Cambrai and in Flanders, illustrate the time of the 'Troubles'. These pieces conclude the series of coins from Flanders exhibited in the case..

Medals

The art of the medal began to flourish in Italy in the mid-15th century. Larger than coins, medals are pure *objets d'art* in which the medallist expresses his talent for the miniature relief portrait. From the 1470s, the dukes of Burgundy called upon Jean Candida (d. 1502). This artist executed the pieces showing Charles the Bold, his brother Anthony, the Grand Bastard, and the medal with the portraits of Mary of Burgundy and Maximilian of Austria, dated 1477.

In the early 15th century, the taste for medals spread to Germany. The museum has on exhibit the portrait of Emperor Charles V and, on the reverse, the grand imperial coat of arms with the heraldic quarters of Spain, Burgundy and Flanders, held by an expressive two-headed eagle, the work of Hans Reinhart. Several German medals show effigies of princes of the house of Habsburg.

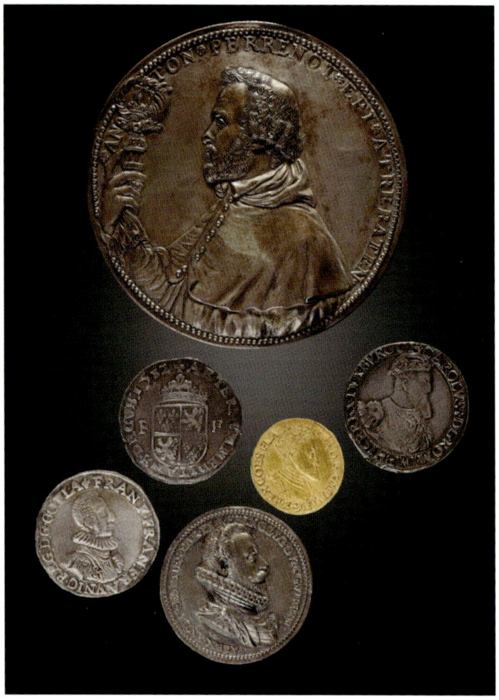

152. Silver florin of Charles V (right)
Double gold *real* of Philip II
Two specimens of the rare half *daaldre* of François d'Alençon (left)
Medal with the bust of Cardinal Granvelle, engraved by Jacques Jonghelinck (above)
Medal with the portrait of Alessandro Farnese (below)

Renowned Italian sculptors spent time in Flanders. Leone Leoni (1509–1590), Jacopo da Trezzo (*c.* 1519–1589) and Poggini placed their talent at the disposal of the Habsburgs, who ruled the Low Countries, Spain and Germany at that time. The model that served to engrave the minting dies for the coins with the portrait of Philip II, King of Spain and sovereign of the Netherlands, is the work of Leone Leoni.

Starting in the second half of the 16th century, sculptors from Brabant and Flanders met the demand of a clientele of sovereigns and illustrious personages. Jacques Jonghelinck (1530–1606) engraved the medals with the head of
152 Cardinal Granvelle, the principal minister of Philip II about 1560. He created
152 the superb medal with the portrait of Alessandro Farnese, Governor of the Spanish Netherlands from 1581 to 1592 and nephew of Philip II. But caught in the reigning political agitation, the artist was also responsible for the prototype of the medal of the *Geuzen* ('the Beggars'), distributed in 1566 when the rebellion against Spain broke out in the Netherlands. Conrad Bloc worked for the Habsburg princes and also for their opponents, the house of Orange-Nassau.

Seals

Matrices, or dies, serve to imprint an impression in wax. They are rare objects, generally in brass, punched and incised according to the same technique used to 'cut' monetary coins.

153 Three matrices are displayed in a glass case. The seal of the Abbot of Mont-Saint-Martin represents the Virgin in Majesty, offering an apple to the infant Jesus on her knee. The scene has the freshness of a medieval statue. A real rarity is the impression of this matrix, certainly created in the 13th century, on a deed dated 1300. Two seals used by the city council of Lille – the large *aux causes* matrix and the counterseal of the aldermen – bear the city's heraldic emblem: a large fleur-de-lis spread over the entire field. DD

153. Seal matrix from the Abbey of Mont-Saint-Martin, 13th century

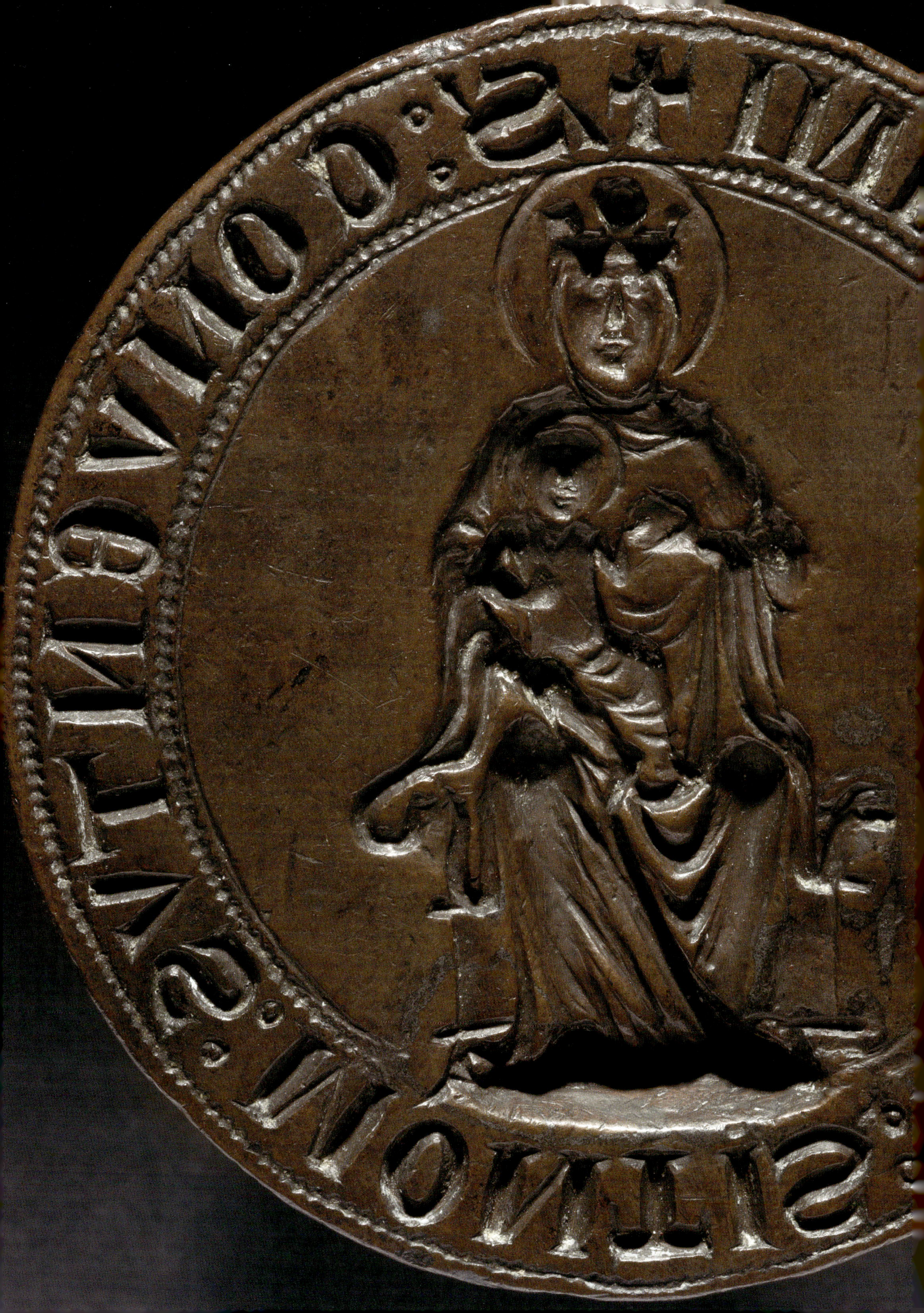

Index

Pagenumbers in italics refer to illustrations

Bibliography

Blanchegorge E., Brejon de Lavergnée A. et B., Castier A., Donetzfoff A., Lavallée M. H. et Scottez-De Wambrechies A., *Guide des collections*, Paris, 1997

Brejon de Lavergnée A. et B., Viatte F. et Zeri F., *Catalogue des dessins italiens. Collections du Palais des Beaux-Arts de Lille*, Paris, 1997

Brejon de Lavergnée A. et Scottez-De Wambrechies A., *Catalogue sommaire illustré des Peintures. I. Écoles étrangères*, Paris, 1999

Brejon de Lavergnée A. et Scottez-De Wambrechies A., *Catalogue sommaire illustré des Peintures. II .École française*, Paris, 2001

Brejon de Lavergnée A., Châtelet A., Donetzkoff A., Dujardin D., Foucart J., Martens D., Merle du Bourg A. et Tapié A., *Maniéristes du Nord*, Paris, 2005

Brejon de Lavergnée B. et Joannides P., *Raphaël et son temps*, Paris, 2002

Brejon de Lavergnée B. Moyne M. et Scottez-De Wambrechies A., *Catalogue des dessins français du XIX*[e] *siècle. Collection du Palais des Beaux-Arts de Lille*, Paris, 2004

Châtelet A. *Cent chefs-d'œuvre du Musée de Lille*, Lille, 1970

Oursel H., *Le Musée des Beaux-Arts de Lille*, Paris, 1984

Oursel H., «Les arts avant la conquête française», «Les arts sous Louis XIV», in *Histoire de Lille*, t.II, Toulouse, 1981

Oursel H., «Les arts sous Louis XV et Louis XVI», «Les arts sous la Révolution et l'Empire» et «Les arts d'un empereur à l'autre» in *Histoire de Lille*, t.III, Toulouse, 1991

Raux S., *Catalogue des dessins français du XVIII*[e] *siècle*, Paris, 1995

Scottez-De Wambrechies A., «La vie artistique à Lille (1851-1914)» in *Histoire de Lille*, t.IV, Paris, 1999

Exhibition Catalogues

1950 *Quarante chefs-d'œuvre du Musée de Lille*, Gand, Musée des Beaux-Arts

1951 *Céramique régionale ancienne*, Lille, musée des Beaux-Arts

1964 *Meisterwerke aus dem Museum in Lille*, Berlin, Schloss Charlottenburg

1967 *Dessins italiens du musée de Lille*, Amsterdam, Rijksmuseum; Brussels, Bibliothèque royale de Belgique; Lille, Palais des Beaux-Arts

1970 *Disegni di Rafaello e di altri italiani del Museo di Lille*, Florence, cabinet des Dessins et des Estampes des Offices

1974 *La collection d'Alexandre Leleux. Grands noms, grandes figures du musée de Lille n°1*, Lille, musée des Beaux-Arts

1974-1975 *From Poussin to Puvis de Chavannes: a Loan Exhibition of French Drawings from the collections of the Musée des Beaux-Arts at Lille*, Londres, Heim Gallery; Cambridge, Fitzwilliam Museum; Birmingham, City Museum and Art Gallery; Glasgow, Glasgow Art Gallery and Museum

1981 *La collection d'Antoine Brasseur. Grands noms, grandes figures du musée de Lille n°2*, Lille, musée des Beaux-Arts

1983-1984 *Autour de David. Dessins néoclassiques du musée des Beaux-Arts de Lille*, Lille, musée des Beaux-Arts; Rome, musée Correr

1985 *Un palais pour un musée*, Lille, musée des Beaux-Arts

1989 *Plans en relief. Villes fortes des Anciens Pays-Bas Français au XVIII*[e] *S.*, Lille, musée des Beaux-Arts

1989-1990 *Renaissance et baroque. Dessins italiens du musée de Lille*, Lille, musée des Beaux-Arts

1990-1991 *L'Europe de la Faïence XVII*[e] *et XVIII*[e] *siècles*, Lille, musée des Beaux-Arts
Raffael und die Zeichen Kunst der italienische Renaissance, Cologne, Wallraf-Richartz Museum

1991 *La Peinture française au XIX*[e] *siècle. Le musée des Beaux-Arts de Lille*, Yokohama, Sogo Museum of Art; Hokkaido, Obihiro Museum; Osaka, Museum of Art Kintetsu; Yamaguchi Prefectural Museum of Art

1992 *Chefs-d'œuvre du musée des Beaux-Arts de Lille. Peintres flamands et hollandais du XVII*[e], Toulouse, musée des Augustins

1992-1993 *Masterworks from the Musée des Beaux-Arts, Lille*, New-York, Metropolitan Museum of Art

1993 *Tradition and Revolution in French Art 1700-1880. Paintings and Drawings from Lille*, Londres, National Gallery
Les Chefs-d'œuvre du musée des Beaux-Arts de Lille, Paris, Grand Palais
Bellezze di Firenze, Lille, musée de l'Hospice Comtesse

1993-1994 *Het Franse Landschap van Corot tot Monet*, Courtrai, Municipal Museum

1994 *De Véronese à Goya. Tableaux et dessins du Palais des Beaux-Arts de Lille*, Tokyo, Tobu Museum of Art; Yokohama, Yokohama Museum of Art; Nagoya, Aichi Prefecttural Museum of Art; Kitakyushu, Kitakuyushu museum of Art

2001 *Delacroix. Médée furieuse*, Paris, musée national Eugène Delacroix

2004 *De Delacroix à Courbet*, Anvers, Musée des Beaux-Arts

Contents

Published with the support of Fondation BNP PARIBAS

Books in print

Agen	The Musée des Beaux-Arts
Albi	The Musée Toulouse-Lautrec
Amiens	The Museum of Picardy
Antibes	The Picasso Museum
Arras	The Musée des Beaux-Arts
Bayonne	The Bonnat Museum
Besançon	The Museum of Fine Arts and Archaeology
Bordeaux	The Museum of Aquitaine
Bourg-en-Bresse	The Monastère Royal de Brou
Caen	The Mémorial de Caen
Caen	The Museum of Fine Arts
Cambrai	The Musée de Cambrai
Castres	The Musée Goya
Colmar	The Unterlinden Museum
Dijon	The Museum of Fine Arts
Douai	The Musée de la Chartreuse
Ecouen	The Château
Grenoble	The Museum of Art
Limoges	The National Museum Adrien Dubouché
Lyons	The Museum of Fine Arts
Lyons	The Textile Museum
Marseilles	The Musée d'Arts africains, océaniens, amérindiens
Montpellier	The Musée Fabre
Mulhouse	The National Automobile Museum (Schlumpf Collection)
Nancy	The Museum of Fine Arts
Nantes	The Museum of Fine Arts
Orléans	The Museum of Fine Arts
Paris	Bibliothèque Nationale
Paris	The Musée des Arts et Métiers
Paris	The Carnavalet Museum
Paris	The Gustave Moreau Museum
Paris	The Musée national du Moyen Age
Paris	The National Museum of Modern Art Cabinet d'Art graphique
Paris	The National Museum of Modern Art Paintings & Sculptures
Paris	The Nissim de Camondo Museum
Poitiers	The Museums of Poitiers
Quimper	The Museum of Fine Arts
Reims	The Musée des Beaux-Arts
La Réunion	The Musée Saint-Denis
Rouen	The Museum of Fine Arts
Saint-Etienne	The Museum of Modern Art
Saint-Germain-en-Laye	The Musée des Antiquités nationales
Saint-Tropez	The Annonciade Museum
Versailles	The Palace
Düsseldorf	The museum kunst palast
Lisbon	The National Coach Museum
Los Angeles	Los Angeles County Museum of Art
Montreal	The Museum of Fine Arts

Series Design Concept
Stéphan Alberty

Design Production
Tony Waddingham

Copyediting
Anagram, Ghent

Photography
Hugo Maertens, Bruges; Gilbert Larmuseau (fig. 10–12); © RMN Paris p. 1, ill. 22, 24

Typesetting
Wilfrieda Paessens

Production
Ludion, Ghent

Library
Annie Oblin, Dominique Declercq, Astrid Willot

Conservation Secretary; Photographic Service
Patricia Truffin

Documentation
Marie-Françoise Bouttemy, Madeleine Schrevelle, Jocelyne De Mets

Museological Service
Denis Villaume, Lucien Ruck

Jean-Jacques Goron
41, Avenue de l'Opéra
75002 Paris
Tel.: +33(0)1 42 98 16 04
Fax: +33(0)1 42 98 14 11

ISBN 2-7118-5223-7
Dépôt légal: September 2006

Printed in Belgium